Loyalty in Time of Trial

The African American History Series

Series Editors:
Jacqueline M. Moore, Austin College
Nina Mjagkij, Ball State University

Traditionally, history books tend to fall into two categories: books academics write for each other, and books written for popular audiences. Historians often claim that many of the popular authors do not have the proper training to interpret and evaluate the historical evidence. Yet, popular audiences complain that most historical monographs are inaccessible because they are too narrow in scope or lack an engaging style. This series, which will take both chronological and thematic approaches to topics and individuals crucial to an understanding of the African American experience, is an attempt to address that problem. The books in this series, written in lively prose by established scholars, are aimed primarily at nonspecialists. They focus on topics in African American history that have broad significance and place them in their historical context. While presenting sophisticated interpretations based on primary sources and the latest scholarship, the authors tell their stories in a succinct manner, avoiding jargon and obscure language. They include selected documents that allow readers to judge the evidence for themselves and to evaluate the authors' conclusions. Bridging the gap between popular and academic history, these books bring the African American story to life.

Volumes Published

Booker T. Washington, W.E.B. Du Bois, and the Struggle for Racial Uplift
Jacqueline M. Moore

Slavery in Colonial America, 1619–1776
Betty Wood

African Americans in the Jazz Age: A Decade of Struggle and Promise
Mark Robert Schneider

A. Philip Randolph: A Life in the Vanguard
Andrew E. Kersten

The African American Experience in Vietnam: Brothers in Arms
James Westheider

Bayard Rustin: American Dreamer
Jerald Podair

African Americans Confront Lynching: Strategies of Resistance
Christopher Waldrep

Lift Every Voice: The History of African-American Music
Burton W. Peretti

To Ask for an Equal Chance: African Americans in the Great Depression
Cheryl Lynn Greenberg

The African American Experience During World War II
Neil A. Wynn

Loyalty in Time of Trial: The African American Experience During World War I
Nina Mjagkij

Loyalty in Time of Trial

The African American Experience during World War I

Nina Mjagkij

ROWMAN & LITTLEFIELD PUBLISHERS, INC.
Lanham • Boulder • New York • Toronto • Plymouth, UK

Published by Rowman & Littlefield Publishers, Inc.
A wholly owned subsidiary of The Rowman & Littlefield Publishing Group, Inc.
4501 Forbes Boulevard, Suite 200, Lanham, Maryland 20706
http://www.rowmanlittlefield.com

Estover Road, Plymouth PL6 7PY, United Kingdom

British Library Cataloguing in Publication Information Available

Library of Congress Cataloging-in-Publication Data

Mjagkij, Nina, 1961-
Loyalty in the time of trial : the African American experience during World War I /
Nina Mjagkij.
p. cm.
Includes bibliographical references.
ISBN 978-0-7425-7043-6 (cloth : alk. paper) — ISBN 978-0-7425-7045-0 (electronic)
1. World War, 1914-1918—Participation, African American. 2. United States. Army—
African American troops—History—20th century. 3. African American soldiers—
History—20th century. 4. African Americans—Social conditions—20th century. 5.
Racism—United States—History—20th century. 6. United States—Race relations. I.
Title.
D639.N4M55 2010
940.3089'96073—dc22   2010047942

This book is dedicated to

Thomas A. Schroeder (1946–2009)
and
Scott J. Ecoff

~

Contents

Acknowledgments   ix

Chronology   xi

Introduction   xix

Chapter 1   The Land of Jim Crow: African Americans on
             the Eve of World War I   1

Chapter 2   From Field to Factory: The Wartime Migration
             of African Americans   23

Chapter 3   Fighting to Fight: The Struggle for Black
             Officers and Combat Soldiers   51

Chapter 4   Raising a Jim Crow Army: The Mobilization
             and Training of African American Troops   73

Chapter 5   Over There: African American Soldiers in France   99

Chapter 6   Closing Ranks? African Americans on the Home Front   121

Epilogue   Returning to Racism   141

Appendix   Documents   149

Notes   197

Bibliographic Essay   201

Index   211

About the Author   225

~

Acknowledgments

I would like to thank my friends and fellow scholars Jacqueline M. Moore and Andrew E. Kersten for reading drafts of the entire manuscript. Their comments and suggestions were invaluable. Equally important was a semester-long sabbatical from Ball State University. Two scholars in particular deserve credit for stimulating my interest in African Americans during World War I: Reinhard R Doerries at the Universität Hamburg and Roger Daniels at the University of Cincinnati. I am also grateful to Michael Joseph Hradesky at Ball State University, who created the maps for this book, and my friends Cynthia Lord, RN, for answering my obscure medical questions, and James Westheider, for sharing his knowledge of the Des Moines Officers Training Camp with me. Special thanks to my graduate assistants Allison Tourville and Stuart A. Keenan, who located numerous articles, books, and documents that were essential to my research. The editor at Rowman & Littlefield, Niels Aaboe, who suggested the title, and his assistants Michelle Cassidy, Sarah David, and Elisa Weeks, who tracked down photos and secured necessary permissions, were helpful in many ways. I am also thankful for the support of Belle T. Choate, Teri L. Merritt, and Dr. Irene Fox, who helped me navigate through the most trying time of my life. My family in Germany—Anatolij I. Mjagkij; Alea, Ben, Christian, and Tatjana Brixel; Steffi Zell; Helga Siebert; Gisela and Jürgen Höhn—though far away, you are always in my thoughts and in my heart. Last but not least, I would like to thank my friends Marion Baljöhr, Oscar Flores, Hadley and Brian Decker, Tre Eisenberg, John M. Glen, Kriste Lindenmeyer, Mollie Spillman, and Mary Syverson, who supported me every step of the way.

~

Chronology

1914
August
1   World War I starts in Europe
November
12   President Woodrow Wilson meets with William Monroe Trotter,
            editor of the *Boston Guardian*

1915
February
8   Release of D. W. Griffith's *The Birth of a Nation*
June
21   *Guinn v. U.S.* declares *grandfather clause* unconstitutional
Summer   Boll weevils and flooding devastate cotton crop in the South
            Great Migration begins
September
9   Carter G. Woodson launches Association for the Study of Ne-
            gro Life and History in Chicago
November
6   Oscar DePriest elected Chicago's first black alderman
14   Booker T. Washington dies
25   Ku Klux Klan reestablished on Stone Mountain, Georgia

1916

Marcus Garvey arrives in the United States.

May

15   Jesse Washington lynched in Waco, Texas

August

24–26   Amenia Conference seeks to reconcile factions among African Americans

November   NAACP appoints James Weldon Johnson as the organization's first field secretary for the South

December

9   National Urban League Conference on Great Migration

27–30   NAACP Conference "The Negro in Wartime"

1917

January

26   National Urban League Conference on Negro Migration, New York City

February

15   Joel E. Spingarn, white chairman of the NAACP's board of directors, publishes an open letter to the "Educated Colored Men of the United States," urging black men to sign up for training in a segregated officers training camp.

March

25   First Separate Battalion (Colored) of the District of Columbia National Guard receives orders to guard the nation's capital

April

6   United States enters World War I

26   President Wilson asks YMCA to provide services for soldiers

27   NAACP leaders meet with Secretary of War Newton D. Baker

May

14   NAACP votes to support the creation of a segregated officers training camp

17–19   NAACP's Washington Conference of black leaders to discuss role of African Americans in the war

18   President Wilson signs the Selective Service Act initiating the draft

19   The War Department announces creation of a black officers training camp

June

5   First draft call registers all men between the ages of twenty-one and thirty

15   The Colored Officers Training Camp opens at Fort Des Moines, Iowa

July

2   Riot in East St. Louis, Illinois

26   The Colored Medical Officers Training Camp opens at Fort Des Moines, Iowa

28   NAACP stages Silent Parade in New York City, 10,000 protest East St. Louis race riot

30   Colonel Charles Young, highest-ranking black officer, forced to retire

31   The War Department's troop mobilization plan provides for the training of black draftees as combat soldiers

August   A. Philip Randolph and Chandler Owen oppose U.S. participation in the war and launch the socialist journal *Messenger*

23   Violent clashes between white residents of Houston and members of the all-black Twenty-Fourth Infantry spark the Houston Mutiny

24   Secretary of War, Newton D. Baker approves Plan 6, limiting black soldiers to service in one combat division and minimal training in arms

31   Secretary of War, Newton D. Baker, meets with black leaders and concerned whites to discuss the role of blacks in the military

September

5   The Selective Service System announces separate "colored" and "white" draft quotas

11   Secretary of War Baker suspends the draft of African Americans

16   104 black physicians and 12 dentists receive their officers commissions at Fort Des Moines, Iowa

22   Secretary of War Baker announces resumption of black draft

October   First black draftees arrive in U.S. training camps
Riot at Camp Mills, New York
Armed black soldiers from Camp Wadsworth march into nearby Spartanburg, South Carolina

5	Baker appoints Emmett J. Scott, former secretary to Booker T. Washington, special adjutant to the secretary of war
15	639 black officers receive their commissions at Fort Des Moines, Iowa
	Congress passes Espionage Act

November
5	NAACP wins victory against segregated housing ordinances in *Buchanan v. Warley*
11	Houston Mutiny court-martial trial of sixty-three defendants
13	Colored Officers Training Camp closes at Fort Des Moines, Iowa
18	First black YWCA Hostess House opens at Camp Upton, New York
23	War Department orders creation of Ninety-third Infantry Division (Provisional)
29	War Department orders creation of Ninety-second Infantry Division

December
11	Secret hanging of thirteen participants in the Houston Mutiny

1918
January
1	369th Infantry Regiment, first black combat unit, arrives in France
29–31	National Urban League Conference on Negro Migration, New York City

February
18	Houston Mutiny court-martial trial of forty defendants

March	Riot at Camp Hill, Virginia,
28	Ballou issues Bulletin #35

April
4	Clifford L. Miller, first black chaplain, arrives at Camp Lee, Virginia
14	372nd Infantry Regiment arrives in France
20	U.S. Department of Labor, Division of Negro Economics, publishes *Negro Migration in 1916–17*

April 23–
June 10   370th and 371st Infantry Regiments arrive in France

May
1   U.S. Department of Labor appoints Dr. George E. Haynes to
            head Division of Negro Economics
16   Congress passes Sedition Act

June
5   Second draft call registers all men between the ages of twenty-
            one and thirty
6–22   Colonel Charles Young rides 497 miles on horseback from Ohio
            to Washington, D.C., to demonstrate that he is physically fit for
            active duty
June 18–
July 12   Ninety-Second Division arrives in France

June
19–21   Government sponsored conference of race leaders convenes in
            Washington, D.C.
24   W. E. B. Du Bois applies for captaincy commission in the Army
24–29   National Liberty Congress meets in Washington, D.C.

July   W. E. B. Du Bois publishes "Close Ranks" editorial
26   President Wilson condemns mob violence

August   Riot at Camp Meade, Maryland
4   A. Philip Randolph and Chandler Owen arrested in Cleveland
7   American Expeditionary Forces headquarters in Paris distrib-
            utes "Secret Information Concerning Black American
            Troops" instructing French officers how to deal with African
            Americans
12   Alice Dunbar-Nelson appointed as Field Representative of the
            Woman's Committee of the Council of National Defense
17   Riot at Camp Merritt, New Jersey
24   Third draft call registers all men between the ages of twenty-one
            and thirty
31   President Wilson commutes the death sentences of ten Houston
            Mutineers to prison terms

September	Riot at Newport News, Virginia
3	German propaganda leaflets target African American troops
12	Fourth draft call registers all men between the ages of eighteen and forty-five
16	Execution of six participants in the Houston Mutiny
	Committee on Public Information accredits Ralph Waldo Tyler as the only African American war correspondent
30	Ernest T. Atwell heads Division of Negro Activities in the U.S. Food Administration
October	Riot at Camp Lee, Virginia
November	
6	Charles Young reinstated
11	World War I ends
13	Army Nurses Corps admits black nurses
December	
9	Robert R. Moton and W. E. B. Du Bois arrive in France

1919

February	
9	370th Infantry Regiment arrives in New York
9-12	369th Infantry Regiment arrives in New York
11	10,000 black soldiers of the 368th, 371st, and 372nd returning from France arrive in Hoboken, New Jersey
17	Victory parade of 369th Regiment in Harlem
May	*Crisis* publishes "We Return Fighting"
5-6	National Conference on Lynching, New York City
June	
15	Emmett J. Scott publishes *Scott's Official History of the American Negro in the World War*
July	Commission on Interracial Cooperation founded
	Claude McKay's poem "If We Must Die" published in *Liberator*
1	Emmett J. Scott resigns from his post in the War Department
14	U.S. Army bans black troops from participating in Paris victory parade

27   Drowning of Eugene Williams triggers Chicago race riot
July 27–
August 1   Chicago race riot begins Red Summer of racial violence

~

Introduction

No, we have not gained all our rights, but we have gained rights and gained them rapidly and effectively by our loyalty in time of trial.

—W. E. B. Du Bois, *Crisis* (September 1918), 217

Prior to World War I, the loyalty of African Americans to their country had been severely tested. Reduced to chattel property during slavery and second-class citizenship in its aftermath, African Americans had little reason to support the nation in time of trial. Nonetheless, they had done so and served in arms during the American Revolution, the War of 1812, the Civil War, and the Spanish-American War. When the United States entered World War I in April of 1917, civil rights advocate W. E. B. Du Bois once again called on African Americans to be loyal to their country, despite the persistence of segregation and discrimination. Du Bois, like many other race leaders, had high hopes that the war would bring about racial equality. After all, President Woodrow Wilson had pledged "to make the world safe for democracy," and was America not part of the world? Racism, Du Bois believed, would have no place in a democratic postwar world, and he urged African Americans to "close ranks" and forgo the struggle for civil rights for the duration of the war.[1] Du Bois's call for black loyalty reflected the optimism of many race leaders who viewed the war as a chance to accelerate racial progress. Black men's willingness to die for their country, they anticipated, would force the nation to reconsider the second-class citizenship status of African Americans.

However, other African Americans were less hopeful. To them, the president's promise of democracy, sounded like smug hypocrisy. Disillusioned by years of racial oppression and the denial of democratic rights, they pointed out that Wilson—the first Southern president since the Civil War—had permitted the deliberate and systematic segregation of African Americans in civil service jobs as well as the introduction of a flood of racist bills into Congress. Moreover, his administration had made no efforts to stop discrimination, end mob violence, or overturn the Army's policy of segregating black troops. Wilson's performance in the years leading up to World War I, they insisted, was a clear indication that the federal government was not willing to grant African Americans anything in exchange for their wartime support. The war, they concluded, was a white man's war from which African Americans had nothing to gain.

Most African Americans shared neither Du Bois's optimism nor the pessimism of those who opposed black participation in the war. The majority of blacks, particularly those who lived in the rural South, were initially indifferent. For them, the war and the complexities of European politics had little meaning. The assassination of some Austro-Hungarian archduke in a strange place called Sarajevo was of no immediate importance to their daily lives. However, that changed when the government initiated the draft in May of 1917, which required all young men, regardless of race, to register for military service. More than 2.2 million black men reported to local draft boards and nearly 370,000 of them were inducted into the Army. Since failure to comply with the Selective Service Act carried stiff penalties, black voices of dissent became less pronounced.

Race leaders who viewed black military service as an important step toward racial equality celebrated the draft as an acknowledgment of black manhood and citizenship. Yet, they remained concerned about the extent of and capacity in which the participation of black men would be permitted in the nation's defense. African Americans had limited opportunity to serve in arms, due to a military policy that dated back to the Civil War. At the start of that war, the Lincoln administration had opposed arming African Americans, largely to appease the slaveholding states of the upper South—Missouri, Kentucky, Maryland, and Delaware—which had sided with the Union. However, pressure from abolitionists and military necessity had forced the administration to reconsider its policy. In 1862, Congress authorized the recruitment of all-black regiments, and in the following year the War Department created the Bureau of Colored Troops, formally introducing military segregation. Eventually, 186,000 black soldiers, constituting roughly 10 percent of the Union Army, served under white command in segregated units.

After the Civil War, the military reduced the size of its peacetime standing army; however, it maintained its Jim Crow policy. As a result, African Americans were limited to service in four all-black regiments: the Twenty-Fourth and Twenty-Fifth Infantry and the Ninth and Tenth Cavalry. In the late nineteenth century, the black cavalry units protected white settlers from Indian attacks on the western frontier, where they acquired the nickname "Buffalo Soldiers." In 1898, when America fought against Spain during the "Splendid Little War," the black regiments took part in the expedition to Cuba, and in the following years black troops helped to suppress the Filipino independence struggle. By the eve of World War I, a total of 10,000 professional black soldiers served in the Ninth and Tenth Cavalry and the Twenty-Fourth and Twenty-Fifth Infantry Regiments, mostly in remote posts in the American West. In addition, 5,000 black men had joined segregated National Guard units in Tennessee, Massachusetts, Maryland, Ohio, Illinois, Connecticut, New York, and the District of Columbia, and another 5,000 worked as cooks, waiters, and coal handlers in the Navy.

However, when the nation entered World War I, the Army did not mobilize the professional black troops for service in Europe but assigned them to the Mexican border, Hawaii, and the Philippines. Likewise, members of the all-black National Guard units received their first service assignments in the United States. Du Bois and other race leaders, who had urged African Americans to support the nation's war effort, were alarmed by the Army's failure to use black soldiers in combat. Moreover, they were troubled when the military relegated the majority of the black draftees to service and labor battalions and forcefully retired Colonel Charles Young, the highest-ranking of only three black officers. African Americans, they concluded, could not demonstrate their patriotism or their courage under fire, if the Army excluded black soldiers from fighting in the front lines or leading men into battle.

Determined to use the war to showcase black loyalty, race leaders pressured Secretary of War Newton D. Baker to give black soldiers and officers a chance to prove themselves in battle. Baker consulted with his staff, who advised him not to train black men in arms, claiming that African Americans lacked the necessary intellect and discipline to become good soldiers. Some Southern whites also voiced objections. Baker weighed his options and caved to black demands. Disregarding the recommendations of his staff, he created two black combat divisions and a black officers training camp and appointed a black man as special racial advisor. Many African Americans applauded Baker's actions. Black men's sacrifices on the battlefield, they hoped, would reinforce black claims for equal rights once the war ended.

Race leaders were equally determined to demonstrate black patriotism and loyalty at home. Urging black civilians to put aside their demands for civil rights while the nation was at war, they reminded them: *"first your County, then your Rights!"*[2] Most African Americans did "close ranks" and contributed money, time, and resources to the nation's war effort. They staged patriotic rallies and supported the various war bond drives. They raised funds for social services organizations, including the Young Men's and Young Women's Christian Associations, which catered to the needs of the black troops in training camps in the United States and in the trenches of France. They organized entertainment for the soldiers on leave, rolled bandages for the Red Cross, knitted socks for the men in the trenches, planted victory gardens, and participated in food conservation campaigns. In addition, 400,000 rural black Southerners took jobs in defense industry centers in the North and helped to furnish the nation and its European allies with military equipment and other necessary supplies.

Although African Americans did not demand civil rights in exchange for their loyalty, they did insist that the government protect them from racial violence and speak out against discrimination. When a deadly race riot erupted in East St. Louis three months after the United States entered the war, African Americans took to the streets. The National Association for the Advancement of Colored People (NAACP), the nation's leading civil rights group, organized the first black protest march in the history of the United States. Drawing on popular wartime rhetoric, protestors challenged the government to address the discrepancy between America's war aims and the persistence of racism in the United States.

The black press, which played a crucial role in publicizing African American demands, used the same strategy to pressure the government to address racial grievances. America's racial practices, black editors insisted, were inconsistent with the nation's democratic ideals. Racist violence and discrimination, they pointed out, undermined black loyalty and patriotism, which endangered home-front unity, demoralized black soldiers, and threatened national security. Afraid that German agents would attempt to capitalize on black discontent, government officials initially tried to stifle black protest. They threatened black editors with censorship and harassed others who were critical of America's racial policy. However, growing concerns about declining black morale and fears of racial unrest also forced the Wilson administration to deal with black complaints. Many African Americans were hopeful that black loyalty had indeed paid off.

However, when World War I ended in November of 1918, African Americans quickly realized that the nation was not willing to grant them civil rights. As the military demobilized, many black workers lost their jobs to returning white veterans, lynchings increased, and numerous race riots erupted in cities throughout the country. African Americans were disappointed. They had helped "to make the world safe democracy," but, despite their loyalty in time of trial, democratic rights eluded them in their own country. Some disillusioned African Americans gave up all hopes for civil rights and instead focused on strengthening the black community. They patronized black businesses, organized black labor unions, and established black self-help groups. Yet others emerged from the war with a renewed determination to challenge Jim Crow. Proud of their home-front support and military service, they joined the ranks of the NAACP, which attracted an ever-growing number of African Americans in the postwar decade and helped pave the way for the modern civil rights movement.

∼

CHAPTER ONE

The Land of Jim Crow

African Americans on the Eve of World War I

In the years prior to World War I, racism, discrimination, and segregation shaped the lives of African Americans in all parts of the country. In the South, where nearly 90 percent of the nation's 10 million African Americans lived, the black population endured racial conditions that did not differ much from slavery. Rural African Americans in particular, who made up almost 79 percent of the black Southern population, were trapped in a system of economic exploitation, political disfranchisement, legal oppression, and violent repression. African Americans living in the Southern cities enjoyed a higher degree of personal freedom, but, just like the rural black population, they lacked the right to vote, did not enjoy legal equality, and were subject to intimidation and violence. In the North, East, and West, which were home to 10 percent of the nation's black population, the majority of African Americans eked out a living, predominantly in cities. Segregation and discrimination relegated them to low-paying jobs and confined them to substandard housing in decrepit neighborhoods. In many states, they had the right to vote, but because of their small numbers, they lacked any political power.

The poor conditions of African Americans, particularly in the rural South, were largely the product of government neglect in the years following the Civil War. The Thirteenth Amendment, adopted in 1865, had freed 4 million slaves, but the federal government had failed to provide them with financial resources to ensure their economic independence from white Southerners. With no money to move North, many African Americans

stayed in the South. Some relocated to Southern cities, while others remained on the plantations where they had worked as slaves. They dismantled
the former slave quarters and used the materials to built small one-room
wooden cabins. Frequently, these were no more than dilapidated shacks with
dirt floors and leaking roofs. They lacked windows and proper furniture and
did little more than provide shelter from the South's sweltering heat or the
occasional torrential rain storms. Here they raised their children and those
of friends who had been sold to other parts of the South prior to the Civil
War. Often the only means of support available to African Americans in the
South was to farm for white plantation owners who had lost their slave workforce but not their lands as a result of the Civil War.

By 1910, nearly 76 percent of black Southern farmers worked as sharecroppers. Under this system, white plantation owners rented parcels of
their land to the former slaves, who promised to pay at the end of the harvest season a share of their crop in lieu of rent. However, until the black
sharecroppers could harvest any crop, they needed seeds, tools, and equipment as well as food and clothing for their families. With no money in their
pockets, they were forced to conduct business with the white landowner,
who provided them with necessary supplies in exchange for putting a lien
on their crop, sometimes charging as much 60 percent interest. Thus, by
the time the black farmer harvested his crop, he owed the white planter not
only a share of his crop for rent, but also for the items he had purchased in
the plantation store. Since white plantation owners routinely defrauded
and overcharged African Americans, black farmers often owed them more
money than their crops generated. As a result, black sharecroppers entered
the new planting season with debt, which incurred high interest rates and
ensured that they owed white planters even more money at the end of the
following year's harvest. Sharecropping and the crop-lien-system kept the
black farmers in perpetual debt and trapped in economic bondage. Unable
to pay off their debts and gain financial independence, black sharecroppers
were bound to the land of white plantation owners, just like the slaves had
been prior to the Civil War.

Sharecropping was subsistence farming that depended on the work of all
family members, including children and women. Children usually performed
various household chores. They helped clean the house, assisted with the
preparation of meals, did the laundry, took care of the younger children, fed
chickens, brought water to their parents and siblings who worked in the field,
and, depending on their age, helped with the harvest. Struggling to support
their families, African American women continued to do what they had
done during slavery. They picked cotton or tobacco with their husbands,

raised their children, took care of their households, and worked as nannies, cooks, maids, or laundresses for white families. In 1910, nearly 97 percent of all black women workers were farm laborers, personal servants, or laundresses. The little amount of money black women earned while working for whites helped alleviate some of the worst suffering of sharecropping families, but it did not end their financial hardship.

The sharecropping system caused appalling economic conditions, which also had a detrimental impact on the health of rural black Southerners. Facing insurmountable debts, black sharecroppers could not afford nutritious food. Their average diet consisted of bread, beans, corn, grits, cornmeal, molasses, yams, okra, collard or mustard greens, and occasionally a piece of pork, chicken, fish, opossum, or raccoon. The food was rich in starches but often short on essential vitamins and proteins. To supplement the meals of their families, black women who worked as domestic servants often took table scraps or castoffs from their white employers—a common practice known as "pan-toting." Nonetheless, the diet of black sharecroppers lacked many essential nutrients.

Poor nutrition took its toll among black Southerners, weakening their bodies, lowering their life expectancy, and raising their morbidity and mortality rate. Many children of black sharecroppers were so hungry that they drank enormous amounts of water to quench their hunger, while others cried themselves to sleep at night. Poverty not only led to inadequate diets that made black Southerners more susceptible to deadly diseases, but also contributed to poor hygiene and sanitation, which further undermined their health. Tuberculosis, hookworms, syphilis, gonorrhea, dysentery, pellagra, rickets, and diphtheria, all caused by poor living conditions, had devastating consequences for rural black Southerners. When epidemics such as smallpox, cholera, typhus, and scarlet and yellow fever swept through the South, they resulted in heavy death tolls among African Americans.

The physical well-being of rural black Southerners was further compromised by the lack of health care and medical services. No public health service offered educational outreach programs that instructed them about proper nutrition, sanitation, and hygiene or the prevention of diseases. Those who became sick and had to seek professional treatment had to travel to towns and cities. There they encountered a health care system that provided only limited services for African Americans. Most white doctors refused to see black patients, and white hospitals either excluded them or treated them in inferior facilities, including basements, attics, and utility sheds. By 1900, only 2,000 black physicians and dentists as well as 40 black hospitals served the nation's nearly 9 million African Americans, however, most were not within reach of the majority of rural black Southerners. Given the lack of adequate nutrition, the prevalence of poor sanitation and hygiene, and limited access to health care providers, it is not surprising that African Americans had a high infant mortality rate and a life expectancy of only thirty-nine years in 1910, compared to fifty years for whites.

Health problems, caused by malnutrition and a lack of sanitation, not only cut short the lives of African Americans, but also undermined their efforts to obtain an education. Learning on an empty stomach, however, was not the only detriment to education. Black schools, particularly in the rural South, were notoriously underfunded and ill-equipped. Prior to World War I, African Americans represented 11 percent of the U.S. population, but they received only 2 percent of the nation's school funds. Many Southern states spent an annual average of $3.81 for each black student enrolled in the public schools, whereas spending for white students averaged $9.37 per year. Salaries of teachers also reflected a racial divide. In 1916, black teachers in the South earned less than half the salary of white teachers. Classes of black students met in poorly constructed one-room school houses, which did not differ much from the shacks the children called home. High student-teacher ratios and outdated instructional materials and equipment further aggravated educational inequities.

The planting and harvest season proved to be another roadblock to education. When farmers needed all hands in the fields, black school attendance suffered and schooling often came to a halt. In 1914–1915, Southern black children attended an average of thirty-five days of classes during the entire school year. Although economic necessity left the sharecropping parents little choice but to use their children as workers, they were nonetheless troubled by the effect it had on their schooling. Education, African American parents hoped, would provide their children with the training and skills necessary to earn a living and break free from the shackles of sharecropping. However, the poverty that was inherent in the sharecropping system slowed the progress of education among African Americans in the South. By 1910, less than 45 percent of rural black Southerners under the age of ten were enrolled in schools, and more than 33 percent of those aged ten or older were illiterate. Without adequate schooling, their future looked grim. Just like their parents, they were doomed to a life of sharecropping, which kept them in utter poverty.

While whites used the sharecropping system to re-enslave black Southerners economically, they also deprived them of their political freedom by disfranchising them. In 1870, Reconstruction Congress had ratified the Fifteenth Amendment, granting African American men the right to vote.

However, Southern black political participation was short lived. In 1872, a General Amnesty restored the right of office holding to virtually all former Confederates, sparking a systematic white backlash. White Redeemers came to power, seeking to reestablish white supremacy by reversing the political gains African Americans had made in the aftermath of the Civil War. They reapportioned voting districts with predominantly black residents, a process known as gerrymandering; set up voting booths in areas hard to reach for African Americans; amended state constitutions to disfranchise blacks; initiated complicated registration and voting procedures; and introduced numerous provisions designed to bar blacks from voting. Among the most notorious were the "grandfather clause," which stipulated that only those men whose grandfathers had enjoyed the right to vote were permitted to cast a ballot; the "literacy test," which allegedly tested the ability to read and interpret a passage from the state constitution in order to qualify for the vote; and the "poll tax," which charged a fee for the privilege of voting. By 1902, all of the Southern states had adopted poll taxes. Since none of these provisions used race as a factor to disqualify blacks from voting, they did not violate the Fifteenth Amendment, at least not in a strictly legal sense. But even when whites blatantly violated the constitutional rights of black voters, the Supreme Court did nothing to defend them. While black men had gained the right to vote, Southern state restrictions made it virtually impossible for them to do so. By the late nineteenth century, the number of Southern black voters reached a nadir, and by 1901 the last remaining Southern black congressman left Washington, D.C. It would take more than seventy years for the next black Southerner to be elected to Congress.

For many white men, black political empowerment represented the ultimate humiliation. In an effort to regain control of the South and reassert their manhood, they used violence and intimidation to strip black men of their masculinity. They burned down the farms of African Americans, flogged the men, raped the women, and tortured and killed those who challenged discrimination, segregation, or black disfranchisement. Lynching, the ritualized slaying of African Americans, reached unprecedented proportions in the late nineteenth century. Some lynchings were spontaneous acts of atrocities committed by small groups of whites under the cover of darkness. Yet others were elaborate public spectacles. Local newspapers advertised upcoming lynchings, and there were special excursion trains to the events, which attracted food and souvenir vendors who catered to thousands of spectators, including women and children. Exuding the leisurely atmosphere of county fairs, replete with family picnics, these public slaughters offered their audiences the thrill of witnessing the prolonged torture and death of a black victim, often inflicted by hanging or burning at the stake. Spectators had the opportunity to have their picture taken with the victim or even purchase parts of the charred body. In many cases, local sheriffs—who had been elected by the white majority with the mandate of upholding white supremacy—not only condoned, but actively participated in the lynchings.

The majority of lynch victims were men, though lynch mobs also targeted women, including pregnant women, and less frequently children. Among the most popular justifications for lynchings were accusations of homicide and allegations that a black man had assaulted a white woman, a charge that covered a broad spectrum of offenses ranging from making improper eye contact to rape. Lynch mobs, claiming that black men were lust-driven beasts with an uncontrollable appetite for white women, often tortured and at times castrated their victims—literally emasculating black men—before killing them. For white men the public display of violence in the defense of white womanhood was an opportunity to demonstrate their manliness. But the public nature of lynching served another purpose. It was a warning to all African Americans that white Southerners would not tolerate any semblance of racial equality. Estimates of the number of victims who died at the hands of lynch mobs vary greatly, ranging from 10,000 between 1878 and 1898 to 2,000 between 1882 and 1901. While figures indicate that the number of lynchings declined in the decade prior to World War I, white mob rule continued to terrorize African Americans in the early twentieth century.

In addition to economic exploitation, political disfranchisement, intimidation, and violence, white Southerners used the legal system to reinvent slavery. Vagrancy laws, which empowered local sheriffs to arrest drifters— those who had no permanent residency or employment—singled out black men. Southern courts sentenced them to long prison terms, placed them on chain gangs, and put them to work to rebuild Southern streets, roads, and public buildings. Many times, corrupt prison wardens supplemented their meager incomes and leased convicts to private companies. The convict-lease system not only provided Southern white business owners with a cheap workforce, but also served as a deterrent for African Americans who considered leaving the plantations.

Other laws sought to create a racial order that placed whites at the top and blacks at the very bottom of Southern society. These so-called Jim Crow laws mandated the complete segregation of the races and at times the exclusion of African Americans. White Southern lawmakers segregated schools, public parks, pools, prisons, drinking fountains, and waiting rooms as well as steamboats, trains, and trolley cars. They excluded African Americans from white hotels, restaurants, shops, theaters, hospitals, cemeteries, public libraries, and schools and banned interracial marriages. In some cities courts used separate Bibles to swear in witnesses and in others prostitutes worked in segregated brothels. White businesses that catered to African Americans forced black patrons to use separate entrances, elevators, and service windows. Signs, indicating "White Only" or "Colored" or "Negro," became popular manifestations of the Jim Crow South and demonstrated white Southern resolve to resist any notions of black equality. Blacks would be free, but the Southern legal system would ensure that whites would control them. When African Americans challenged the constitutionality of the Jim Crow laws, the Supreme Court sided with the Southern states. In the infamous *Plessy v. Ferguson* (1896), the justices ruled that segregation did not violate the constitutional rights of African Americans, arguing that separate facilities were not inherently unequal. Thus, African Americans were free but had no economic power, no political rights, and no legal recourse.

Facing dreadful conditions, many rural black Southerners sought refuge in their churches. For a few hours each Sunday black sharecroppers could escape the unbearable realities of their lives and find comfort among those who suffered the same plight. Away from the scrutiny of whites, parishioners gathered to hear their ministers preach the Gospel and to meet with neighbors and friends. Their preachers promised them salvation from the poverty and violence that consumed their existence and assured them of a better afterlife in heaven. But sermons were also celebrations of life, expressed by emotional worship that was punctuated by singing, shouting, and clapping. The churches were an important source of strength for African Americans, offering them hope as well as spiritual, moral, and emotional support. Moreover, they provided the black community with social spaces, where those who farmed in isolation for much of the week could interact with others. Religious ceremonies such as baptisms, weddings, and funerals further extended opportunities to socialize, while Sunday schools sought to furnish children with religious and moral guidance as well as education. Nonetheless, the churches provided only a temporary refuge from the racial violence, economic exploitation, political disfranchisement, and legal oppression that permeated the lives of all black Southerners.

Compared to the rural black Southern population, African Americans who lived in the nation's cities generally enjoyed a higher degree of personal freedom as well as a higher standard of living. In 1910, more than 83 percent of the Northern black population and about 18 percent of black Southerners lived in urban centers. By 1910, a dozen cities, eight of them in the South, had a black population in excess of 40,000 (see table 1.1).

Table 1.1   Cities with Largest Black Population, 1910

Southern Cities		Northern and Western Cities	
Washington, D.C.	94,446	New York City	91,709
New Orleans	89,262	Philadelphia	84,459
Baltimore	84, 749	Chicago	44,103
Birmingham	52,306	St. Louis	43,960
Memphis	52,411	Pittsburgh	25,623
Atlanta	51, 902	Kansas City	23, 566
Richmond, VA	46, 733	Indianapolis	21, 816
Louisville	40,522	Cincinnati	19,639
Nashville	36, 523	Boston	13,564
Savannah	33,246	Columbus, OH	12,739

Many of the black urban residents were rural migrants who had managed to break free from the oppressive sharecropping system through hard work, thrift, and often sheer luck. Between 1890 and 1910, approximately 200,000 African Americans migrated from the South to the North and West, settling primarily in cities. The majority of these pre–World War I migrants came from the border states and the upper South, including Maryland, Kentucky, Missouri, Virginia, Delaware, and Tennessee. Many more, however, headed for the cities of the South, where smaller numbers of European immigrants created less labor competition. As a result of this migration, the Southern black urban population grew by 34 percent in the first decade of the twentieth century.

Moving from the countryside to the cities, African Americans hoped to improve the quality of their lives. The urban centers lured the migrants with the promise of a less racially oppressive climate, enhanced economic opportunities, better schools for their children, and access to health care. In addition, they offered a variety of conveniences including restaurants and stores and commercial entertainment venues such as theaters, pool halls, juke joints, and taverns. In addition, the cities were home to vibrant black communities that supported a variety of churches, mutual aid societies, fraternal orders, and social clubs as well as black-owned businesses.

Although city life often represented a considerable improvement over rural sharecropping, black urban residents were not immune to discrimination, segregation, and racial violence. Racism forced most black city residents into low-paying unskilled and menial occupations that often entailed backbreaking, dirty, and dangerous work. African American men loaded and unloaded trains, ships, and warehouses; built roads and railroads; hauled furniture; worked as janitors, porters, gardeners, coachmen, grave diggers, butlers, and waiters; and performed various odd jobs that required physical strength and endurance. Only a few worked as skilled artisans, such as shoe-makers, carpenters, or blacksmiths. In Northern cities, they found additional employment as dining car attendants for railroad companies and as service personnel in white-owned hotels. Heavy industries in the North generally barred black men and only employed them temporarily to replace striking white workers. However, as soon as white workers returned to the factories, black strikebreakers lost their jobs.

The majority of African American women who worked in the cities, North or South, found jobs in the service industry. They worked as cooks, nannies, maids, and laundresses. Doing white people's laundry was poorly paid and exhausting work, but, in the eyes of many black women, better than working as servants inside white homes. White employers often expected their domestics to serve them around the clock, which left black women little time to spend with their own children. Moreover, since whites required their constant presence, black domestics frequently had to live in the servant quarters of white households, which afforded them little privacy and at times subjected them to unwanted sexual advances from their male employers. As one black nursemaid complained, "nearly all white men take, and expect to take, undue liberties with their colored female servants—not only the fathers, but in many cases the sons also."[1] Sexual harassment was so common that many black parents did not permit their young daughters to work in white households. However, working in white households did have advantages. The "service pan," the general term for kitchen leftovers, became a main source of food for many black homes. Whether African Americans worked as common laborers in construction, washed and ironed the laundry of whites, or found employment as live-in domestics, paltry wages and long hours characterized the work of the vast majority of the black urban residents.

Those who lived in the cities used much of the money they earned to pay for overpriced housing. In 1910, only 23 percent of African Americans owned their homes. For the majority, living conditions in the cities did not differ much from those in rural areas. Black migrants who had left the cotton and tobacco fields for the cities, traded in their dilapidated one-room wooden sharecropping shacks for decrepit shanties in the South or run-down multiple-family dwellings in the North. Particularly in the South, buildings often lacked sewage connections, adequate fresh water supply, and proper ventilation. One sanitary inspector of a Southern city described conditions as "a crying disgrace to any civilized people."[2] Unsanitary conditions were aggravated by overcrowding and the fact that black homes were usually located in the most undesirable areas of the cities, often in or near red-light districts, adjacent to railroads or cemeteries, or close to manufacturing plants.

Municipal governments took little interest in improving housing conditions in black residential areas. Many black neighborhoods lacked adequate police and fire protection and sanitary services. Garbage accumulated outside the buildings and in the back alleys, attracting flies and rats. In the Southern cities, where many of the streets were not paved, roads became impassible during rainstorms, leaving behind pools of stagnant water that provided ideal breeding grounds for mosquitoes. Poorly serviced outhouses added their distinct scent to the filth and stench that characterized many of the black residential areas. Not surprisingly, diseases often plagued black neighborhoods. Epidemics spread rapidly, due to appalling unsanitary conditions and the close proximity of residents, whose weakened immune system was the product of nutrient-deficient diets.

Despite poor housing conditions, white landlords charged their black tenants outrageously high rents. African Americans had no option but to pay the asking price, because they could not find housing elsewhere, either because whites refused to rent to them in predominantly white neighborhoods or as a result of municipal codes. By 1910, a number of Southern cities with large black populations—such as New Orleans, Baltimore, Richmond, Louisville, and Atlanta—passed residential segregation ordinances to ensure that African American housing would be legally confined to specific parts of the cities. In the North, white property owners organized neighborhood improvement associations to prevent African Americans from taking up residence. Moreover, they resorted to the restrictive covenant, a clause which they inserted into a property sale contract that prevented home owners from renting or selling to African Americans. By the early twentieth century, housing discrimination increasingly pushed African Americans into well-defined urban areas, which led to the emergence of ghettos. In New York City African Americans lived in "San Juan Hill" and Harlem, in Chicago along State Street, in Philadelphia in the Seventh Ward, in Washington, D.C., in the city's northwest neighborhood, and in Baltimore on Druid Hill Avenue. Since space was limited and rents were high, many black city residents took in boarders to make ends meet. As the population density in black neighborhoods increased, housing conditions deteriorated further and sanitary problems worsened.

Whether North or South, black city residents who ventured outside their squalid neighborhoods, faced discrimination and segregation. In the North, where African Americans constituted a relatively small portion of the overall population, manifestations of racism were less obvious than in the urban South. In many Northern cities, restaurants, theaters, hotels, hospitals, and public schools did not segregate African Americans in the prewar years.

However, discrimination was on the rise. As the number of black city residents grew, African Americans found it harder to obtain adequate housing, white businesses ceased to serve black patrons, and incidents of police harassment increased. In Southern cities, blatant discrimination dominated the black urban experience. White businesses either did not cater to African Americans or provided them with segregated and inferior services. Trolley cars relegated them to the back and movie theaters to the balcony. Municipal libraries and pools excluded them and at post offices, town halls, court houses, banks, and stores, they had to wait in line until clerks finished serving white patrons. When African Americans encountered white pedestrians in the streets they had to move off the sidewalks, and when whites talked to them they addressed them as "Boy," "Uncle," "Mammy," or "nigger."

In addition to these daily degradations, black city residents lived with the constant fear of racial violence. Although lynchings happened less frequently in urban than in rural areas, the cities were not safe havens from the wrath of white racists. Lynchings did occur in cities and, at times, racial violence erupted into full-scale riots, in Southern as well as Northern cities. In 1898, escalating racial tensions exploded in Wilmington, North Carolina. A white mob took to the streets, randomly killing more than 20 African Americans and forcing nearly 1,500 black residents into exile. In 1900 a white mob, assisted by policemen attacked blacks in New York. In 1906, nearly 10,000 whites ran amok for four days in Atlanta, burning and looting, killing 25 African Americans, wounding hundreds of others, and forcing about 1,000 black residents to flee the city. Even Springfield, Illinois, hometown of President Abraham Lincoln, became the site of racial violence. In 1908, acting on rumors that a black man had raped a white woman, an armed white mob killed 8 African Americans and destroyed the town's black neighborhood, forcing 2,000 black residents to flee.

Regardless of racial violence, Jim Crow facilities, inadequate housing, and poor working conditions, cities continued to attract growing numbers of rural migrants in the years prior to World War I. Although working in the cities did not seem to offer much of an economic advantage over sharecropping, there was a crucial difference: urban workers earned money—even though the amount was usually very small—whereas sharecroppers earned debt.

The urban shanties may have been run-down and the tenements tightly packed, but for the migrants they signaled personal freedom. Living in the city meant not living under the watchful eyes of the white plantation owner and not having to submit to his economic oppression or his verbal, physical, and sexual abuse. City life offered ample opportunities for social interactions and, at least in the Northern cities, the chance to participate in local and state politics. The physical conditions of black urban neighborhoods may have been poor, but there was strength in numbers, which instilled a sense of communal fellowship and allowed black residents to live with a certain degree of dignity and self-respect. And despite the dreadful poverty, black city residents, more so than their rural counterparts, were likely to get medical attention, wear decent clothing, and send their children to school.

Not all African Americans lived in decrepit dwellings, performed menial labor for whites, or lacked education. A small group of black elites enjoyed relative prosperity, which provided them with the means to live very comfortably. These so-called "Aristocrats of Color" were descendants of the small communities of free blacks that had existed prior to the Civil War. They were lighter skinned—many of them were the offspring of white masters—better educated, and had more money than the majority of black urban residents. Prior to the Civil War, when the vast majority of African Americans still labored as slaves, they had started to accumulate wealth through hard work, wise investments, and sometimes with the help of their white fathers.

The "Aristocrats of Color" lived in stately mansions in respectable well-kept black neighborhoods and in some cities in black enclaves in predominantly white residential areas. Their homes had indoor bathrooms, ornate fireplaces, and spacious parlors, which they decorated with elegant furniture and fine art. They employed domestic servants, in the South largely African Americans, but in the North they often hired recent immigrants from Germany or Scandinavia. They dined on gourmet food, drank expensive wine, owned exquisite china, wore high-quality tailor-made clothing, listened to classical music, and read the great works of world literature. They took pride in their sophistication and cultural refinement and fostered the same in their children. They hired governesses and tutors—some of them white—to instruct their children and teach them the rules of proper etiquette. And they sent their children to private academies, finishing schools, and select universities that emphasized classical curricula, including instruction in Latin and French. In the summers they toured Europe or vacationed with families and friends in Saratoga Springs, New York; Newport, Virginia; and Atlantic City, where black-owned inns provided room and board for the vacationers. Others headed to Maryland's Arundel-on-the Bay, developed by Charles Douglass, the son of famous abolitionist Frederick Douglass; and Michigan's Idlewild, also known as the "Black Eden." Both were exclusive black holiday resorts that served as the summer playgrounds for the upper class.

Whether vacationing at a resort or staying at home, the black elites liked to socialize with their peers. They hosted musical recitals, receptions, formal teas, and lavish balls. When they entertained, they usually did so in the privacy of their homes, in black-owned clubs, or in private ballrooms, to avoid exposure to racial discrimination and segregation. When they did appear in public, they were always impeccably dressed, walked with poise, and generally exuded an air of respectability and refinement that was beyond reproach. The public image they tried to convey was that of a perfect gentleman or lady, because "the way to defeat racism," they believed, "was to obey every rule of proper behavior to the letter, to offer no provocation for discrimination."[3]

Not surprisingly, members of the black elite often looked down on lower-class African Americans, blaming them for reinforcing racist prejudices and stereotypes. They claimed that their crude and vulgar conduct, their loud demeanor, their lack of personal hygiene, and their cheap clothes, were responsible for much of the racial discrimination that all members of the race had to endure. Some black elites, driven by a sense of *noblesse oblige*—which held that their privileged position in society obligated them to help the less fortunate rise to their level of respectability and sophistication—tried to aid and reform lower-class blacks. Others, for less self-serving reasons, launched a variety of philanthropic and charitable efforts. Particularly upper-class women, in conjunction with their churches, became involved in organizing neighborhood health clinics, kindergarten facilities, and educational classes, and providing homes for the elderly, orphans, and single mothers.

Yet other members of the black elite were afraid that the inappropriate behavior and the careless appearances of the black masses would undermine their own status in society. They tried to avoid associating with the lower classes and instead retreated into an exclusive world, populated by the privileged few. They pursued intellectual stimulation in literary and historical societies, honed their oratorical skills in debating clubs, joined secret and fraternal orders, and attended churches that did not invite the noisy emotional participation of congregants. And, just like European aristocrats, they guarded the integrity of their group and selected their spouses from the ranks of the nation's leading black families. Because they viewed themselves as members of a class that had descended from a common lineage, they placed more emphasis on proper pedigree than on money. Those who shared their heritage, even if they had lost their wealth, were nonetheless members of their elite circle, and those who did not, like the emerging black middle-class, they eyed with suspicion.

The black middle-class consisted of those who had risen to prominence and acquired wealth following the Civil War. This group was largely composed of professionals, such as doctors, teachers, and lawyers, as well as businessmen who catered to the growing black urban populations. By 1900, more than 40,000 black business owners offered a variety of services, particularly in the cities of the South. Some of them had made a fortune in real estate speculations, but many more had earned it through hard work and frugal living. Many of them had started out working for whites, until they had saved enough money to open their own businesses. These businesses not only catered to the growing number of black city residents but also provided them with a variety of employment opportunities and helped to infuse capital into the black communities. African American entrepreneurs ran their businesses with the help of black workers, managers, and office clerks; they advertised their products and services in black newspapers; and employed black lawyers, barbers, undertakers, and domestic servants. The majority of black-owned businesses were small grocery and retail stores, followed by barbershops, publishing and printing houses, funeral homes, and saloons. Other profitable ventures included banks and building and loan associations, which provided African Americans with the necessary capital to launch their own businesses and build their own homes. In 1913, African Americans could open accounts, deposit money, and apply for loans in sixty-two black-owned banks, most of them located in the South. However, by far the largest black enterprises were insurance companies, boasting combined assets of $7,500,000. Among the most successful ones was the North Carolina Mutual Life Insurance Company, which used the investments of its more than 100,000 policyholders to help establish a hospital, a library, and three newspapers in Durham, North Carolina.

While black business leaders provided a crucial source of wealth, black professionals rendered critical services for the African American community. Teachers, doctors, and lawyers made up the core of the black middle class. In 1910, there were 34,000 black teachers working in the nation's public schools, including 141 exclusively black high schools. In the same year, the census recorded 3,077 physicians, 478 dentists, and 779 lawyers, two of whom were women.

Editors who published black newspapers and journalists who worked for them were also part of the black middle class and played an important role in the African American communities. In the early twentieth century more than 150 black newspapers reported about racial conditions throughout the country, celebrated the achievements of African Americans, advertised black businesses, and exposed lynchings and race riots.

Many of the professionals had received their training at what we now call Historically Black Colleges and Universities (HBCUs), which had emerged in the aftermath of the Civil War. The HBCUs were founded by the missionary associations of white Northern churches and, to a lesser extent, by black denominations, which had only limited financial resources. In addition, a handful of independent nondenominational schools as well as several state-funded agricultural, mechanical, and teachers colleges offered degrees in higher education. By 1915, nearly 100 black colleges, many of them staffed by white administrators and white faculty, served the nation's African American population. However, only one-third of the schools offered college-level courses and only two of them—Meharry Medical College in Nashville and Howard University in Washington, D.C.—trained black physicians and dentists. Instead, many of the HBCUs focused on vocational training in order to provide their students with useful skills that would make them more competitive in the job market. Others, known as normal schools—a quaint term for teacher training institutes—churned out large numbers of teachers to meet the high demand for education among African Americans, particularly in the South.

The decision to emphasize vocational training rather than college-level work was largely the product of racism. In 1890, a group of white philanthropists had gathered at Lake Mohonk, New York, to discuss the so-called Negro Question. Without soliciting the input of African Americans, the men concluded that industrial education was best suited to aid blacks in their struggle for improvement. Many of the white philanthropists as well as school administrators and faculty, believed that blacks simply did not have the intellectual capacity to succeed in academic courses. Others were convinced that the most immediate need of African Americans was to gain practical skills, which would allow them to break out of the exploitive sharecropping system. Nonetheless, some black schools tried to offer a challenging liberal arts curriculum that encouraged students to excel in scientific and academic subjects. But, their work was hampered by insufficient funding, which resulted in outdated equipment, inadequate supplies, and faculty that often lacked proper preparation.

Despite financial troubles and academic shortcomings, black colleges played a crucial role in the lives of all African Americans. Not only did the schools provide a few select members of the race with the opportunity to achieve professional and financial success, but the sheer existence of each graduate served to debunk the racist myth that black people were intellectually inferior. A black lawyer who opened an office in Nashville or a black physician who started a practice in Atlanta not only provided important services for the black community, but also challenged white racist claims of black inferiority. Consequently, the pursuit of formal education was not merely an individual quest for personal fulfillment and professional achievement. In the eyes of many African Americans, education became an important stepping-stone toward racial equality for all members of the race. Those who succeeded had a chance to undermine racism and prove that African Americans were intellectually equal to whites.

While most African Americans regarded education as the key to racial progress, they disagreed about strategy. Should educated African Americans challenge Jim Crow and demand racial equality? Or should they focus on improving the economic and social conditions of the black community and prove to whites that African Americans deserved civil rights? The dispute over strategy is best illustrated by the two most influential black leaders of the early twentieth century: Booker T. Washington and W. E. B. Du Bois. Washington, the more conservative of the two men, advocated a gradual approach toward obtaining civil rights. He insisted that African Americans learn vocational skills, which would allow them to find jobs, earn a steady income, acquire property, and gain financial independence. Washington believed that, at least for the time being, economic advancement was more important than legal, political, or social equality. Du Bois rejected the idea and demanded immediate equality. African Americans, he argued, were citizens of the United States and therefore entitled to enjoy all rights granted by the Constitution. There could be no economic advancement without equality. The philosophical differences between Washington and Du Bois dominated the struggle for racial advancement and divided the black community in the years leading up to World War I.

Washington's racial advancement philosophy, which exhorted economic success rather than universal voting rights or integration, was popular with whites, especially white Southerners. In 1895, they invited him to speak at the Atlanta Cotton States and International Exposition. Washington delivered his so-called Atlanta Compromise speech, urging blacks to stay in the South and assuring whites that African Americans would not demand social and political equality, if whites would not exclude them from economic progress. He cautioned skeptics, that unless whites aided African Americans, black poverty and ignorance would continue to drain Southern resources and drag down the region. Whites applauded Washington's plan to provide African Americans with job skills, rather than mobilizing them to pursue racial equality. Likewise, many blacks regarded his racial advancement strategy as a realistic and pragmatic approach to lift the race from poverty. While Washington accommodated to Jim Crow in public, he secretly funded legal challenges to segregation and discrimination. However by accommodating to the racial realities of the South, Washington was able to reach deep into the pockets of white philanthropists and by the turn of the twentieth century he controlled virtually every dollar they donated to black causes.

Washington used his financial ties to white philanthropists to enhance Tuskegee Institute, the school he had founded, and those organizations that embraced his racial advancement philosophy, but he saw white money merely as a means to an end. The ultimate goal was black economic self-sufficiency. For that purpose, Washington launched the National Negro Business League (NNBL) in 1900. The NNBL sought to promote black businesses, by providing entrepreneurs with a forum for professional networking. Business owners gathered to exchange information about sound business practices and to share ideas for advertising and marketing their products to black consumers. By 1910, more than 200 NNBL-affiliated organizations operated in the United States, many of them funded by white industrialist and philanthropist Andrew Carnegie, who funneled his money through Washington.

In the eyes of many Americans, both black and white, Washington was the national spokesman for the race. Black organizations sought his seal of approval before applying for funds from white philanthropists and white politicians started to consult Washington on all racial matters, including President Theodore Roosevelt, who invited him to dinner in the White House. Washington's powerful position attracted the admiration of many African Americans who were in awe that a man born into slavery associated with the country's wealthiest citizens and the nation's most prominent politicians. The "Wizard of Tuskegee," as his allies began to call him, personified the viability of his racial advancement strategy.

However, not all African Americans agreed with Washington's plan. Among the most vocal critics of Washington was W. E. B. Du Bois, who urged African Americans to protest discrimination and segregation and demand civil rights instead of trying to earn the respect of whites. Du Bois graduated from Harvard the same year Washington delivered his "Atlanta Compromise" speech. Du Bois praised Washington's speech because he was convinced that the majority of blacks who lived as sharecroppers in the South needed vocational training. However, he also insisted that African Americans needed civil rights and that the gifted among them—the so-called Talented Tenth— should pursue higher education, to prepare them for their leadership role in the struggle for racial equality. Du Bois himself started to gain a national reputation as a well-respected scholar of sociology, but his Harvard diploma did not protect him from racism. When he joined the staff of Atlanta University in 1898, he faced daily reminders of white supremacy.

Growing increasingly impatient with racial conditions, Du Bois publicly attacked Washington's accommodationist and gradual approach in his book *The Souls of Black Folk* (1903). Instead of accepting an inferior status in society and waiting for whites to bestow civil rights on African Americans, Du Bois called on the "Talented Tenth" to organize and systematically challenge Jim Crow. In 1905, he gathered his supporters at Niagara Falls in Canada and established the Niagara Movement. The organization pledged to fight for the right to vote and to end segregation and discrimination in the United States. However, plagued by lack of money and pro-Washington forces, who made a concerted effort to undermine the group's work, the Niagara Movement was largely limited to public denouncements of racism.

In 1909, Du Bois found another and much more influential forum for his protest activities, when he helped create the National Association for the Advancement of Colored People (NAACP). Unlike the Niagara Movement, which was composed of members of the black "Talented Tenth," the NAACP was a biracial organization. It emerged in the aftermath of the race riot that occurred in Springfield, Illinois, in 1908. Northern white reformers, shocked by the outbreak of racial violence in President Lincoln's home town, called for a meeting with black leaders—including Washington, who declined to attend, and Du Bois, who did—to discuss the race question. This meeting and subsequent gatherings led to the formation of the NAACP in 1909. The NAACP, funded to a large degree by its white founding members, set up its headquarters in New York City. Committed to civil rights, the association launched publicity campaigns against lynchings, disfranchisement, segregation, and educational and employment inequality. It hired attorneys and initiated lawsuits that challenged Jim Crow and used its monthly journal, the *Crisis*, to attack discrimination. In 1910, Du Bois became editor of the *Crisis*. For Du Bois, this was the opportunity of a lifetime. He was finally able to leave the South, relocate to New York, and work with a national organization that was dedicated to securing equal rights for African Americans. The NAACP provided Du Bois with resources and an organizational structure that allowed him to challenge accommodation and gradualism. More importantly, Du Bois was now beyond the reach of the Tuskegee Machine, which had used the vast network of Washington loyalists and access to white philanthropic funds to crush all opposition to the Wizard of Tuskegee.

Within a few years, the NAACP attracted an ever-growing number of black members, who found the organization's protest and civil rights agenda much more appealing than Washington's reliance on accommodation and gradual change. Washington's death in 1915 further helped the NAACP to establish itself as a powerful force in American race relations. Although Washington left behind large numbers of disciples who shared his vision of racial uplift, his failure to groom a charismatic successor who could take charge of the Tuskegee Machine, led to the gradual demise of his influence during World War I.

The NAACP's growing appeal was perhaps also due to the deterioration of race relations that characterized the administration of Woodrow Wilson. Elected in 1912, Wilson became the first Southern president since the end of the Civil War. Wilson, born in Virginia and raised in Georgia, had earned a reputation for endorsing segregation and racial exclusion. Between 1902 and 1910, when Wilson served as president of Princeton University, he had effectively barred African Americans from attending the school, making it the only Ivy League institution that denied admission to black students. Fearful that racial tensions would disrupt campus life, Wilson convinced prospective black students to withdraw their applications, claiming that members of their race would not feel comfortable at Princeton. Wilson's subsequent career as governor of New Jersey did little to assure African Americans that he was interested in improving race relations. Between 1911 and 1913, while Wilson was governor of New Jersey, the state enacted no legislation that addressed black concerns. In 1912, when Wilson decided to run for the White House, most African Americans found the nominee of the Democratic Party less than appealing, but neither of the other candidates had established stellar records in the area of race relations.

At the time of the 1912 presidential election, black voters who had not been disfranchised—mostly those living in the North—had the choice to cast their ballots for four candidates: the incumbent Republican, William H. Taft; Theodore Roosevelt, who headed the newly organized Progressive Party; Southern white Democrat Woodrow Wilson; or socialist Eugene V. Debs. Since the Civil War, African Americans had traditionally voted for the Republican Party, in reverence for the "Great Emancipator," Abraham Lincoln. However, by 1912, many African Americans had become disillusioned with the Republican Party's failure to protect their rights, condemn racial violence, and work for equality. Tapping into black discontent, Democratic candidate Wilson promised African Americans that they could expect absolutely fair treatment if he were elected president. Given the choice of candidates, it is not surprising that some prominent blacks endorsed Wilson's bid for the White House. Both W. E. B. Du Bois as well as his friend William Monroe Trotter, editor of the *Boston Guardian*, encouraged their readers to vote for the Democratic Party. Wilson, who promised a "New Freedom" and campaigned on a ticket that emphasized reform, won the election, but his black supporters soon realized that it was not a victory for African Americans.

When Wilson took office in 1913, he quickly gained notoriety for supporting the agenda of white supremacists. He appointed five Southerners to his ten-man cabinet, permitted the introduction of nearly two dozen racist bills into Congress, took no steps to stop the economic exploitation of Southern sharecroppers or black workers, and made no efforts to outlaw lynchings. Moreover, Wilson abandoned the practice of making patronage appointments, government jobs traditionally given to African American party supporters. Afraid to alienate white congressional leaders from the South, Wilson withdrew the nominations of prominent blacks to high government posts when Southern senators blocked their appointments.

African Americans were bitterly disappointed with the new president, especially when his administration started to segregate African Americans in civil service jobs. For the first time since the Civil War, federal government agencies segregated lavatories, lunchroom facilities, and working spaces of black civil servants, reversing "a fifty year tradition of integrated civil service."[4] Appalled by these indignities, some black government workers resigned in protest. Those who endured the conditions were demoted or removed from their posts. Concerned about the deterioration of race relations and the steady decline in the number of African American civil servants, advocates of racial equality appealed to the president. Oswald Garrison Villard, grandson of famous white abolitionist William Lloyd Garrison and chairman of the board of the NAACP, took the lead and met with Wilson in August of 1913. Unsatisfied with the results of the meeting, the NAACP filed an official protest two days later. In addition, the civil rights organization mobilized the press and launched a massive letter-writing campaign to persuade the president to stop the discriminatory practices; however, to no avail.

Dismayed that Wilson had broken his campaign promise to African Americans, William Monroe Trotter, the black editor of the *Boston Guardian*, confronted the president. Trotter and members of his National Independent Political League met with Wilson in November 1913 to express their outrage with the segregation of black civil service employees. Trotter reminded Wilson that African Americans had helped to build the nation and presented him with a petition signed by 20,000 Americans who demanded an end to the government's Jim Crow policy. The president asked Trotter to be patient and assured him that he had not issued a segregation policy. Wilson was not lying, but he was not speaking the truth either. The heads of the various civil service departments and not the president were responsible for initiating the controversial policy changes; however, Wilson had done nothing to reverse them. The impact Trotter's argument had on the president is unclear, but in the months following his meeting with Wilson some of the more blatant discriminatory practices ceased, at least temporarily.

In May of 1914 new concerns about racial discrimination surfaced, when the Civil Service Commission asked prospective employees to attach their photographs to job applications—a requirement that was not revoked until the 1930s. In addition, news of the dismissal and demotion of several black government clerks attracted the renewed attention of African Americans. Trotter once again called on Wilson in November 1914. This time, however, the president was less amiable—perhaps because he was grief stricken by the death of his wife of thirty years, who had died just a few days prior to the meeting. Wilson informed Trotter that segregation in the civil service was intended to eliminate racial frictions and designed to create a comfortable work environment for both races. It was not discrimination, the president reasoned paternalistically, because it served to protect African Americans from white hostilities. Trotter fired back, "Have you a 'new freedom' for white Americans and a new slavery for your Afro-American fellow citizens?"[5] When Trotter reminded Wilson that black voters might not support him in the future, the president lost his temper. He objected to Trotter's political "blackmail," refused to discuss the matter any further, and virtually kicked him out of the White House. Upon his departure, Trotter held an impromptu press conference and related details of the meeting to reporters who were waiting in the White House. The clash between Trotter and Wilson became national news and made the front page of the *New York Times*, generating a massive public outcry against the government's segregation policy. But once again, the appeals fell on deaf ears. By the end of Wilson's second year in office, the president's relationship with African Americans had suffered irreparable damages.

However, black discontent with Wilson did not reach a low point until 1915. That year, film director D. W. Griffith released his racist movie epic *The Birth of a Nation*, which was largely based on Thomas Dixon's novel *The Clansman*. In an effort to boost movie attendance, Dixon, an unabashed Southern racist and former student of Wilson's, sought an official endorsement from the president and arranged for a private screening of the film in the White House. Following the showing of the movie, which liberally quoted from Wilson's five-volume *History of the American People*, Dixon claimed that the president had praised the film. Although the records do not substantiate that claim, Griffith and Dixon used the White House screening as a marketing device, suggesting that the president had given *The Birth of a Nation* his seal of approval. Wilson informed his private secretary that he had done no such thing; however, he did nothing to dispel that myth in public. To African Americans, the president's silence spoke louder than words. They were shocked that he did not publicly condemn the film's racist depiction of blacks and its glorification of lynchings as a legitimate means of maintaining law and order. Under the leadership of the NAACP and the black press, African Americans launched nationwide protests. Seeking to ban the film, they appealed to the National Board of Censorship of Motion Pictures, which ordered the cutting of a few scenes but otherwise endorsed the film. Ironically, all the protest activities were good publicity for the movie, which played to audience-packed theaters and became the highest grossing film in the years leading up to America's involvement in World War I.

Wilson's decision to remain silent in response to the controversy sparked by *The Birth of a Nation*, his refusal to stop segregation in the Civil Service, his hostile confrontation with Trotter, and his failure to condemn racial violence, illustrated to African Americans the president's callous indifference to black concerns. Not surprisingly, they withdrew their support from the Democratic Party when Wilson ran for reelection in 1916. Some prominent African Americans as well as influential black newspaper editors declared their support for Republican Charles E. Hughes, who had served on the Supreme Court when it struck down the infamous "grandfather clause" in *Guinn v. U.S.* in 1915. However, Hughes was reluctant to support racial equality during his presidential campaign. When the NAACP sent the Republican candidate a letter, asking him to state his position on racial matters, Hughes ignored the request. Frustrated with the choice of candidates, the NAACP's *Crisis* instructed black voters to abstain or cast their ballot for the Socialist candidate. But the size of the black vote was too small to wield political leverage and Wilson was reelected in 1916.

Thus, on the eve of World War I, the economic, social, political, and legal conditions of African Americans did not differ much from those during slavery. The vast majority of blacks continued to live in utter poverty in the rural South, where they had limited access to health care, proper nutrition, and education. Their daily lives were characterized by white economic exploitation, intimidation, and violence, as well as Jim Crow laws. Unable to exercise the right to vote, African Americans were at best second-class citizens. Although a small number of black urban elites and members of the black middle class enjoyed relative economic prosperity, they too faced discrimination and segregation as well as a hostile federal government and a Supreme Court that was largely indifferent to the plight of African Americans. Nonetheless, while racism remained firmly entrenched in American society for decades to come, the start of World War I in Europe in 1914 did ring in a new era for African Americans.

~

CHAPTER TWO

From Field to Factory

The Wartime Migration of African Americans

The onset of World War I in Europe brought about dramatic changes for African Americans. Stimulated by the war, many rural blacks left the plantations of the South and migrated to the factories of the North. The so-called Great Migration was one of the largest population shifts in the history of the United States. Between In 1916 and 1917, nearly 500,000 black Southerners moved to cities in the North, comprising roughly 5 percent of the total black Southern population. The mass exodus resulted in a black Northern population increase of more than 43 percent. In addition to a significant growth of the black urban population in the North, the Great Migration also introduced large numbers of African Americans to factory work, which led to the formation of a black industrial working class. Between 1910 and 1920, the number of blacks employed in manufacturing and other industries grew by 40 percent. Wartime employment opportunities in the North offered African Americans a chance to escape the racially oppressive South and improve their economic conditions. However, the resulting black population growth in the cities of the North also contributed to numerous problems, including housing shortages, a lack of recreational facilities, and growing tensions between black city residents and the rural newcomers as well as interracial strife.

When the war started in Europe in August 1914, the United States remained initially neutral. After all, President Woodrow Wilson insisted it was a European conflict that had erupted as a result of entangling diplomatic alliances and Americans had no reason to mobilize their forces and join the hostilities. Nonetheless, the war had immediate repercussions for Americans, particularly African Americans. War-torn European nations, often with the help of U.S. government loans, purchased large quantities of defense goods and other industrial products from American manufacturers. Industrialists, eager to make a profit, had a difficult time meeting increased export demands because their immigrant workforce started to diminish as a result of the war. Millions of Europeans, who had flocked to American factories in the late nineteenth and early twentieth centuries had been their main source of cheap labor, but many of the prospective new immigrants were now drafted to serve in the European armies while others already living in the United States returned to their homelands to fight. During the first year of the war, the number of immigrants dropped from 1.2 million in 1914 to 326,000 in 1915, contributing to a severe labor shortage in the United States.

To boost the dwindling workforce, American industries opened their doors to African Americans. Prior to the war, industrialists had largely excluded African Americans from their manufacturing plants, fearing that their employment would ignite unrest among the immigrant white workforce. But when World War I created new economic realities—the prospect of making a lot of money while facing a dearth of white workers—entrepreneurs reconsidered their Jim Crow policy. Their initial response was to hire African Americans who lived near the defense industry plants in the cities of the Northeast. However, the number of black Northerners proved to be too small to meet the demands, and manufacturers started looking elsewhere. Aware that the majority of African Americans barely eked out a living as sharecroppers on Southern plantations, Northern industrialists sent labor agents to the South to recruit black workers. Large numbers of African Americans embraced the opportunity to leave the South for well-paying jobs, shorter workdays, and a less racially oppressive climate in the North.

For black Southerners there were plenty of reasons to leave the South. Following the start of the war, Southern cotton producers lost access to most of their European markets and cotton prices tumbled. At the same time, the boll weevil, a destructive insect that made its way north from Mexico, devoured much of the South's cotton crop. In Alabama, Mississippi, Louisiana, Oklahoma, Arkansas, Georgia, Florida, and South Carolina, the boll weevil devastated agricultural regions where farmers had relied almost entirely on cotton cultivation. In other areas, floods washed away the remaining crops, leaving black farmers in utter despair and ready to jump at any opportunity to leave the South.

Desperation had driven many African Americans out of the South even prior to World War I. In 1877, Benjamin "Pap" Singleton, a former slave from

Nashville, had urged black Southerners to move to Kansas, claiming that the West offered African Americans economic and political autonomy. But relocating to the western frontier entailed many risks. Life on the prairie meant an uncertain future characterized by unfamiliar terrain, harsh winter storms, frequent tornadoes, and lack of shelter. In 1877, less than one hundred African Americans heeded Singleton's call to move West and claim free land under the provisions of the 1862 Homestead Act. During their first winter in Kansas, the initial group of black settlers faced tremendous hardships. They lived in dugouts or brush shelters and many teetered on the brink of starvation. However, within a year they started to build homes and news of the rural black settlements spread throughout the South. By 1879, 20,000 African Americans from Mississippi, Louisiana, and Texas joined the Kansas settlers, and Singleton came to be known as the "Moses of the Colored Exodus."

Singleton was not the only African American who urged blacks to leave the South. In 1889 thousands of black Southerners headed for the newly opened Oklahoma Territory, seeking to escape political repression and economic exploitation and driven by a desire to establish independent black communities. In 1892, the numbers of the so-called Exodusters swelled, when Ida B. Wells-Barnett, a black journalist and antilynching activist, exhorted blacks in Memphis to go West to stave off mob violence. Yet others, disillusioned with Jim Crow, propagated emigration to Africa. The American Colonization Society, which had tried to resettle free blacks and manumitted slaves in Liberia since 1816, received a flood of inquiries from African Americans who were eager to leave the South. However, by 1900, only about a thousand black southerners had managed to raise sufficient funds to emigrate to Africa. Until the eve of World War I, the most popular destination for black migrants continued to be the West. As late as 1910, more than 52 percent of black Southern migrants crossed the Mississippi River in search of a better future.

A slightly smaller percentage of black Southerners headed for the urban North. By 1910, they had settled in a few select cities, including New York, Philadelphia, and Chicago, which were home to nearly 25 percent of the North's total black population. Virtually all of these prewar migrants came from the rural areas and small towns of the upper South. Most were young and single and many were unskilled or skilled workers. Yet others were members of the educated black Southern elites—the "Talented Tenth"—who were disenchanted with the deterioration of race relations and the lack of professional advancement opportunities in the South. In New York City, for example, which had the largest black population of any Northern city on the eve of World War I, the vast majority of black lawyers, physicians, ministers, politicians, and businessmen had been born in the South.

When the war started in Europe, a flood of new migrants joined the black residents of the urban North. Large numbers of farmers and agricultural workers from the rural South as well as unskilled residents of Southern towns and cities, made their way north. Unlike the prewar migrants, many came from the Deep South—Mississippi, Georgia, Alabama, South Carolina, and Louisiana—and had little more than the clothes on their backs. Although many of them were literate or semiliterate, the majority had less education than the migrants who had preceded them. Unable to make a living in the South and unwilling to accept Jim Crow, they took advantage of the labor shortage generated by the war and moved North in search of industrial employment. The principal destinations of the wartime migrants were a handful of large cities, some of which already had significant black populations, including New York, Chicago, Philadelphia, and St. Louis, while others, like Detroit, Cleveland, and Newark, saw the number of black residents explode, virtually overnight. Smaller Midwestern cities with wartime production industries, like Gary, Indiana, and Akron, Ohio, also attracted a large portion of the migrants. During the war, Gary's tiny prewar black population of 383, grew by nearly 1,300 percent and Akron's 657 black residents faced a nearly 850 percent black population increase (see table 2.1).

The prospect of earning decent wages was one of the most important factors that drove African Americans out of the South. However, economic considerations were not the only impetus for the migrants. Equally important were concerns about racial injustices and violence, the lack of educational opportunities for their children, and gaining personal autonomy. A black woman in Florida explained that Southern blacks "are not so greatly disturbed about wages. They are tired of being treated as children."[1] The North, which had been a beacon of hope for runaway slaves in the years prior to the Civil War, now became the destination of hundreds of thousands of black Southerners who flocked to the "Promised Land" in search of freedom, equality, and economic advancement.

The initial group of migrants often moved with the help of white labor agents, who had been active in the South since the end of the Civil War. In the late nineteenth century, they had been recruiting African Americans to work for plantations and railroad camps in other parts of the South as well as rural Southern industries, such as lumber, mining, and turpentine. With the onset of World War I, labor agents started to shift their focus and began to recruit African Americans for jobs in the North. They provided information about specific Northern cities and industries and offered train fare as well as labor contracts. In many cases, contracts stipulated that migrants had to reimburse their future employers for the cost of railroad tickets. At times,

Table 2.1 Impact of the Great Migration on Northern Cities

| | 1910 | | 1920 | | |
	Black Residents	Percent of Population	Black Residents	Percent of Population	Increase
New York	91,709	1.9	152,467	2.7	66.3
Chicago	44,103	2.0	109,458	4.1	148.2
Philadelphia	84,459	5.5	134,229	7.4	58.9
St. Louis	43,960	6.4	69,854	9.0	58.9
Detroit	5,741	1.2	40,838	4.1	611.3
Pittsburgh	25,623	4.8	37,725	6.4	47.2
Indianapolis	21,816	9.3	34,678	11.0	59.0
Cleveland	8,448	1.5	34,451	4.3	307.8
Kansas City	23,566	9.5	30,719	9.5	30.4
Cincinnati	19,739	5.4	30,079	7.5	53.2
Columbus	12,739	7.0	22,181	9.4	74.1
Newark	9,475	2.7	16,977	4.1	79.2
East St. Louis	5,882	10.0	7,437	11.1	26.4
Youngstown	1,936	2.4	6,662	5.0	244.1
Gary	383	2.3	5,299	9.6	1,283.6
Toledo	1,877	1.1	5,691	2.3	203.2
Akron	657	1.0	5,580	2.7	749.3
Buffalo	1,773	0.4	4,511	0.9	154.4

however, industrialists were so desperate that they paid for the migrants' transportation.

Despite the desire of many African Americans to leave the South, they were initially skeptical of white labor recruitment agents. African Americans, for obvious reasons, had little confidence in whites who told them about the abundance of employment opportunities in the North. Indeed, many agents misrepresented wages and working conditions. Moreover, African Americans were painfully aware that industries had recruited them in the past only as strikebreakers and that black workers had always lost their jobs when unions negotiated new contracts and whites returned to the factory floors. African Americans became even more suspicious, when con men, who posed as agents, asked black Southerners for advance payment and in return promised to provide them with transportation, jobs, and housing, but then took off with their money. Yet, it was not only whites who defrauded the migrants. In Mobile, Alabama, a black man, claiming to be a preacher, passed around a collection plate, allegedly to raise funds for train fare. Both the man and the money vanished.

White Southerners were another obstacle to black migration. At first, many of them paid little attention to African Americans leaving the South. Indeed, most were baffled when they learned that a growing number of African Americans were heading North. After all, white Southerners had assumed that blacks were quite happy in the South, because that was the response they got every time they had asked them. Since Southern whites had deluded themselves into believing that black discontent was not a cause of the migration, some suspected foul play. The migration, a white publication in Texas speculated, was a Republican Party ploy designed to move large numbers of black voters North to maintain political control of that region. Likewise, the chairman of the Ohio Democratic Party claimed that Republicans who sought to increase their presence in the state were responsible for the migration. However, initial shock and denial soon gave way to genuine concern about losing the black Southern workforce. Always troubled by outside agitators, white Southerners tried to curtail the activities of labor agents. So-called enticement laws prohibited employers and labor agents from recruiting black workers. South Carolina, for example, adopted a law that made the solicitation of labor a misdemeanor. Other states forced agents to purchase prohibitively expensive operating licenses. Georgia, Virginia, and Alabama required a $500 state licensing fee (the equivalency of more than $11,000 in 2009), and the latter an additional $250 for each county. Many Southern cities and counties passed ordinances that imposed additional fees. Savannah and Jacksonville sold municipal permits for $1,000; Birmingham charged $500; and Macon County a jaw-dropping $25,000 (the equivalency of $582,000 in 2009). To avoid paying for costly licenses, labor agents often used black assistants who were less likely to attract the attention of whites. Disguised as salesmen and insurance agents they visited black homes and businesses and recruited prospective migrants. Southern states and municipalities soon became aware of the practice and prosecuted black and white agents who failed to purchase labor recruitment permits. Alabama, for example, imposed a $500 fine and a sentence of one year of hard labor on any agent who operated without a license. In Montgomery, labor agents who recruited workers for out-of-state jobs without valid permits faced an additional $100 fine and six months of hard labor. And Jacksonville imposed a fine of $600 or a sixty-day jail term for the same offense. Finally, whites threatened agents with violence, beat them up, literally ran them out of town, or arrested them.

While some Southern whites created legal roadblocks and resorted to coercive measures to stop the work of labor agents, others were less alarmed by the migration. Some Southern whites even applauded the mass exodus, hoping that it would solve the South's race problem, by ridding the region of all African Americans and opening up jobs for white workers. Others were confident that only shiftless, idle, and discontented blacks were leaving the South, those who were either nonproductive forces in the Southern economy or undesirable troublemakers. Yet others, certain that African Americans would be unable to withstand the harsh winters in the North, predicted that the black migrants would return to the sunny South within a few months. The influential *New Orleans Times-Picayune*, trying to ease the minds of its white readers, proclaimed: "The negro does not like cold."[2] Convinced that gullible blacks had been lured to the North by clever labor agents, some whites assured themselves that the migrants would soon realize their terrible mistake and return to the South. To prepare for their anticipated homecoming, Mississippi and Louisiana established state commissions that sought to provide train fare to those who wanted to return. However, when the migrants failed to return after the first winter in the North, white Southerners discussed possible reforms to prevent a further exodus.

Leading Southern white university and college administrators issued an open letter declaring that the only remedies for the mass exodus were enhanced economic opportunities as well as fair treatment of blacks. Many Southern white newspapers also speculated that African Americans would remain in the South if whites gave them a square deal. As one paper put it bluntly, "the truth is that the treatment of the Negro in the South must change or the South will lose the Negro."[3] Addressing that concern, white papers cautioned that lynchings were likely to drive the black Southern workforce out of the region. For that reason, many white Southerners were particularly troubled by the gruesome lynching of Jesse Washington in Waco, Texas. On May 15, 1916, spectators numbering 15,000 watched, as a white mob castrated Washington, tied him to a car and dragged him through the streets, and then slowly roasted him to death. Racial violence like this, reform-minded papers warned, was sure to cause more African Americans to leave the South. To stem the mass exodus of black workers, they urged white Southerners to refrain from lynchings, offer higher wages, reduce rents, improve educational opportunities, and construct comfortable and inexpensive housing for African Americans. Some communities even raised charitable funds and distributed them among the most destitute black residents, while others raised wages and cut rents. Not surprisingly, their limited efforts neither stopped nor slowed the exodus.

White southerners were not the only ones voicing concern about the mass migration. Some black southerners also tried to convince African Americans to stay in the South. When the disciples of Booker T. Washington convened for the annual Tuskegee Negro Conference in 1917, they adopted several declarations, reminding African Americans that their place was in the South. Robert R. Moton, who had succeeded Washington at Tuskegee Institute, even dispatched speakers from his school to discourage prospective migrants from going North. Moton remained true to Washington's ideology, which held that the South provided African Americans with the best chance of becoming landowning farmers and acquiring wealth. In the North, they would have to compete with white labor, which in the past had resulted in the exclusion of black workers from industrial employment, whereas in the South, whites depended on their labor. Moton may have been truly convinced that the future of black Americans was in the South, but it is also possible that his opposition to migration was influenced by the fact that he was in charge of a black school. He undoubtedly feared that the mass exodus would deprive him of potential students as well as white financial support, unless he publicly opposed migration. Likewise, Southern black businessmen and ministers, whose livelihood depended on patronage from the black community, often urged prospective migrants to stay in the South. Their less-than-altruistic motives, however, backfired. As one prominent black man noted, public opposition to migration "is the most unpopular thing that any professional or business Negro can do."[4] Black ministers who tried to dissuade their congregations from leaving often faced empty pews. Those who opposed migration not only ran the risk of losing their clients or their parishioners, but also their lives. When a black preacher in Tampa used the pulpit to discourage his flock from leaving the South, he was stabbed the following day for doing so. Aware of the danger of either condemning or endorsing the Great Migration in public, many of the Southern black leaders did neither.

While some black southerners actively tried to deter African Americans from going north, others merely cautioned them "not to expect to find everything rosy. There will be considerable disappointment if they think they will not encounter prejudice in the North."[5] Northern blacks also voiced concern that many migrants had unrealistic expectations and were ill-prepared for life in the North. While the black-owned *Pittsburgh Courier* was not opposed to migration, the paper insisted that each migrant know "exactly where he is going; for whom he is to work, the conditions of the community to which he goes, and just what advantages and disadvantages he may expect to find."[6] The National Urban League, a biracial social service agency that sought to aid black urban residents, echoed these concerns. In 1916, the League organized a National Conference on Migration and issued several recommendations to prospective migrants. Troubled by the influx of "indolent inefficient men" who would "soon become a burden to the northern communities and bring reproach and humiliation to thrifty Colored citizens in communities where white people have not hitherto considered Negroes undesirables," the National Urban League urged prospective migrants not to rush north without considering the ramifications.[7]

Despite these warnings, the systematic exodus of black Southerners, sparked by World War I, not only continued but intensified. To a large degree the increase in the number of migrants was due not to the work of white labor agents—a U.S. Department of Labor study estimated that only 10 to 20 percent of the migrants were solicited by recruiters who worked for Northern industries—but the migrants themselves. Those who had migrated north wrote letters home praising the working and living conditions and encouraging others to follow them. A Southern man who had moved to Philadelphia expressed the feelings of many migrants when he wrote: "I Don't have to work hard. Don't have to mister every little white boy who comes along I haven't heard a white man call a colored a nigger."[8] In addition, many migrants enclosed money in their letters: indisputable evidence that life was better in the North. Proud relatives and friends shared the letters of successful migrants with other members of the community. They read them aloud on street corners, in grocery stores, at the local barbershops, and in their churches. Other powerful apostles of the exodus were migrants who returned to the South to visit families and friends. Often sporting expensive clothes, they raved about opportunities in the North, and took with them others as they headed back. Once the migration started, these letters and visits, played a more important role in bringing additional migrants to the North than the work of the labor agents.

The chain migration did not go unnoticed by white Southerners. They eyed with suspicion black migrants who returned for visits to the South. In order to avoid invoking the wrath of white Southerners, some migrants tricked them, claiming that they had returned because they did not like the North and wanted to live out the rest of their lives among family and friends in the South. In reality, though, they came back to recruit new migrants. To discourage a further drain of their workforce, white Southerners tried to enlist the help of influential blacks, and at times, succeeded in bribing them to speak out against migration. And, like vultures white Southerners descended upon migrants who returned South, dissatisfied with their experience in the North. They used the white press and pressured black Southern newspaper editors to publish their stories of disappointment as a lesson to those who considered leaving the South. Moreover, the papers carried news of poor housing conditions and migrants who were allegedly starving or freezing to death in the North. But Southern blacks paid little attention to those reports. They knew that the white press had its own agenda and that Southern black newspapers could be easily manipulated by whites, who either withheld profitable advertisements to punish black editors who did not comply with their demands or rewarded those who did.

A much more reliable source of information about living and working conditions in the North were black Northern newspapers, such as the *Chicago Defender*, the *Pittsburgh Courier*, the *Cleveland Gazette* and *Cleveland Advocate*, the *New York Age*, and the *Philadelphia Tribune*. Unrivaled in its importance was the *Chicago Defender*, which made its way south with the help of African Americans who worked on the railroads. The editor of the *Defender*, Robert S. Abbott, was a Southern migrant himself. Born in Georgia in 1868, he had trained as a printer at Virginia's Hampton Institute, Booker T. Washington's alma mater. Abbott first visited Chicago as a member of the Hampton Quartet, which performed at the World's Columbian Exposition in 1893. Three years later he graduated from college and moved to Chicago, where he earned a law degree in 1899. Unable to establish a career as a lawyer—because he was too dark-skinned, another black attorney informed him—Abbott pursued his interest in publishing. With an initial investment of twenty-five cents, he launched the *Defender* in 1905, with a press run of three hundred papers.

During the first five years of publication, the *Defender* had a limited readership and consisted of only four pages that covered local interest stories and gossip. However, that changed in 1909, when Abbott exposed the municipal government's failure to clear Chicago's red-light district located in the city's black neighborhood. Casting himself as a race leader who was fighting to improve the living conditions of Chicago's black population, Abbott attracted large numbers of new readers and garnered the support of black reporters, artists, cartoonists, and editorial writers, who were eager to volunteer their services for such a worthy cause. In 1910, Abbott further expanded the paper's staff when he hired J. Hockley Smiley as managing editor. Abbott and Smiley restructured the paper. They copied the general layout of white daily newspapers, introduced eye-catching headlines and political cartoons, and adopted a sensationalist style that appealed to many new readers. More importantly, Abbott departed from his previous emphasis on society chitchat and redefined the paper's mission. Exposing racism nationwide, the paper became the defender of the race and its editor a crusader for racial justice. Never afraid to resort to hyperbole, Abbott now dubbed the *Defender* the "World's Greatest Weekly." But despite Abbott's grandiose claim, the *Defender* remained essentially a local newspaper paper, aimed at black residents of the Windy City.

It was not until 1910, that the *Defender's* readership started to expand beyond Chicago's city limit. That year Abbott launched a column that carried news coverage of black railroad workers, particularly Pullman porters. Company founder George Pullman had started to hire blacks as attendants for his white railroad clientele in the years following the Civil War because he believed that African Americans projected an image of servility to white customers. By 1915, the Pullman company, headquartered in Chicago, had become the nation's single largest employer of black workers. The black porters made up the berths of white travelers, served them food, pressed their clothes, shined their shoes, and tended to a host of other needs of their white patrons. More importantly, though, the porters traveled across the nation and had ample access to black communities in the South. Abbott realized the potential of expanding the *Defender's* readership and gave copies of his papers to the porters as well as itinerant black entertainers to distribute during their journeys into the South. Abbott's strategy paid off. By 1916, the *Defender* had a circulation of 50,000, two-thirds of it outside of Chicago. Particularly in the South, African Americans eagerly awaited the arrival of the paper from the North. Those who could afford to buy a copy of the *Defender* read it and passed it on to family members and friends, who circulated it until the pages were worn out. And, like the letters of migrants, those who were literate, read the paper aloud at barbershops, pool halls, and after church services or wherever large numbers of African Americans gathered. As a result of this informal circulation system, the paper reached many more black readers than the sales figures indicate. By the end of World War I, the *Defender*, with a weekly circulation of nearly a quarter million, was the most widely read black paper in the nation.

The *Defender's* mass appeal was largely the product of its bold and uncompromising style. Unlike the Southern black press, which often had to kowtow to whites, the *Defender* used a frank, critical, and often militant tone. For example, when Abbott learned that a black woman had frozen to death in Atlanta, he asked his readers provocatively: "If you can freeze to death in the North and be free, why freeze to death in the South and be a slave."[9] Much to the satisfaction of its readers, the *Defender* mimicked the practice of white papers, whose columns identified African Americans as "colored" or "negro." Abbott blatantly mocked this practice when he did the same in his coverage of President Woodrow Wilson and other well-known politicians, identifying them as "white." In addition, Abbott and his correspondents covered lynchings and other incidents of racial violence in the South in lurid detail and contrasted them with reports about better living conditions in the North. It was a simple choice: black life in the South was bad, while the North was full of unbridled opportunities for the race. Articles focused on better jobs, housing, and education in the North, but the *Defender* also highlighted Chicago's numerous black leisure time amenities and entertainment venues. Moreover, it published advertisements for black-owned businesses and its society section featured elaborate descriptions of lavish social events hosted by the city's prominent and wealthy black elites. Accounts of black movie houses, theaters, restaurants, hotels, social clubs, sport teams, and dance halls filled the pages of the paper and created in the minds of black Southerners an image of Chicago and other northern cities as the Mecca of economic opportunity, racial equality, and vibrant black culture. Fueling the already existing desire of black Southerners who wanted to leave the South, the *Defender* played a crucial role in the wartime migration.

Abbott became an ardent proponent of migration when the economic boom triggered by the war in Europe left Northern industrialists little choice but to hire blacks. The decrease of the immigrant workforce, he realized, created unprecedented employment opportunities for African Americans in the industrial centers of the urban North and a chance for them to escape the racially oppressive South once and for all. Of course, Abbott was also an astute businessman. He knew that the influx of blacks into Northern cities would likely increase the number of *Defender* readers, which would undoubtedly raise profits generated from the sale of additional papers as well as advertisements. Beginning in 1916, Abbott urged all blacks to leave the South and announced that he had negotiated special group discount rates with the railroad companies. Soon white employers in the North became aware of Abbott's access to Southern black communities and started to place Help Wanted ads in the *Defender*. In addition to ads specifically aimed at potential migrants, the paper carried boarding house notices, printed the schedules of trains departing the South, and reminded black Southern entrepreneurs to take advantage of the growing black consumer market in the North. In 1917, Abbott went a step further. He informed his readers that masses of blacks were ready to leave the South during a "Great Northern Drive" on May 15. While Abbott created the illusion that concerted and well-planned migration efforts were underway for that date, the "Great Northern Drive" was not an organized group departure. Indeed, some scholars have speculated that Abbott invented the story to raise circulation of his paper. Nonetheless, large numbers of black Southerners heeded Abbott's advice and headed north.

White Southerners, alarmed by the mass exodus that Abbott appeared to have orchestrated, tried to suppress the distribution of the *Defender*. In Alabama, whites killed two local sales agents. In Arkansas, a legal injunction barred circulation of the paper in two counties. In Georgia, the state governor instructed the postmaster to stop its distribution through the mail. In Mississippi, the Meridian chief of police confiscated the paper from local dealers. In Louisiana, whites tried to exclude the *Defender* and all other Northern black papers from the mails. These coercive efforts forced the *Defender* underground in the South. However, contrary to what white Southerners had hoped to achieve, the clandestine circulation of the *Defender* gave Abbott's call to leave the South even more credence. Throughout the war, hundreds of black Southerners continued to write Abbott, asking for money to finance their trips, help in finding jobs and housing, and general information about living and working conditions in the North.

While some African Americans spontaneously packed their bags and left the South, moving north usually entailed careful planning. Some African Americans, especially single young men, received free passes or prepaid railroad tickets from labor agents; however, the majority of black Southerners were not as fortunate. Most had to save money and sell their belongings, including furniture, clothing, and other personal items, to raise sufficient funds to pay for their train fare. Given the poverty of Southern blacks, many potential migrants could only afford to purchase a ticket for one member of their family or for part of their trip. En route to their final destination in the North, many migrants stopped in various cities of the South and worked until they had saved enough money to move on. Others joined informal migration clubs, which often had ties to migrants in the North who provided useful information, established connections to prospective employers, and promised to furnish newcomers with initial shelter. Most migration clubs were relatively small groups composed of family, friends, and neighbors or those who belonged to the same church. However, some clubs claimed as many as 1,000 members. Migrants joined these clubs because traveling with a group of familiar faces was less traumatic than making the trip alone, and some club leaders managed to negotiate group discounts that made train fare more affordable. Many migrants made the journey with the financial assistance of relatives and friends who had moved north and sent money or train tickets to those who remained in the South.

Not surprisingly, single young men and women in their physical prime—between the ages of twenty and forty-five—were among the first to leave the South. The U.S. Labor Department estimated that approximately 70 to 80 percent of the migrants had no family ties in the North. Large numbers of unmarried black men started to take advantage of free train passes handed out by labor agents who sought to fill vacant positions in the railroad industries and steel mills of the North. In 1916, railroad companies ran special eighty-foot steel coach migration trains that picked up young men at secret locations outside Southern train stations. This initial group of migrants often moved into quickly constructed company labor camps that were specifically built for the all-male black workforce. The camps varied in size and in quality. Some provided lodging for as little as 25 workers, while others housed nearly 800 men. Typically, camps consisted of wooden sheds that were packed with cots or bunk beds and allowed for little privacy. Additional camp buildings were equipped with kitchens, mess halls, wash rooms, and toilet facilities. Sanitary conditions were good in some camps, where the workers enjoyed access to clean showers, bathrooms, and flush toilets. However, in others, conditions were appalling. One railroad camp in Pennsylvania, for example, had no indoor plumbing and the men had to sleep on filthy, vermin-infested mattresses. In other camps, the men slept in converted passenger coach or windowless freight cars. The quality of food also varied greatly. Some camps had well-staffed and clean kitchens that offered inexpensive nutritious meals or packed lunches, while others were filthy, teeming with flies, and reeking with stench. Only a few of the camps had any kind of recreational facilities, consisting at best of a few pool tables and a couple of checkerboards. Not surprisingly, many camps had problems with drunkenness and disorderly conduct. Lodging fees were nominal and ranged from one to two dollars per month, whereas meals averaged four to eight dollars a week. Both expenses were minor, given that Northern black industrial workers earned between three and five dollars a day. Thus, even if the men ventured into nearby towns and splurged occasionally on entertainment, drinks, and clothing, they still had enough money left to save for themselves or to send to relatives in the South.

Single women soon followed the men, however, their numbers were generally smaller, at least at the outset of the Great Migration. Since many of the jobs in the North were in heavy industries, which traditionally did not hire female workers, employment opportunities were less abundant for black women than for black men. However, labor shortages created by the war soon opened jobs for black women in hotels, restaurants, steam laundries, garment factories, textile mills, food and meat processing plants, and other light industries. Despite these new employment opportunities, the overwhelming number of black women working in the North continued to be concentrated in the areas of personal and domestic service. Black women who migrated North largely performed the same type of work they had done in the South. Though black women remained at the bottom of the economic ladder, the prospect of earning higher wages in the North certainly played a crucial role in their decision to move. In the North domestic workers could earn in a day the same amount of money they got paid for a week of labor in the South. While economic motives lured many single women to the North, others left the South to escape sexual harassment by white employers, abusive boyfriends, or domineering parents. An equally powerful force was the desire to get away from racial oppression, experience greater personal autonomy, live with dignity, and enjoy the urban amenities they had read about in the *Defender*. Most of the single female migrants, concerned about their personal safety, traveled in groups composed of family members and friends, particularly other women. And they usually traveled directly to specific cities in the North, without stopping while en route. Upon their arrival, many joined kin, friends, or neighbors who had preceded them north.

The number of families migrating together was initially small, due to high transportation costs. Some African Americans living along the coastal Southeast traveled by steamboat, which was the cheapest way of traveling north. However, for the majority of black Southerners the railroads were the only means of transportation. In 1915, the railroads charged passengers two cents per mile. Thus, a ticket from Mobile, Alabama, to Cleveland cost about twenty-one dollars. Since black Southern farm workers made between fifty and seventy-five cents a day, it would have taken roughly four to six weeks of earnings to pay for one ticket. Train fare continued to increase throughout the war. In 1918 the same ticket cost twenty-five dollars and by 1919 the price rose to twenty-seven dollars. Thus families often pooled their resources to send one individual north, usually an unmarried adult male, whose task was to serve as a scout and to earn the necessary funds to pay for the train fare of relatives who were awaiting their departure in the South. After the first wave of migrants moved north and sent money back home, the number of families following them started to accelerate. As more and more migrants left the South, black professionals and businessmen packed their bags and followed their customers north. Pastors, who witnessed the number of their parishioners dwindle, joined them, at times relocating with their entire congregations.

Whether migrants traveled alone or in groups, the decision to leave almost always triggered mixed emotions. Many were ecstatic about moving to the North, with its promise of abundant economic opportunities, better living conditions, and freedom from racial oppression. However, their joyful anticipation was dampened because their departure meant that they had to leave behind familiar surroundings as well as family, friends, and neighbors. Some of those who stayed in the South intended to follow the migrants North as soon as they had saved enough money to purchase their own railroad tickets.

However, most African Americans did not leave the South. Indeed, the overwhelming majority of African Americans continued to live in the

South until World War II sparked another wave of migration. Those who remained in the South were no less discontented with the racial status quo than those who left for the North. But various factors influenced their decision to stay. Many saw the departure of large numbers of black workers as an opportunity to improve their own economic conditions. The ensuing labor shortage, they hoped, would provide them with leverage to pressure whites for economic concessions and perhaps even fairer treatment. Their reasoning was justified, at least to a certain degree. The mass exodus did stimulate many Southern whites to lower rents and raise wages in order to maintain their black workforce. Moreover, America's entry into the war in 1917 generated a dramatic increase in the demand for cotton and a subsequent doubling of Southern farm wages. The wartime mobilization also created numerous new jobs in Southern industries. African Americans found growing employment opportunities in coal and iron ore mining, lumber and turpentine industries, and the construction of military camps, most of which were located in the South. Others who stayed in the South took advantage of the departing migrants' need to raise money for train tickets. Many migrants, eager to go North as quickly as possible, were willing to sell their personal property at a considerable financial loss, allowing those who stayed behind to purchase tools, wagons, furniture, homes, and real estate at prices that were well below market value. Yet others, who had farmed all of their lives, simply could not imagine living in big cities and working in industrial jobs or leaving their familiar environment for the unknown. Large numbers of African Americans remained in the South due to family obligations. They took care of elderly or sick relatives and small children who were not as mobile as other segments of the population and would have had great difficulty making the journey north.

While the departure of the migrants created economic and emotional turmoil in the Southern black communities, it also aroused the anger of white Southerners. Those who prepared to go north had to use great caution to evade whites who were trying to stop them from leaving.

Whites ordered local railroad offices not to honor prepaid tickets or closed them altogether. They instructed trains to run through their towns without stopping and imprisoned African Americans who showed up at the stations on charges of vagrancy. In Georgia, whites collaborated with local authorities on a number of occasions in an effort to stop blacks from boarding the northbound trains. In Albany, policemen tore up the railroad tickets of migrants. In Macon, they evicted hundreds of migrants from the railroad station. In Savannah, they used their clubs to prevent 200 African Americans from entering the railroad station, indiscriminately beating men, women, and children. To avoid potentially dangerous encounters with whites, prospective migrants tried to conceal their intentions, particularly sharecroppers who owed white landlords money. Many did not even tell their own ministers for fear that word would get around to whites. They left for the railroad stations under the cover of darkness, sometimes walking several miles to catch a train in a neighboring city, or jumped onto running trains outside of town.

Once on the trains, the migrants faced a strenuous and uncertain journey. Crammed into overcrowded substandard Jim Crow cars, many migrants had to stand for much of the trip. Moreover, as they passed through the South, the migrants remained apprehensive about the possibility of whites stopping the trains and removing them. It was not until the migrants crossed the Mason-Dixon Line, which divided the North and the South, that they knew beyond a doubt they had arrived in the "Promised Land." For many this was an intensely emotional event that signaled their symbolic liberation from Jim Crow. As the trains cut across the Ohio River into the North, many migrants tested and celebrated their newfound freedom. Some left the segregated railroad cars to find seats next to white passengers, while others kissed the ground or knelt down in prayer.

After a physically and emotionally exhausting trip, the migrants got their first glimpse of urban industrial life when the trains pulled into the Northern cities. Initially, many of the newcomers must have been disappointed. What they knew about the North, they had learned from the letters of migrants, the stories of returning visitors, and the pages of the *Defender*, all of which had portrayed Northern city life in extremely positive terms. Based on these glowing and often exaggerated depictions that tended to omit any negative aspects, it is likely that many of the new arrivals from the South had unrealistic expectations. However, reality set in as soon as they caught sight of the cities. Instead of finding the paradise they had hoped to see at the end of their long journey, they were greeted by dirty factories, fuming smoke stacks, tall buildings, strange odors, unprecedented noise levels, unfamiliar dialects, huge crowds of people of various racial and ethnic backgrounds, and possibly, depending on the season, bone-chilling temperatures. But there was little time to contemplate the choice they had made.

As the cars rolled into the Northern train stations, the migrants' frantic search for familiar faces began. Many of the newcomers, carrying their belongings in suitcases or pillowcases, had arranged to meet a relative, friend, or member of their migration club who would help them get settled during their first few days in the cities. Those who had friends or acquaintances waiting among the people who crowded the terminal had a much smoother entry to urban life than those who had come North without any personal contacts. Usually their friends provided them with temporary shelter, showed them around the black neighborhoods, introduced them to friends, took them to church, helped them get jobs, and acquainted them with Northern racial etiquette. Migrants who had no personal contacts were lucky if a chance encounter on the train provided them with a bed for the first night. Otherwise they had to find their way around town alone or hire a "professional" guide to locate adequate and inexpensive sleeping quarters by nightfall. Those who were literate and could read the sign that identified the services of the Travelers Aid Society at the train station might have asked one of its staff members for help. However, since white women made up the bulk of the Society's representatives, it is unlikely that many black Southerners, particularly men—who dominated the first wave of migrants—would have dared to approach them. In some cities the National Urban League sent delegates to the train stations to greet and assist the new arrivals with general information as well as boarding house registers. In addition, black churches opened their doors, accommodating stranded and destitute migrants and offering them food and clothing. Newcomers who had more money at their disposal than the majority of migrants could stay at the black branches of either the Young Men's Christian Association or Young Women's Christian Association or pay for a room at the growing number of boarding houses and hotels that catered to African Americans. Those who could find no accommodations spent their first night outside—under bridges, on park benches, and in back alleys—or in abandoned buildings or railroad cars.

Following the migrants' arrival in the North, their most pressing need was to find adequate and affordable housing, which was not readily available. The influx of massive numbers of new black residents caused severe housing shortages, which were aggravated by racial discrimination. Prior to World War I, clearly defined ghettoes already existed in Northern cities with very large black populations—such as New York, Chicago, and Philadelphia— whereas in other cities racial residential demarcation lines had begun to emerge. The black population explosion sparked by the Great Migration led to a further concentration of African Americans in certain urban areas, particularly low-income sections, and resulted in the emergence of distinct black neighborhoods in all Northern cities. This was due largely to a tightening of the housing market. As more and more migrants flocked to the cities, white landlords, for fear of lowering property values, became increasingly reluctant to sell or rent homes to African Americans outside of the black districts. Tacit "gentlemen's agreements" ensured that white realtors steered black clients away from certain neighborhoods and the restrictive covenant, a property sales clause that prohibited the owner of a home to rent or sell to

THE SURVEY FOR MAY 4, 1918

Courtesy Newark Evening

Photo 2.1 *This Florida family was among 400,000 black migrants who left the rural South in search of a better life in the urban North. Source: Newark Historical Society*

African Americans, effectively excluded blacks from white residential areas. Although the Supreme Court in *Buchanan v. Warley* (1917) ruled unconstitutional municipal ordinances that mandated residential segregation, the decision did not address the constitutionality of the restrictive covenant. Thus, white city residents confined the black population into congested ghettos—cities within cities— that offered substandard dwellings in the most undesirable neighborhoods. Homes inside the ghettos often lacked running water, electricity, and adequate ventilation. Roofs were leaking, and kitchen appliances, bathrooms, and windows were broken.

Greedy white as well as black landlords were eager to profit from the housing shortages in the black neighborhoods. They did so by dividing large homes into small kitchenette units and raising rents for their tenement apartments. A U.S. Department of Labor study estimated that during the war the rents of black tenants in Northern cities increased between 10 and 100 percent. Facing exorbitant rents, many migrants worked overtime for time-and-a-half pay, while others devised an ingenious way of raising money. They hosted catered parties at their homes, charged admission and sold food and drinks to help pay for their rent. In addition to "rent parties," another popular way of making ends meet was to take in lodgers. Utilizing all available space, migrants slept in attics, basements, garages, sheds, store fronts, kitchens, and bathtubs, or they shared a bed with another lodger who worked a different shift, a common practice known as renting a "warm bed." However, not all residents took in boarders merely to make money. Many opened their homes to recently arrived friends and family members who needed temporary shelter.

Taking in boarders, whether for financial or personal reasons, helped contribute to severe overcrowding. Soon the black neighborhoods were bursting at their seams and the ghettos started to deteriorate into slums. As the population density increased, so did sanitation and health problems as well as crime and delinquency rates. Black communities in the Northern cities witnessed a dramatic increase in tuberculosis, pneumonia, infant mortality, and venereal diseases. Particularly pneumonia and tuberculosis, caused by exposure and enhanced by exhaustive labor, inadequate nutrition, and poor hygiene, contributed to African American death rates that were twice as high as those of white city residents. High infant mortality rates also plagued the black communities. During the war years, nearly 15 percent of black infants died before their first birthday, compared to roughly 9 percent of white babies. Limited access to hospitals and physicians, inadequate sanitation, and lack of confidence in the white medical establishment as well as rural black Southerners' reliance on folk remedies worsened health conditions among African Americans. Black crime rates in the Northern cities also increased in the wake of the Great Migration. While the migration certainly attracted its share of crooks and con artists, most black delinquents were arrested for petty offenses such as vagrancy, drunkenness, disorderly conduct, gambling, and loafing on street corners. Many of the arrests were due to the lack of wholesome recreational and leisure time facilities in the black communities, because saloons, pool rooms, and "blind pigs"—illegal drinking and gambling establishments—were frequently the only sources of entertainment that were readily available to the migrants.

Longtime black urban residents, those who had lived in the Northern cities for several decades and in many cases several generations, were alarmed by the physical and alleged moral decay of black neighborhoods. Blaming the Southern migrants for the deterioration of living conditions in the urban North, well-educated light-skinned black elites often viewed the newcomers with contempt and expressed disdain for their unsophisticated and "uncivilized" behavior. They were appalled by the migrants' choice of clothing, their lack of education, their Southern drawl, and their unrefined tastes for "down-home cooking," that included fried chicken, barbecued pork, chitterlings, and pigs feet. While members of the black upper class did not discourage black Southerners from moving North, they expressed doubts about the migrants' ability to adjust to urban industrial life. Mostly, however, they were concerned about their own status in society.

Prior to the Great Migration, the old guard, which had made a living by catering to an almost exclusively white clientele, had enjoyed lives that were relatively free from racial tensions. Northern states had legally barred racial discrimination in schools and public accommodations—though the legislation was seldom enforced and no Northern cities had ordinances that excluded African Americans from renting or owning property in any urban neighborhoods. While the majority of African Americans lived in black enclaves, some members of the black elite lived in integrated neighborhoods. Their children attended schools with whites and a few even married white spouses. Although many of the cities' white-owned restaurants discriminated against black patrons, others catered to them regardless of the color of their skin. All of this, they believed, was evidence that integration was not only desirable but possible. They were convinced that their hard work, restrained life style, exemplary public deportment, and unassailable manners—Victorian values shared by upper-class white Americans—had earned them the respect of whites and allowed them to live in racial harmony. However, the arrival of large numbers of seemingly backward migrants threatened to destroy their world. The uncouth conduct of the Southerners, they feared, would offend and alienate whites and inevitably heighten racial discrimination, which would affect all members of the race, including them. Worried about the deterioration of race relations, some of the old settlers distanced themselves from the migrants to preserve their lifestyles. Whites, they hoped, would realize that the old elites had nothing in common with the uncultured riffraff from the South and would therefore continue to treat them with the respect and courtesy they deserved.

Other members of the old black elite sought to ease the transition of the Southern migrants to urban life and joined forces with the emerging black middle class. Composed of skilled artisans, clergymen, journalists, physicians, lawyers, teachers, dentists, and business leaders who had migrated to the cities at the turn of the century, members of the middle class owed their fortunes largely to the expanding black urban population. Like the old settlers, they challenged racial discrimination. However, instead of pursuing integration, they advocated self-help and supported the creation of separate black-controlled institutions. Old elites, who were ardent integrationists, were dismayed, because to them any form of self-segregation signaled acceptance of Jim Crow. Indeed, members of the black urban middle class did not surrender to racism, instead they embraced both Booker T. Washington's call for racial solidarity and black economic empowerment as well as W. E. B. Du Bois's insistence on protesting discrimination and segregation. While their concern for the migrants was sparked, at least in part, by ulterior motives— after all, every new black city resident was a potential client, customer, or patron who could contribute to the growth and prosperity of black institutions—they also shared the belief that the better class of African Americans had an obligation to aid the less fortunate and lift the race.

Middle-class blacks and their old settler allies provided important social services and welfare programs for the migrants. In cities across the North, they launched civic groups that aided newcomers, but in many cases they worked through existing black community organizations, such as fraternal orders, affiliates of the Association of Colored Women's Clubs, and branches of the YMCA and YWCA. Local churches, especially the nation's two largest black denominations, Baptists and Methodists, also played a crucial role in easing the migrants' transition to urban life. The *Christian Recorder*, the newspaper of the African Methodist Episcopal church reminded its ministers to "get these Negroes in your churches; make them welcome; don't turn up your nose and let the saloon man and the gambler do all the welcoming."[10] Wilhelmina Lewis Means, a member of Detroit's Second Baptist Church, recalled that her minister urged members of the community to meet the migrants "from the South, at train stations, to bring them in, to see that they had housing and food" and to help them get jobs.[11] The services these black institutions provided for the migrants varied from city to city. Most organizations maintained employment bureaus for those who had come north without a work contract, and kept lists of vacant homes, furnished rooms, and boarding houses. Some operated dormitories, kindergarten, and nursery facilities as well as reading and game rooms. Yet others distributed food and clothing and offered temporary housing, vocational training, and educational classes, as well as entertainment, athletic, and recreational programs. Moreover, volunteers helped migrants read and understand job and rental contracts and wrote letters home for those who were illiterate.

In addition to these self-help efforts, members of the black middle class collaborated with white racial liberals and philanthropists to aid the migrants. The single most important biracial organization that assisted black newcomers during World War I was the National Urban League. Established in 1911 in New York City, the League was composed of black community leaders, social workers, and white progressives, who were concerned about poor housing, sanitation, and health conditions in the black urban neighborhoods as well as the deterioration of race relations. When World War I opened the floodgates and the influx of thousands of black newcomers threatened to worsen living and racial conditions in the urban North, the League invited representatives of industry, labor, government, churches, and the press to discuss the ramifications of the migration. Delegates convened for a National Conference on Negro Migration in Cleveland in 1916 and in the following year in New York City. Both conferences decided not to discourage or deter prospective migrants, but urged them to take proper steps to prepare for their move north by securing jobs and housing prior to their departure. Once the migrants arrived in the North, the Urban League pledged to assist them. Though the League was only in its infancy at the start of World War I, the wartime migration contributed to its nationwide growth. By 1919, more than thirty cities had League affiliates, including many of the cities that were the principal destinations of the Southern migrants: New York, Chicago, Detroit, Cleveland, Newark, Philadelphia, Pittsburgh, St. Louis, Milwaukee, Columbus, and Youngstown, Ohio.

Although most migrants did not encounter the Urban League until after their arrival in the North, large numbers of black Southerners were aware of the League's work through the *Defender*, even prior to their departure from the South. Many of the migrants took the *Defender*'s advice to contact local League branches and flooded their offices with requests for information about housing, employment, and addresses of landlords and boarding homes. League officials supplied a host of informational materials, including advice on what to wear and warnings about pickpockets and other crooks who often descended upon the newcomers and took advantage of the naive country rubes. Moreover, the League cautioned the migrants not to leave the South unless they had secured a labor contract and at least temporary shelter in their destination city.

Upon the migrants' arrival in the North, League workers who served as travelers' aid agents were often the first to greet the newcomers at the train stations. They gave them directions, sent young single migrants to reputable boarding homes, and provided free temporary lodging to those who needed a bed for the night. They distributed cards with the League's address, informing the migrants about available services such as employment bureaus and housing registers. And they dispensed warm clothes and hot meals to newcomers who had failed to bring proper clothing or were hungry and had run out of money. At the League's local branches, paid staff and volunteers assisted those who were looking for a job, a home, or wholesome recreational opportunities. They offered vocational courses and educational programs, trained domestics in the use of modern kitchen appliances, and organized kindergartens, baby clinics, playgrounds, and day care. In addition, League staff visited factories in an effort to open new or better employment opportunities for black workers. Some League officials were especially ingenious in their effort to address housing shortages. The Detroit League, for example, convinced two foundries to build low-priced homes for their black employees. In addition, the Motor City League purchased the leases of brothels that had been closed by police and then converted them to house migrants. The League also collaborated with other black civic groups and organized community centers that hosted dances, basketball and baseball tournaments, book clubs, and debating societies. After the migrants had settled in their new urban homes, a cadre of League volunteers, largely drawn from the ranks of the women's clubs, visited the newcomers. They instructed them about sanitation and health care, urged them to get vaccinated, and sent visiting nurses to those who required medical assistance.

Although the League's work provided the newcomers with much-needed practical assistance and useful information, its staff and volunteers, composed of middle-class blacks, were often as condescending and patronizing in their interaction with the migrants as the old elites. Many regarded themselves as the better class of blacks and looked down on the migrants' food choices, their clothing, and their conduct, which they considered to be vulgar and uncivilized. Intent on fostering middle-class values and ideals, League officials lectured the migrants on the standards of proper dress, nutrition, public deportment, thrift, work habits, recreational pursuits, and cleanliness. They discouraged migrants from loafing on street corners; sitting on front porches or stoops; visiting red-light districts; frequenting saloons, juke joints, or pool halls; using vulgar language; or speaking loudly in public. These kinds of

behavior, the League insisted, were public nuisances that were sure to increase white prejudices and racial hostilities. Instead, the League urged the
Southern newcomers to become a credit to their race. They encouraged them
to join reputable churches, seek out wholesome recreational venues, con-
sume nutritious food, save money, and practice proper personal hygiene. And
in lunchtime talks in factories they reminded them to be punctual, efficient,
clean, productive, sober, and thrifty workers.

The Urban League's middle-class leadership was not alone in its concern
about the migrants. Robert S. Abbott, editor of the Chicago *Defender*, was
also worried that their rustic appearances and behavior would contribute to a
surge in racial discrimination. Abbott repeatedly reminded the migrants to
behave and dress appropriately. He published lengthy etiquette manuals that
admonished them not to "use vile language in public places . . . act discourte-
ously to other people . . . encourage gamblers, disreputable women or men to
ply their business . . . congregate in crowds on the streets . . . spend . . . time
hanging around saloon doors or poolrooms . . . appear on the street with old
dust caps, dirty aprons and ragged clothes."[12] Abbott, whose profits from flour-
ishing newspaper sales among the migrants had allowed him to develop and
sustain an appetite for the finer things in life, also disapproved of their food
choices and eating habits. Chicken shacks, barbecue wagons, and other street
and sidewalk vendors selling Southern foods, he believed, were unsightly sores
on the urban landscape. The *Defender* advised against the consumption of
distinct Southern foods, claiming that they were unhealthy and lacked nutrition. However, Abbott's real concern was that Southern foods, just like
Southern garments, would reflect poorly on all members of the race and contribute to a deterioration of race relations in the cities of the North.

Despite black middle-class efforts to eliminate manifestations of Southern
culture that they deemed backward and objectionable, the migrants retained
some of their customs and traditions. They adopted new urban dress codes,
but largely held on to their food, music, and religious preferences. In the years
following World War I, Southern "down-home cooking" became one of the
most profitable business ventures in the Northern black urban communities.
Blues performers as well as jazz musicians—many of whom left the South in
the aftermath of the 1917 closing of legendary Storyville, the red-light district
and music center in New Orleans—enjoyed tremendous popularity among
the migrant population. While many of the migrants joined existing black
urban churches, others established new ones that celebrated their Southern
origins. Storefront churches that embraced traditional black Southern forms
of active worship, including shouting, singing, and other emotionally demon-
strative expressions, appealed to large numbers of migrants.

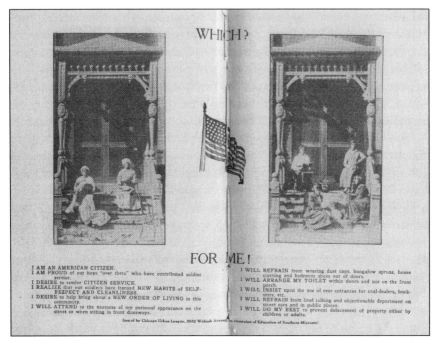

Photo 2.2 *The Urban League urged Southern black migrants to dress and behave appropriately in the cities of the North. Source: National Urban League, Annual Report 1919 (January 1920): 20–21*

While the wartime migration sparked tensions between the black elite and middle-class residents of Northern cities and the working-class migrants, it also amplified already existing interracial hostilities. White Northerners were alarmed by the flood of Southern black migrants, especially rural, un-educated, single men who lacked the moral guidance of families and churches. In the eyes of white residents, the migrants seemed to overrun their cities. They threatened to lower property values and contribute to rising crime rates and increased sanitation and health problems. Although some white Northern newspapers were sympathetic to the migrants, characterizing them as victims of Southern racism, many more portrayed them as a threat to civic order. As white Northern concerns about the negative impact of the black migrants began to surface, the release of D. W. Griffith's epic motion picture *The Birth of a Nation* (1915) added fuel to the fire. Griffith's film, commemorating the fiftieth anniversary of the end of the Civil War, de-picted the aftermath of slavery from a Southern white perspective and used the most vicious racist stereotypes to portray African Americans. Although the movie blamed white Northerners for ending slavery and thereby creating racial chaos in the South, the film was extremely successful in the North, where it struck a chord with white audiences who feared that the black migrants were about to destroy their way of life. Whites in the North were determined not to let that happen and some even resorted to violence.

In several Northern cities, white residents harassed and beat up migrants and attacked the homes of those who dared to rent or purchase property in previously all-white neighborhoods. In Detroit, a mob of 200 whites forced black residents who had moved into a white section of town out of their home. The thugs then demolished the house and threw out the furniture and destroyed it. In Cleveland, white gangs used stones to smash the windows of black homes, and in Chicago hoodlums detonated twenty-four bombs at black residences.

In the summer of 1917, mounting white opposition to the migrants escalated into a full-fledged riot in East St. Louis, Illinois, the bloodiest and deadliest race riot of the twentieth century. Like other industrial cities, East St. Louis had attracted its share of Southern black migrants. Although their numbers were relatively small—compared to those who had moved to Cleveland, Detroit, Chicago, or nearby St. Louis—nonetheless, their arrival triggered white hostility. Unscrupulous Democratic politicians exploited the situation. They spread rumors claiming that the Republican Party was responsible for the influx of the migrants, insinuating that the party had brought Southern blacks to the city to increase the Republican vote and to work as strikebreakers. As fears of job competition grew, white residents began to use force against the black migrants. Beginning on May 28 and lasting throughout June of 1917, whites regularly assaulted black residents, set their houses on fire, and randomly shot at them. These incidents of racial violence paved the way for the riot that erupted on July 2. When African Americans fired back at their tormentors, white crowds armed themselves and marched through the city, instigating an orgy of violence and destruction. They brutally tortured and killed black men, women, and children and torched black homes. Local police and National Guard troops refused to act and some even encouraged and aided the mob. When the rioting died down, thirty-nine African Americans lay dead, hundreds were wounded, entire city blocks in the district known as "Black Valley" had been reduced to ashes, and thousands of black residents had fled across the Mississippi River to seek shelter in St. Louis.

African Americans throughout the country were stunned by the devastation and the atrocities. The bloodbath had happened in a city that had attracted thousands of Southern migrants with the promise of a better life. Was this the "Promised Land," where economic opportunities and racial equality abounded? Until the events in East St. Louis, many migrants had considered the North a safe haven from racial violence. It was a place where Southern blacks could find well-paying jobs in industries, enroll their children in good schools, and enjoy a higher degree of personal autonomy and better living conditions than anywhere in the South. But East St. Louis was a reminder that even in the "Promised Land" they were second-class citizens. Lacking civil rights, African Americans were ambivalent about their role in the world conflict as America started to mobilize for war in the spring and summer of 1917.

~

CHAPTER THREE

Fighting to Fight

The Struggle for Black Officers and Combat Soldiers

When the United States entered World War I in April of 1917, African Americans were divided in their response to America's involvement. Some African Americans were indifferent. In their eyes it was a white man's war from which African Americans had nothing to gain. Others were disillusioned with their second-class-citizenship status or resentful of the Army's segregation policy and opposed black military service. However, many influential black leaders viewed military service as an important step toward racial equality. They argued that if African Americans demonstrated their willingness to make the ultimate sacrifice for their country, the nation could no longer deny them civil rights. Although troubled by segregation in the armed forces, they decided that it was more important to secure combat and officer training for African Americans than to challenge the Army's Jim Crow policy. Throughout 1917 they launched concerted efforts to ensure that the Army would not relegate black men to labor battalions but prepare them for combat duty and train black officers to lead them into battle.

From the outset, the prospect of black men serving in combat under the command of black officers was grim. The Army excluded African Americans from the nation's fourteen officers training schools and decided not to mobilize the four all-black Regular Army units—the Ninth and Tenth Cavalry and the Twenty-Fourth and Twenty-Fifth Infantry—for service in Europe. Although the professional black troops were seasoned soldiers whose training and experience had prepared them for combat, the War Department assigned the men to the most remote and isolated military outposts in the West and along the

Mexican border as well as Hawaii and the Philippines. Likewise, the War Department initially did not send members of the all-black National Guard units to Europe but assigned them to service in the United States. In the spring of 1917, the War Department summoned the First Separate Battalion of the District of Columbia to guard strategic positions in the nation's capital, fully aware that German spies would find it impossible to infiltrate them.

Black hopes for combat duty were further crushed when the War Department, which initially sought to raise the necessary manpower through voluntary enlistment, limited the number of black volunteers. Immediately following America's entry into the war, 4,000 black volunteers enlisted in the Army, filling the ranks of the four segregated all-black Regular Army units. Since it was Army policy not to accept black men for service in white regiments the War Department suspended any further black enlistments. As Army recruitment offices turned down black men, some African Americans were wondering why they should volunteer to fight for a nation that had treated them so badly. Black Presbyterian minister Francis J. Grimké put it bluntly: "A government that is so blinded by prejudice, so lacking in sense of justice . . . is not worth serving . . . Let them fight their own battles, and go to the devil."[1]

However, the War Department's decision to limit black military participation was short-lived. Within a month after declaring war, the Wilson administration realized that the War Department's call for volunteers had generated a less-than-satisfactory response among white Americans. As one scholar noted: "the U.S. government announced a war, and American men declined the invitation."[2] Some white Americans were slow to volunteer because they had European roots and were apprehensive about potentially facing relatives, friends, or former fellow countrymen in battle. Yet others were reaping the benefits of a booming economy. Wages in industry were higher than military pay and factory jobs seemed far less dangerous than frontline duty, even though industrial accidents caused the deaths of numerous workers each year. Moreover, many men could not get excited about the war's abstract goal of fighting imperialism, despotism, and autocracy. In addition, large numbers of men who lived in isolated communities in the rural South, had only limited access to information about world politics and had never heard of Germany or the Kaiser. Finally, particularly in the South, white men were often not willing to volunteer for military service because it meant leaving their families without proper protection from alleged sexual advances of black men.

The lack of white volunteers, as well as allied appeals for troop reinforcements, forced the American government to resort to compulsory military service in May of 1917. President Wilson had instructed Secretary of War

Newton D. Baker to prepare for a military draft on February 22, 1917, several weeks prior to America's declaration of war. Indeed, preparedness had been on the minds of many Americans after the outbreak of hostilities in Europe in 1914. Military and government officials had discussed revising the nation's defense system and counseled against reliance on state militia units and volunteers. Instead, some of them advocated universal military training for all American men, arguing that it was the most democratic way of raising an army. However, that suggestion generated a lot of opposition, particularly among farmers, specifically white Southerners who feared losing their black agricultural workforce. Wilson also had misgivings about universal military training, because it had the potential to undermine America's industrial workforce and weaken defense production. The War Department opted for a compromise solution. On April 6, 1917, the administration introduced a bill that called for a selective draft. All men between the ages of twenty-one and thirty would have to register for military service. But the bill granted exemptions to a number of individuals, including legislators; high-ranking government officials; clergymen; pacifists; essential agricultural and industrial workers; and those who were physically, mentally, or morally unfit or had dependent families. Conscious of the controversy that had plagued the Civil War draft, which had allowed rich men to hire substitutes to fight for them, the 1917 Selective Service bill permitted no substitutions.

While the proposed legislation sought to put to rest working-class concerns that poor men would do all the fighting, the bill's inclusion of African Americans raised racial concerns among Southern whites. In 1916, anticipating U.S. involvement in the war, Southern members of the House of Representatives had already introduced a bill to prevent the enlistment of African Americans. However, Secretary of War Newton D. Baker, perhaps the most racially liberal member of the Wilson administration, had opposed the bill and it gained little support in Congress. The 1917 draft bill revived the debate about black participation in the military, and Southern Democrats, ironically members of Wilson's own party, launched a massive campaign to defeat it. They argued that the training of black men in arms would at best threaten white supremacy and at worst ignite a race war. However, others reasoned that exempting African Americans from the draft would not only be unfair to whites but also dangerous. If African Americans were relieved from military service, white men would have to shoulder the entire burden of fighting while black men would be allowed to stay at home and out of harm's way. Thus, neither arming black men nor exempting them from military service was appealing to white Southerners. Despite considerable race-based opposition from Southern Democrats, members of Congress—

perhaps motivated by a desire to demonstrate their patriotism and loyalty— passed the Selective Service Act on May 18, 1917. The law initiated a draft, requiring all men, regardless of race, to register for military service. States that failed to select black draftees would have to meet their manpower quota by inducting whites.

While some African Americans praised the draft as a recognition of black citizenship, others had doubts that it would indeed be color blind. To maintain segregation in the military, draft administrators would have to identify the race of draftees on their registration cards. This, many civil rights activists feared, would allow the War Department to single out black draftees and assign them exclusively to labor units. They wondered how African Americans could prove their patriotism and demonstrate their courage under fire if they saw no frontline duty, but were relegated to building latrines and peeling potatoes. Thus, the training of black men as combat soldiers and officers was a crucial concern of race leaders during the spring and summer of 1917. The all-important question was: could they achieve both goals without compromising the struggle for racial equality?

The National Association for the Advancement of Colored People (NAACP) addressed that question three days after the United States declared war. On April 9, its board of directors passed a unanimous resolution pledging to continue the fight for racial justice and announcing the NAACP's opposition to discrimination in the armed forces. However, within a few short weeks, the NAACP retreated from its original position and started to endorse the creation of a segregated black officers training camp. The two men who were largely responsible for changing the NAACP's course were Joel E. Spingarn, the white chairman of the association's board of directors, and W. E. B. Du Bois, the organization's highest-ranking black official and editor of its *Crisis* magazine.

Spingarn, though an outspoken integrationist, had started to agitate for an all-black officers training camp prior to U.S. entry into the war. In 1915, he had attended a private volunteer training camp, run by preparedness advocate General Leonard Wood. Spingarn initially tried to convince Wood to admit black cadets to his camp in Plattsburg, New York. However, Wood refused to consider Spingarn's suggestion. When the 1916 National Defense Act established reserve officers training camps that barred African Americans, Spingarn concluded that the War Department would under no circumstances agree to integrate the armed forces. Thus, African Americans were left with two unenviable choices: either forgo officer training entirely or demand a segregated camp. Spingarn decided that the latter was the lesser of two evils. A black officer corps, Spingarn hoped, was best positioned to lead the fight against military segregation. In early 1917, he approached Wood about opening a camp for black officer candidates. Wood promised to do so if Spingarn secured the signatures of 200 college-educated black men who were willing to enroll in the training program. In February, Spingarn took his campaign to the black public. In an open letter, Spingarn urged the "Educated Colored Men of the United States" to sign up for training in a segregated officers training camp. He admitted that his proposal was not ideal and reminded African Americans that support of the camp did not mean that they should stop agitating for racial equality and justice.

Not surprisingly, the plan generated fierce opposition among the NAACP's leadership, leading Spingarn to offer his resignation as chairman of the board. Although Spingarn remained at the helm of the NAACP, his call for a segregated black officers camp divided the association's membership and triggered a flood of harsh criticism from the black press. Numerous black papers, including the influential *Chicago Defender*, the *Cleveland Gazette*, the *Baltimore Afro-American*, the *New York Age*, and the *Washington Bee*, condemned Spingarn for promoting a Jim Crow camp. It was bad enough that African Americans had to accommodate to segregation imposed by whites, they argued, but for blacks to demand a segregated officers camp was infinitely worse. It legitimized discrimination and set back the struggle for racial equality. Robert S. Abbott, editor of the *Chicago Defender*, categorically opposed the camp, insisting that "If we are good enough to fight, we are good enough to receive the same preparatory training our white brothers receive."[3]

While most black editors and NAACP activists initially opposed Spingarn's plan, black colleges and universities responded with enthusiasm. On March 20, one month after Spingarn published his open letter to the "Educated Colored Men of the United States," he visited Howard University, the nation's leading black school in Washington, D.C. In a speech he sought to drum up support for the camp and even offered to pay personally for 100 uniforms. Inspired by Spingarn's speech, black fraternities spread the word to campuses around the country, and Howard students, faculty, and administrators organized the Central Committee of Negro College Men. Howard's president authorized academic leaves for all committee members who worked to convince African Americans to support the camp and lobbied Congress to overcome white opposition. The committee raised funds to print and mail officers training camp applications to all black colleges and universities, and soon Spingarn received letters of support from the presidents of Hampton Institute, Fisk University, Morehouse College, and other black schools. The solitary voice of objection came from Robert R. Moton, who had become principal of Tuskegee Institute after Booker T. Washington's death in 1915.

Though not opposed to the camp, Moton declined to distribute the applica-tion forms because he feared that his support would alienate one of the school's white trustees, who was attempting to raise a black cavalry regiment composed of Tuskegee men. In addition to mobilizing black students, mem-bers of the Central Committee visited churches and civic groups to sign up recruits, flooded Congress with letters, and distributed an appeal, titled "Training Camp for Negro Officers," to all members of Congress. Comple-menting the work of the students, Dr. George W. Cabaniss, a prominent D.C. physician, and Dr. J. Milton Waldron, former president of the NAACP's Washington branch, launched the Committee of 100 Colored Citizens on the War. The Committee of 100 raised public awareness and initiated a let-ter-writing campaign aimed at swaying white politicians and government officials to support the creation of a black officers training camp.

Emboldened by the enthusiastic response among the black colleges, Spin-garn led a delegation of his supporters, including Kelly Miller, dean of How-ard University's College of Arts and Sciences, and NAACP cofounder Ar-chibald H. Grimké, to meet with Secretary of War Newton D. Baker on April 27. Baker informed Spingarn and his men that the admission of Afri-can Americans to the existing fourteen officers camps was out of the ques-tion, due to the racial prejudice of many of the military brass. Baker assured the delegation that he did not share those racist sentiments and that he was supportive of a black officers training camp, but that he had not yet made specific plans. While Spingarn's supporters were disappointed with Baker's lukewarm response, the Secretary of War was not stalling. Indeed, he had instructed the Office of the Chief of Staff to study the matter and present recommendations for the creation of a black officers training camp. Military leaders voiced serious reservations about preparing black men for combat duty, let alone officers training. Reiterating racist stereotypes, they insisted that black men lacked discipline, were lazy and intellectually inferior to whites, and should only be used in labor battalions under white command.

As the Secretary of War was weighing his options, the black students and educators who had lobbied for the creation of a black officers training camp were losing their patience. On May 7, the Central Committee of Negro Col-lege Men tried to force Baker into action and presented the War Department with a list of 1,500 names of black volunteers who were eager to start their officer training. Four days later the Committee of 100 asked Wilson to inter-vene, however, their request elicited no response from the president. As usual, Wilson remained mum.

Meanwhile, NAACP leaders, witnessing the surge of support for a black officers training camp among the black colleges started to reconsider their initial opposition to segregated military facilities. The first NAACP official to endorse Spingarn's proposal for a black officers training camp was W. E. B. Du Bois, editor of the association's *Crisis* magazine. Du Bois's endorsement of the camp seemed uncharacteristic, since he was an ardent proponent of integration and opposed to anything that smacked of accommodation. Several reasons help explain Du Bois's controversial decision to back Spingarn. Du Bois and Spingarn, perhaps more so than other NAACP leaders, had established a close personal relationship. Though their friendship was at times fraught with tensions, they were similar in temperament and considered themselves to be intellectual equals. Following the death of Booker T. Washington in 1915, both men had collaborated in an attempt to unite Washington's former supporters and NAACP activists. In 1916, they invited 200 representatives to a meeting at Spingarn's summer estate in Amenia, New York. Approximately 50 prominent black leaders, representing accommodationist and integrationist forces, attended the Amenia Conference, including Emmett J. Scott, Booker T. Washington's former secretary at Tuskegee Institute; Mary Church Terrell, cofounder of the NAACP; Howard University's Kelly Miller; and James Weldon Johnson, NAACP field secretary and co-composer of the "Negro National Anthem," *Lift Every Voice and Sing*. Attendees adopted a "Unity Platform" that sought to appease both factions, by acknowledging the importance of vocational as well as academic education in the struggle for racial advancement. Yet, the platform also stressed political freedom as a prerequisite for racial equality. Although attendees made no plans for implementing their agenda, the conference was a symbolic victory for Du Bois and Spingarn, whose organizing efforts helped to establish the NAACP as the nation's foremost civil rights group on the eve of World War I. Moreover, the conference cemented the friendship that Du Bois and Spingarn had established over the course of several years. Indeed, when Du Bois needed money to pay for a kidney operation in early 1917, the independently wealthy Spingarn loaned him the necessary funds.

But it was not only the friendship between the two men that helped sway Du Bois to support Spingarn's call for a separate black officers training camp. Du Bois also agreed with his friend's assessment that the War Department was unwilling to consider integration of the armed forces. Du Bois, who was known for using the *Crisis* as a platform for his eloquent attacks on discrimination, explained his controversial decision in the April 1917 issue of the magazine. Supporting a segregated black officers training camp, he conceded, was not ideal, but merely a necessary evil. Addressing opponents, he admitted that a separate camp was indeed an insult to African Americans; however, he insisted that the "choice is as clear as noonday. . . . It is a case of camp or no officers."[4] Other prominent African Americans as well as white NAACP members came to Du Bois's aid, including Mary White Ovington, influential white cofounder of the NAACP; Major Charles R. Douglass, son of black abolitionist Frederick Douglass; and Lieutenant Colonel Charles Young, the Army's highest-ranking black officer. Opposition within the NAACP dissipated, and the association's board of directors voted to support the campaign for a segregated black officers training camp on May 14.

By the time the NAACP officially endorsed Spingarn's call for a black officers training camp, the Secretary of War had made up his mind. On May 12, he instructed his personal secretary to inform the president of Howard University that he had approved the creation of the camp. However, Baker's unofficial letter did not reveal any specifics, such as the camp's location or the name of the commanding officer who would be in charge of training the black recruits.

Three days later, the NAACP invited 700 representatives from black newspapers, businesses, schools, and churches as well as civic and social welfare organizations to a conference in Washington, D.C. Between May 17 and 19, participants gathered at Howard University to discuss the role of African Americans in the war. Although many delegates had misgivings about accommodating to Jim Crow, they decided not to challenge segregation in the armed forces. In exchange, however, they asked the government to provide combat and officer training for black troops. The delegates adopted a lengthy list of resolutions that illustrated their determination to reconcile their accommodationist recommendations with their integrationist aspirations. They pledged to support the war effort, despite the military's Jim Crow policy, but also vowed to continue their fight for racial justice. They assured the nation of black loyalty and patriotism, yet at the same time, they reminded the government that a victory for world democracy had to include democratic rights for African Americans. "Absolute loyalty in arms and in civil duties," Du Bois explained, "need not for a moment lead us to abate our just complaints and just demands."[5]

Those who met in Washington had high hopes that their willingness to accommodate would garner results. They did not have to wait long. On May 19, the last day of the conference, the War Department officially announced the creation of the black officers training camp.

Spingarn, with the help of the Central Committee, had achieved his goal: African Americans would have the opportunity to become officers and lead black troops into battle. It appeared as if African Americans had won a victory, albeit a bittersweet one. They had sacrificed their demands for military integration, but they had secured a training camp for black officers. Despite initial black opposition to the camp, the vast majority of African American activists, including the editors of the most influential black newspapers who had at the outset objected to self-segregation, eventually accepted the camp and celebrated it as an unprecedented opportunity for black men to assume leadership positions in the Army.

But before the camp could open, it would take another round of recruiting qualified black candidates. In early May, the Central Committee had presented the Secretary of War with a list of 1,500 volunteers who were ready to start officer training. However, now the War Department insisted on enrolling only mature men between the ages of twenty-five and forty-four, with a preference for those thirty and older. Since all of the Central Committee recruits were college students or recent graduates, none of them met the new age requirement. Once again, the Central Committee dispatched its recruitment crews and by mid-June managed to sign up a sufficient number of qualified black men. Not surprisingly, students and faculty who had worked so hard to make the officers training camp a reality hoped that the Army would train the black cadets on the grounds of one of the black college campuses. Instead, the War Department selected Fort Des Moines, Iowa, as the site for the nation's first and only black officers training camp.

The decision to train the men at Fort Des Moines, the War Department explained, was based solely on considerations of military efficiency. The campuses of Howard University and Hampton Institute were too small to accommodate the cadets, while Alabama's Tuskegee Institute was inappropriate because of its location in the Deep South, where the sight of black officers was sure to arouse white hostility. Fort Des Moines, military leaders argued, was a large 400-acre camp with easy access to rail lines, and they pointed out that Iowa had an excellent record in racial matters. Obviously, the state's clean bill of health in the area of race relations was due to the fact that Iowa had only a tiny black population. In 1910, black residents of Iowa numbered roughly 15,000, constituting less than 0.7 percent of the state's total population. Indeed, the War Department picked Iowa, at least in part, to suppress white Southern opposition to the black officers camp and to prevent the eruption of interracial violence, which would have been detrimental to military efficiency. While the majority of the nation's military training camps were located in the South, the training of black officers in Southern states would have, without a doubt, incited racial violence, as white rank-and-file soldiers would have been forced to salute black officers. In Iowa, on the other hand, which was home only to Camp Dodge, encounters between white soldiers and black officers could be kept to a minimum. The War Department's plan was to train the black cadets in a remote part of the country with as little publicity as possible. After completion of their training, the black officers were to be shipped immediately to France in order to protect white American soldiers from any embarrassing contacts with African Americans who outranked them.

On June 15, 1,250 black officer candidates, 1,000 of them civilians and 250 noncommissioned officers from the Army's four black regiments, arrived in Iowa to begin their three-month training program. Black advocates of the camp had hoped that the War Department would put one of the three black commissioned officers—Charles Young, John E. Green, or Benjamin O. Davis—in charge of the Des Moines camp. But instead, the Army questioned Young's physical fitness and bogged him down with medical tests, dispatched Green to Liberia, and posted Davis in the Philippines. A white man, Lieutenant Colonel Charles C. Ballou, who had in the previous five years served with the all-black Twenty-Fourth Infantry, assumed command of the camp. Although black supporters of the camp would have preferred an African American commander, Ballou was not the worst choice for the job. However, he was not the best one either.

Ballou was firmly committed to segregation, but he also believed that separate facilities could be truly equal. When whites voiced doubts about the ability of black officers to lead black men into battle, Ballou praised the performance of the black cadets. However, his praise was not genuine, but merely intended to maintain morale among the men and to avoid racial conflicts. Despite his public statements in support of the black officer candidates, Ballou shared the racist views and paternalistic attitudes of many white contemporaries. Reporting to the War Department, he insisted that African Americans lacked the mental and moral capacity to lead black soldiers. When some of the local restaurants and theaters refused to serve black men in uniform, Ballou cautioned the men under his command to avoid any controversial conduct, reminding them that the nation was watching them and that their success or failure was bound to reflect upon all members of their race. And when Des Moines residents staged patriotic rallies in the stadium of Drake University, Ballou ordered the black cadets to entertain the white spectators with spirituals.

Ballou had little faith that the black men under his command would become capable and efficient officers, and he exposed them only to minimal training. White officers and black noncommissioned officers from the Army's all-black regiments, conducted daily drills, exercises, and class work, which kept the black rookies busy from 5:30 AM until 10:45 PM. Yet, despite this intense schedule, some black officer candidates became suspicious when the camp provided only infantry instruction and none of the prescribed artillery courses offered at the white camps. George S. Schuyler, a disillusioned twenty-two-year-old black noncommissioned officer, noted that many of the recruits "sensed that we were just marking time for some high-echelon purpose."[6] Not only did the training of the black cadets at Des Moines differ from that of white officer candidates, but so did the size of their class and their educational background. Doubtful that African Americans could raise a sufficient number of qualified black applicants, the War Department had decided to start classes at Des Moines at approximately half the size of a standard officers training class. Moreover, the military had lowered educational admission standards for black men. While a college diploma was required of white cadets who were enrolled in the nation's fourteen officers training camps that excluded blacks, at Des Moines the minimum requirement was a high school diploma. Although the military gave preference to those who had attended college, only 40 percent of the Des Moines men had earned their degrees.

Most of the civilians who had signed up for officer training at Des Moines were members of the "Talented Tenth." They were students, lawyers, engineers, businessmen, physicians, dentists, journalists, teachers, university professors, and other highly skilled professionals. They hailed from more than fifty black colleges and universities, with Howard leading enrollments at nearly 200 students and faculty. Among the men were well-known individuals, including the founders of two black fraternities as well as men who rose to fame after the war, most notably the journalist and author George S. Schuyler; the cofounders of the National Bar Association; and Howard Long, who became the first African American to earn an EdD from Harvard. But perhaps the camp's most famous student was Charles Hamilton Houston, who would later serve as Dean of Howard University's Law School. In the 1930s, Houston was responsible for training Thurgood Marshall, the NAACP attorney who helped overturn segregation in the 1954 *Brown v. Board of Education* decision and who became the first black Supreme Court justice in 1965.

In addition to training black officer candidates in the art of commanding infantry troops, Fort Des Moines was also home to the Colored Medical Officers Training Camp. Opening on July 26, the medical training camp was under the supervision of white camp commander Lieutenant Colonel E. G. Bingham, who prepared black physicians, dentists, and other health care professionals for service with the Army Medical Corps. Plagued by an initial shortage of qualified applicants, Bingham convinced 33 of the physicians and 12 of the dentists who trained under Ballou to transfer to the medical camp. Soon the camp boasted 116 medical professionals as well as 900 enlisted men who trained for various health care posts.

While the training of black officers at Des Moines raised the hopes of many African Americans, who anticipated full democratic rights as a just reward for their support of the war, black expectations were dampened when the War Department forcefully retired Charles Young in the summer of 1917. At the time the United States entered World War I, Young, the highest-ranking black officer in the Army, was the obvious choice to lead a black division. The son of former slaves from Kentucky, he had graduated from the U.S. Military Academy at West Point, New York, in 1889. He was one of only nine black cadets and only the third black man to graduate from West Point. Following his graduation, Young served in various military capacities with the all-black Ninth and Tenth Cavalry in the West and along the Mexican border. In 1894, the Army assigned Young to Wilberforce University in Ohio, one of the oldest historically black colleges and universities. At Wilberforce he taught military science and established his permanent home, the "Youngsholm" estate, where he entertained many visitors, including poet Paul Laurence Dunbar and W. E. B. Du Bois, who started teaching at Wilberforce in the same year as Young. During the two years that Du Bois taught at Wilberforce, he was a frequent guest at Youngsholm, and the men established a lifelong friendship. In 1898, when the Spanish-American War erupted, Young left his post at Wilberforce University to supervise and train the Ninth Ohio black volunteer battalion. In 1902, the War Department dispatched him to command black troops in the Philippines, and two years later he became the first black military attaché to Haiti. Between 1911 and 1915, he served in the same capacity in Liberia. In 1916 he resumed his service with the Tenth Cavalry and joined General John J. Pershing's Punitive Expedition to Mexico. Pershing was so impressed with Young's performance that he personally arranged for his promotion to lieutenant colonel. When the United States entered World War I, Young was in charge of Fort Huachuca in Arizona. Given Young's credentials, many African Americans hoped that he would be promoted to colonel, or perhaps even general, and assume command of a black combat division. Instead, Young spent the first three months following U.S. entry into the war in various military medical facilities, as the Army was trying to determine his physical fitness.

Young's trouble began on May 7, 1917, when he reported to a medical examination board in preparation for his promotion to the rank of colonel. The medical examiners determined that Young had high blood pressure and ordered him to undergo further tests at Letterman General Hospital in San Francisco, where he remained throughout June and into July. While undergoing tests and waiting for the results at the hospital, Young learned of the establishment of the black officers training camp at Des Moines and became increasingly convinced that the War Department had orchestrated his time-consuming medical exams not because of health concerns but because the military brass wanted to prevent his promotion. His suspicion was well founded.

Although Young did have high blood pressure, which contributed to his death in 1922, the medical examiners were willing to disregard his health problem because the nation was at war and in dire need of experienced officers. However, Young's rise to military fame had incensed white officers who served under his command in Fort Huachuca. Captain Albert B. Dockery, a white Mississippian who was steeped in Southern racial etiquette, complained to his father that he had to take orders from a black commander. Dockery's outraged father appealed to the senator from Mississippi, a staunch supporter of Woodrow Wilson, who then approached the president. Concerned about appeasing white Southerners, Wilson asked the Secretary of War if it was possible to transfer Dockery to another camp, but since other Southern senators had filed similar complaints, removing one white soldier would not have solved the problem. Instead, Secretary of War Baker informed Wilson that Young was in ill health and that the problem might resolve itself. It did, though it appears that racial concerns rather than health problems were the motivating force behind Young's involuntary retirement.

In June, Young, who was awaiting the final decision of the military medical board, appealed to Du Bois. He informed his old friend from Wilberforce that he was fit and ready to serve and that one of the nurses believed that his case was a joke, given the nation's wartime need for experienced officers. Du Bois quickly responded and mobilized public opinion. A deluge of letters and telegrams flooded the White House; however, as he had done previously, the president ignored the protests. In July 1917, the doctors at Letterman Hospital certified Young unfit for active service. The surgeon general of the Army concurred with the medical findings. On July 30, with the approval of President Wilson, the Army promoted Young to the rank of colonel and retired him from the military. African Americans were shocked, and many agreed with the *Chicago Defender*'s claim that the Army had railroaded Young to prevent his promotion. Although Young was disappointed, his forced retirement did not diminish his patriotism. Instead he urged African Americans "not to agitate or protest in my favor. The administration must not be embarrassed. . . . We all love the country too well for that."[7] Young returned to his home in Ohio—however, not without stopping at the Des Moines camp, where the black officer candidates treated him like royalty.

For the remainder of the war, Young challenged his retirement. He maintained that he was physically fit and tried to prove that he was in good health by riding horseback from his home in Ohio to Washington, D.C. in the summer of 1918. But, despite his widely publicized 497-mile journey and the efforts of the NAACP, the Army did not reinstate Young until November 6, 1918, five days before the end of World War I. Young's retirement was a personal blow to his friend Du Bois, and a bitter disappointment to many African Americans. It called into question the sincerity of the Secretary of War, who had assured race leaders that black men would have the opportunity to serve as commissioned officers. Moreover, it raised doubts about the War Department's willingness to continue the training of black officer candidates in Des Moines. Many African Americans suspected that the Army's decision to retire Young indicated that the military had no intentions of either granting black men officer's commissions or utilizing black soldiers in combat.

Black morale hit another low with the outbreak of the East St. Louis race riot on July 2, less than three months after the United States had entered the war and President Wilson had proclaimed that America would make the world safe for democracy. African Americans were wondering if America was safe for democracy, and if Wilson would take steps to improve race relations, initiate a federal investigation of the riot, or at least condemn the savagery. However, Wilson remained silent. Several distinguished African Americans traveled to Washington and tried to appeal to the president, asking him to speak out against the atrocities and to support antilynching legislation. All of them were turned away.

Appalled by the mob violence and the president's silence, black morale dropped sharply. The riot and the government's inaction undermined the faith of African Americans who had hoped that black support of the war would bring about civil rights. In the aftermath of East St. Louis, black loyalty and patriotism gave way to disillusion and despair. Reverend Adam Clayton Powell, Sr., the influential black pastor of Harlem's Abyssinian Baptist Church, urged African American men not to take up arms in defense of the nation. "While we love our flag and our country," he explained, "we do not believe in fighting for the protection of commerce on the high seas until the powers that be give us at least some verbal assurance that property and lives of the members of our race are going to be protected . . . from Maine to Mississippi."[8] Yet other black leaders encouraged African Americans to take up arms—however, not in defense of the nation. Several black newspaper editors exhorted their readers to arm themselves and defend their lives and property with guns. However, most black editors advocated a nonviolent approach.

The NAACP, seeking to arouse the conscience of the public, organized the first black protest march in the history of the United States. On July 28, 10,000 African American men, women, and children gathered near the

NAACP's headquarters in New York City for a "Silent Parade." Among the protestors were doctors, lawyers, teachers, ministers, and black veterans of the Spanish-American War. Impeccably dressed, they marched silently to the sound of muffled drums, carrying banners that read "Mr. President, why not make America safe for democracy?" and "Mother, do lynchers go to Heaven?" The decision to dress well and march in silence was deliberate. While the NAACP tried to arouse the American conscience in hopes of gaining support for federal antilynching legislation, civil rights leaders knew that the public might turn against the protestors and accuse them of being unpatriotic. To deflect those charges, the NAACP called the protest march a parade and made sure that it exuded an air of respectability and order. When the police inspector in charge of public safety objected to a banner that depicted President Wilson looking at a mother crouching protectively over two children, with the ruins of East St. Louis in the background, organizers withdrew it immediately. In the aftermath of the march, NAACP delegates called on the president to seek his support. However, like previous black protestors, the group failed to gain entry into the White House.

Photo 3.1 *In response to the East St. Louis race riot, the National Association for the Advancement of Colored People organized the Silent Parade, the first black protest march in U.S. history. On July 28, 1917, 10,000 black men, women, and children marched down Fifth Avenue in New York City. Source: Photographs and Prints Division, Schomburg Center for Research in Black Culture, New York Public Library*

In the weeks following the Silent Parade, the NAACP launched a concerted effort and flooded the president with protests and petitions, seeking
his support for racial justice and asking him to authorize a federal investigation of the riot. The black press published many of the letters, including that
of a young black man who declared that he would refuse to serve in the
military unless the president gave his assurance that he would protect African Americans from mob violence. Kelly Miller, Dean of Howard University's College of Arts and Sciences and one of the nation's leading black intellectuals, wrote the most highly publicized letter. Miller charged that Wilson's
failure to speak out against the East St. Louis mob, lynchings, and other racial atrocities, was an indication of his hypocrisy and insincerity. Miller's
scathing criticism of the president made his fifteen-page letter very popular
with black audiences. Published as a pamphlet, titled *The Disgrace of Democracy*, it sold more than 250,000 copies. While Miller's letter expressed the
anger and frustrations of African Americans, it did not generate a response
from the White House.

Though the president remained mum, Congress appointed a special committee to investigate the causes of the bloody massacre. Republican representatives William Rodenberg and Leonidas C. Dyer, who later introduced an
antilynching bill, initiated the investigation. The riot, they argued, had ob-
structed interstate commerce, which posed a serious threat to the nation's
security during wartime production and transportation of defense goods. The
committee compiled nearly 5,000 pages of testimony in the fall of 1917. The
final report, published a year later, blamed intense labor competition between white workers and recently arrived black migrants as well as graft,
corruption, bigotry, and racism among city government officials, politicians,
and union organizers for the violence. Despite strong words of condemnation, Congress took no further action. Given the government's apathy and
the president's silence in response to the East St. Louis riot, many African
Americans had doubts that the men training at Des Moines would receive
their officers commissions and that the War Department would train black
men to serve in arms.

In the month following the riot, hopes for black combat assignments were
further crushed by the outbreak of racial violence in Houston. On August 23,
1917, soldiers of the all-black Twenty-Fourth Infantry, stationed near Houston, attacked members of the local white police force in retaliation for discriminatory treatment and police brutality. Houston was not the first city in
Texas where black soldiers had clashed with whites. On August 13, 1906, the
First Battalion of the all-black Twenty-Fifth Infantry, stationed at Fort
Brown, had allegedly fired 250 rounds of ammunition into several buildings

in Brownsville. The federal government investigated the allegations and despite the black soldiers' insistence that they were innocent, all members of the First Battalion were discharged without honor. African Americans appealed to Congress, and the Senate initiated hearings. In March 1910, the Senate committee upheld the dishonorable discharge decision, claiming that at least some of the members of the First Battalion had instigated the shooting. Although it was unclear if some of the black soldiers were indeed involved in the shooting spree, there was not sufficient evidence to discharge all of the men. Meanwhile, white officers commanding the black troops were cleared of all charges.

The Brownsville incident was on the minds of many Texans, when the War Department dispatched the all-black Third Battalion of the Twenty-Fourth Infantry to Houston to guard the construction of nearby Camp Logan. The black troops who arrived on July 28, 1917, immediately encountered a racially hostile environment. Houston's white residents as well as white construction workers at Camp Logan harassed and insulted the black soldiers. To appease whites, who felt threatened by the presence of armed black men, the white commander of the black battalion disarmed all of the black soldiers, except those who served on guard duty at Camp Logan. The fact that the black troops were unarmed, contributed to the escalation of violence on the night of August 23.

The so-called Houston Mutiny was sparked when local white police officers pistol-whipped two black soldiers who protested the beating of a black woman. When other soldiers of the all-black Twenty-Fourth Infantry learned that two of their comrades had been arrested on charges of interfering with the police, smoldering tensions erupted. Rumors of an imminent attack by a white mob and alleged gunshots outside the military camp spread among the unarmed black soldiers. Seeking to defend themselves, approximately 100 of the men seized their weapons and marched into town. On their way, they shot and killed sixteen individuals, before they finally attacked the police station, where the two arrested black soldiers had been taken. Within two hours the rampage was over and the black troops returned to camp.

Military investigators quickly determined that 156 black soldiers had missed roll calls during the rioting and concluded that all of them had participated in the upheaval. However, upon closer examination, Army prosecutors decided to charge only 118 of the men, resulting in the largest court-martial in U.S. history. In three separate trials, military courts sentenced twenty-eight soldiers to death and forty to life in prison for mutiny and premeditated murder. Seven of the men were acquitted, while others received sentences for lesser crimes, including desertion. The Army transferred the remaining members of the Twenty-Fourth Infantry to the Philippines for the duration of the war.

The "Houston Mutiny" confirmed the fears of many whites, particularly Southerners, who opposed the training of black men in arms. The white press condemned the bloodshed and Southern congressmen demanded the removal of black troops from the South. Not surprisingly, the black press took a different stand. The Chicago *Defender* admitted that the violence was deplorable but conceded that it was difficult for African Americans to tolerate racism. Other black papers went a step further. The *Philadelphia Tribune* applauded the black soldiers for displaying proper manhood and for refusing to stand quietly by and seeing "our women slapped in the face by rough-necks and illiterate Southerners."[9] The *Crisis* even celebrated the soldiers as "martyrs for the cause of democracy."[10]

The racial clash at Houston sent shockwaves through the black community. African Americans were outraged that the convictions had been based largely on the testimony of seven black soldiers whom the military had pressured to testify in exchange for leniency. Moreover, African Americans were incensed that none of the white officers in charge of the black troops were held accountable and that thirteen of the men were secretly executed and

Photo 3.2 *In the wake of the Houston Mutiny, the Army charged 118 black soldiers with murder. The resulting courts martial were the largest in U.S. history. Source: National Archives. ARC identifier 533485/Local Identifier 165-WW-127(1)*

buried in unmarked graves before their cases could be reviewed by the Secretary of War. In response to the public outcry, the War Department issued General Order No. 7, mandating that future military death sentences were to be carried out only after proper review by the president.

Black anger about the treatment of the soldiers charged with participation in the "Houston Mutiny" was accompanied by concern. African Americans who had lobbied for the training of black combat troops and black officers feared that the mutiny would provide the War Department with a perfect excuse to disband any plans to train black soldiers in the use of weapons and to dissolve the Des Moines officers training camp. Indeed, prior to the violence in Houston, the Army had been willing to train black men for combat duty as long as they served in segregated units. However, after the incident, military leaders changed their tune and the Secretary of War caved to white Southern pressure. Only one day after the "Houston Mutiny," Baker approved a new policy that addressed white Southern concerns. To avoid any further racial disturbances, he restricted black military service opportunities. Henceforth, black soldiers were limited to one combat division. Moreover, he stipulated that once black men were drafted, they were to be used predominantly in service or labor units, receive only minimal training in arms, and be sent overseas as quickly as possible.

While the new military policy appeased bigoted military personnel and Southern whites, Baker also realized that restricting black combat opportunities was sure to generate African American opposition and increase racial frictions, which had the potential of undermining military efficiency. To placate African Americans, the Secretary of War met with Tuskegee's principal, Robert R. Moton, and a group of concerned black and white educators in the week following the "Houston Mutiny." On August 31, Baker assured the group that black men would continue to receive training in arms, though he failed to reveal that the training would be minimal. Concerned about maintaining racial harmony and preventing any disruption of the mobilization of troops, Baker listened to Moton, who recommended the appointment of Emmett J. Scott as special racial advisor to the Secretary of War. Houston-born Scott had been Booker T. Washington's personal secretary at Tuskegee Institute from 1897 until Washington's death in 1915. He had been one of Washington's closest consultants and friends and had helped to organize and sustain the Tuskegee Machine, the school's vast network of supporters. Scott, a devout accommodationist, had hoped to succeed Washington as Tuskegee's principal, but instead the school's board of trustees had appointed Moton. Scott stayed at Tuskegee, but his presence created an awkward situation for both men, which Moton hoped to resolve when he suggested that Baker appoint Scott to the War Department. Seeking to avert disruptive racial strife, Baker agreed to consider Scott's appointment. But, just in case African Americans could not be appeased, the Secretary of War also authorized the Military Intelligence Branch to expand its efforts to gather information about "Negro subversion."

Following his meeting with Moton, Baker conferred with Tasker H. Bliss, the Army's chief of staff, who recommended the formation of a combat division composed entirely of black draftees. This, Bliss argued, would lift black morale and ensure black support of the war effort, despite the fact that most African American draftees would be relegated to service or labor units. Baker, however, was reluctant to alienate Southern whites and informed his generals that the induction of black draftees was on hold. For many African Americans, Baker's decision was proof that black men would not be allowed to lead black troops in battle.

Already disappointed by the War Department's decision to suspend the conscription of black draftees, African Americans suffered another blow on September 16. That day 104 physicians and twelve dentists, most of them holding degrees from the all-black Meharry Medical College in Nashville, Tennessee, and Howard University's Medical School, received their medical officer's commissions at Des Moines' Colored Medical Officers Training Camp. However, none of the black officer candidates who had been training to command black troops in combat received their commissions. Instead, the War Department announced that it was going to extend the training program of the black cadets and postpone the commissioning of black officers until mid-October. Following the announcement, several hundred disillusioned black cadets left Des Moines, convinced that the unexpected extension of the training course signaled the government's unwillingness to commission any black officers.

But just as the prospect for black combat troops serving under the command of black officers seemed bleak, African Americans found a new and unlikely ally. In the aftermath of the moratorium on black inductions, white Southerners quickly realized that delaying the conscription of black men meant that white men would have to be called up for service in disproportionately large numbers to meet the state quotas. Angry white Southerners, charging racial inequity, protested to their congressmen, forcing Baker once again to change policy. On September 22, Baker announced that the induction of African Americans would resume. By then the Selective Service System had established separate "white" and "colored" quotas for each state, to address charges that the burden of the draft had rested unfairly on the shoulders of whites. In an effort to avert renewed white opposition to black military training, Baker assured concerned whites that black soldiers would be strictly segregated within each cantonment and that their troop strength would not exceed 30 percent of the total soldier population of each camp.

While catering to white Southern demands, Baker also juggled to pacify black activists. In mid-September, Baker met with W. E. B. Du Bois, who reassured him that he could count on the support of African Americans. However, Du Bois did not miss the opportunity to remind the Secretary of War that incidents of discrimination tended to undermine black loyalty. Aware that racial tensions in the armed forces had the potential of compromising troop performance, Baker appointed Emmett J. Scott as Special Assistant to the Secretary of War. On October 5, 1917, Scott assumed responsibility for all matters involving black troops. Serving as a liaison between the African American community and the War Department, Scott's job was to apprise Baker of any morale issues among the black soldiers and to alert him to racially charged problems. However, Baker made clear that Scott's appointment did not reflect the War Department's intention to end segregation in the military. He assured Scott that he discouraged racial discrimination, but reminded him that "there is no intention on the part of the War Department to undertake at this time to settle the so-called race question."[11] While the War Department looked upon Scott's employment largely as a concession to African Americans, and rarely heeded his advice, it was nevertheless an important symbolic gesture that generated widespread praise from the black community. African Americans wrote hundreds of letters to the Secretary of War, applauding Scott's assignment. Even Kelly Miller, who had openly attacked the Wilson administration for its silence following the East St. Louis riot, proclaimed that it was "the most significant appointment that has yet to come to the colored race."[12] The black press was equally laudatory. Even white Southern newspapers, concerned about preventing incidents similar to the "Houston Mutiny," deemed the selection of the accommodationist Scott, a wise move.

In the wake of Scott's appointment, the Secretary of War also made good on his promise to commission black officers and to create black combat divisions. On October 15, 639 black cadets successfully completed their training program at Des Moines and received officer commissions. Following graduation, the newly minted black officers enjoyed a fifteen-day leave before reporting to several military camps—all of them, with the exception of Camp Meade, Maryland, located in the North—to help train the black draftees they would lead in battle. Meanwhile, the War Department closed the Des Moines camp and announced that for the remainder of the war African Americans would be admitted to the previously all-white officers training camps. However, given the racial climate, relatively few black men were. Finally, in November, the War Department organized two black combat divisions. The Ninety-Second Infantry Division, under the command of General Ballou, was composed of black draftees as well as the black officers and black medical officers who had trained at Des Moines. The Ninety-Third Infantry Division (Provisional) consisted largely of black National Guard units who never assembled or trained together in the United States.

Thus, after fighting for the right to fight throughout much of 1917, African Americans had wrought several concessions from the Secretary of War by the end of that year. They had secured black officers, the appointment of Scott as a special assistant to Baker, and two black combat divisions. Those achievements, while important, were overshadowed by the fact that the Wilson administration continued to discriminate against African Americans and that the War Department remained firmly committed to military segregation. The war, as many black leaders had hoped, would provide African Americans with the opportunity to fight for their country and demonstrate their loyalty and patriotism under fire. However, the ability of black soldiers to fight in the war was limited significantly by the racism they encountered during their mobilization and training in the United States and their deployment overseas.

~

CHAPTER FOUR

Raising a Jim Crow Army

The Mobilization and Training of African American Troops

On the eve of World War I, few African American men had any military background. In the spring of 1917, when the nation went to war, approximately 10,000 black men were professional soldiers who served in the Army's all-black Twenty-Fourth and Twenty-Fifth Infantries or the Ninth and Tenth Cavalries. An additional 5,000 African Americans had received military training in eight segregated National Guard units. However, the overwhelming number of the more than 380,000 black men who served during World War I were civilians: 4,000 of them volunteers and 367,710 draftees. The vast majority of black draftees, 89 percent of the men, served in stevedore or labor battalions. They loaded and unloaded ships, trucks, and trains; built roads and barracks; dug ditches; took care of livestock; removed manure; washed laundry; cleaned facilities; and prepared food. Black men did so in disproportionately large numbers. Although African Americans made up less than 10 percent of the population of the United States, they comprised more than 30 percent of the laborers in the armed forces. Only 42,000 African Americans prepared for combat service with the all-black Ninety-Second and Ninety-Third Divisions. Regardless of their rank or whether they served in combat or in labor units, discrimination and segregation characterized the experience of all black soldiers during World War I. But despite racism, the military experience also created unprecedented opportunities for African American men that helped to heighten their expectations for racial change after the war. Determined to raise a fit and efficient fighting force, the federal government started to pay attention to the health and education of black men. It provided medical care to the men in uniform, instructed them in proper hygiene and sanitation, and, with the help of the Young Men's Christian Association (YMCA) launched educational classes that instilled in many men a new sense of pride, self-confidence, and self-consciousness.

The overwhelming majority of black men entered the military as a result of the draft, which was responsible for raising 72 percent of the nation's armed forces and 96 percent of its black troops. The task of procuring the nation's eligible men for military service fell to the Selective Service System, which supervised a decentralized conscription that was administered by local and state officials who staffed the registration and draft boards—virtually all of them lily-white. The draft was a three-step process that began with the registration of eligible men, continued with their screening and selection, and ended with their exemption from service or their induction into the military.

The registration of the nearly 24 million American men, among them some 2.3 million African Americans, took place during four national draft calls. On June 5, 1917, the first group of men between the ages of twenty-one and thirty registered for military service. On June 5, and August 24, 1918, those who had turned twenty-one since the previous registration had to report. And on September 12, 1918, the final group of men, which included those who were between eighteen and forty-five, registered. On draft call days, eligible men reported to their voting precincts, where registration boards, consisting of three county officials—the sheriff, the court clerk, and the medical officer—supervised the registration. The boards, appointed by state governors, were white, as were the thousands of volunteers who helped with the registration process. Upon their arrival at the polling places, the men filled out draft cards which asked them for their citizenship status, date of birth, address, marital status, height, military background, and occupation as well as the name of their employer, the number of dependents, and any physical impairment that might preclude them from military service. And, to implement the military's segregation policy, each registrant had to identify his race.

The fact that the draft registrations were administered at the nation's voting precincts could not have been lost on black leaders who had argued all along that military service and civil rights went hand in hand. However, for the majority of black men, most of whom lived in the rural South, registering for the draft must have been a daunting ordeal. The government had ordered them to go to the voting precincts, places that they usually avoided for fear of attracting the wrath of whites. Moreover, many of the men were illiterate and had to rely on white volunteer staff at the registration sites to help them fill out their draft cards. Finally, black sharecroppers and others who worked for whites were uncertain how white landowners or employers would react.

After all, registering for the draft not only meant taking time off from work, but was also the first step toward induction into the military, which could potentially deprive whites of their black workforce for an indeterminate time. Some white landowners, in an effort to keep their black workers in the fields, prevented African Americans from registering for the draft. However, there were also many black men who did not register because they were indifferent or unaware of the draft call. Yet others did not know if they were eligible because they did not have birth certificates or knew their exact birth dates. Whatever their reason, some black men did not register for military service, even though failure to do so carried a prison sentence of up to one year. Nationwide, approximately 2 to 3 million men did not register and were branded "slackers." Among them were many African Americans; however, their exact number is impossible to determine, since the government used voter registration lists to identify eligible men and, in most cases, these did not include the names of African Americans.

To process the registration forms, the president, drawing from a list of names provided by each state governor, appointed 14,416 white men to serve on 4,647 draft boards—one for each county and one for every 30,000 city residents. The composition of draft boards varied widely, but usually one member was a physician. The boards ploughed through a mountain of registrations and called up men to question, examine, and select those they deemed mentally and physically fit for military service. Draft board physicians often examined black and white men on different days or segregated them. As one black draftee observed, the room reserved for whites had hooks for the men's clothing, whereas African Americans had to get undressed in a corner furnished with a carpenter's bench. In addition to administering physical exams, local draft boards also determined if any of the men had grounds for deferment, due to a disability, religious conviction, employment in crucial war industries, or because they had dependents. Based on a classification system provided by the Selective Service System, local draft boards placed the draftees in four categories to meet their state's "white" and "colored" quotas. Class I included men whom the government would draft first. These were single as well as married men who were not employed in essential industrial or agricultural production and whose families were not dependent on their income. Those who did not meet the criteria of Class I were assigned to three different categories and less likely to be called up for military service. Eventually, the War Department inducted only draftees in Class I.

Overall, the draft boards placed 52 percent of black men, but only 33 percent of whites in Class I. Moreover, they found that nearly 75 percent of African Americans were fit for military service, a surprisingly high percentage, given the poor nutrition, sanitation, and health conditions as well as the lack of medical care that characterized the lives of most black Southerners. White draft board physicians clearly applied medical standards to the disadvantage of black men, which became obvious when the black doughboys reported to the training camps. There Army physicians reexamined them and rejected large numbers of those whom draft boards had deemed fit. Some camp commanders sent more than 30 percent of their newly arrived black draftees home because medical entrance exams determined that the men were not suitable for service. In comparison, the military discharged nationwide only 8 percent of all draftees for medical reasons. Particularly in the South, draft boards sought to meet their "colored" quotas with African Americans who were least likely to deprive white planters of a healthy and strong black workforce. For some whites in the South, the draft also provided an excellent opportunity to rid their communities of black troublemakers, especially those who challenged Jim Crow. In several cases the racism was so blatant that the Selective Service System intervened and removed draft board members from their posts.

While the majority of registered black men responded to their draft call, many others did not. To what degree these so-called delinquents either consciously avoided or unintentionally failed to report to the draft boards is not clear. However, Selective Service administrators suspected that many African Americans, particularly those living in the rural South, became inadvertent "delinquents." They failed to report to local draft boards because they were illiterate and unable to read their draft notifications. In other cases, white landlords intercepted the mail and either neglected to deliver draft notices or did not read them to their illiterate black tenants. Many other African Americans never received their draft letters because they had moved after registering and had not left forwarding addresses with the Selective Service. Since it took several months to process registrations and send out draft calls, it was impossible to track down those who had relocated without notifying their draft boards.

As a result of the biased administration of the draft, African Americans had a much higher induction rate than whites. The War Department inducted more than 34 percent of all black men who had registered for the draft, but only 24 percent of whites. In five Southern states— including Florida, Louisiana, Mississippi, South Carolina, and Georgia—the number of black draftees even exceeded those of whites. Selective Service administrators explained that not racial bias, but the large number of white volunteers was responsible for the higher induction rate of African Americans. At the start of the war, 650,000 whites, but only 4,000 black men had enlisted, since the Army had limited the number of black volunteers. The larger number of white enlistees, according to the Selective Service System, had reduced the pool of qualified white men and accounted for a higher white deferment rate.

Racial prejudice was clearly a factor that contributed to the high percentage of black inductions, but so was the lack of education among African Americans and the fact that many of them lived in poverty. Illiterate black men were unable to fill out the forms required for deferments and those who were literate often did not know how to request an exemption and had no money to get legal counsel. Moreover, African Americans were underrepresented in industrial defense occupations that would have qualified them for exemptions from military service. Likewise, black men had little hope of getting a deferment on religious grounds, since few of them belonged to well-recognized pacifist religious groups, such as the Quakers. But even religious objectors were drafted and assigned to perform noncombatant work in the camps. African Americans who applied for deferments, claiming that they had dependents, did not fare any better. Draft boards often denied their applications, pointing out that the monthly soldier pay of thirty dollars was more than most black men were able to earn in civil life to support their families. African Americans who obtained exemptions, often did so because white employers or landlords, interested in maintaining their black workforce, intervened on their behalf.

In addition the government classified nearly 106,000 African Americans as "deserters," an offense that carried a term of thirty years of imprisonment at hard labor. The vast majority of "deserters" were men who had received induction notices from their draft boards but had failed to report for military duty. According to military officials, roughly 10 percent of the black men who had registered for the draft were "deserters," compared to only 4 percent of white registrants. The high desertion rate among African Americans was, like the high delinquency rate, often due to a lack of education, black mobility, and white collusion. An illiterate black draftee who could not read his draft notice was also not able to read his letter of conscription. Likewise, a black man who had moved since registering for military service, without informing the post office of his new address, received neither his draft call nor his induction notice in the mail. And white landowners who relied on black workers were as eager to prevent their black tenant farmers from responding to the draft call as they were determined to stop them from departing for distant training camps. What made matters worse was that the government offered a $50 reward to individuals who apprehended "deserters." Some whites, particularly Southern landowners, not only concealed draft notices from their black tenant farmers while they were tending the crops, but after

Table 4.1 Black and White Registration and Induction Rates

	Total Registration	Black Percent of Registration	Total Induction	Black Induction	Black Percent of Induction	White Induction
United States	10,640,846	10.1	2,666,813	367,656	13.8	2,299,157
Alabama	206,210	39.7	59,755	25,874	43.3	33,881
Arizona	40,179	0.7	8,113	77	0.9	8,036
Arkansas	168,287	30.4	49,312	17,544	35.6	31,768
California	316,302	1.0	67,067	919	1.4	66,148
Colorado	91,556	1.2	22,804	317	1.4	22,487
Connecticut	174,820	2.0	32,539	941	2.9	31,598
Delaware	24,559	15.5	4,993	1,365	27.3	3,628
District of Columbia	36,670	30.1	9,631	4,000	41.5	5,631
Florida	94,585	41.2	24,916	12,904	51.8	12,012
Georgia	260,197	43.3	66,841	34,303	51.3	32,538
Idaho	45,478	0.6	12,566	95	0.8	12,471
Illinois	707,070	3.1	177,483	8,754	4.9	168,729
Indiana	283,731	4.0	69,749	4,589	6.6	65,170
Iowa	240,703	1.2	66,864	929	1.4	65,935
Kansas	167,266	3.3	41,905	2,127	5.1	39,778
Kentucky	215,910	12.0	58,330	11,320	19.4	47,010
Louisiana	179,941	42.4	56,205	28,711	51.1	27,494
Maine	68,104	0.2	15,266	50	0.3	15,216
Maryland	136,501	19.4	33,867	9,212	27.2	24,655
Massachusetts	397,698	1.5	76,567	1,200	1.6	75,367
Michigan	411,019	1.7	96,480	2,395	2.5	94,085
Minnesota	294,291	0.6	73,680	511	0.7	73,169
Mississippi	157,525	51.8	43,362	24,066	55.5	19,296
Missouri	334,902	6.8	92,843	9,219	9.9	83,624
Montana	97,073	0.3	27,340	198	0.7	27,142
Nebraska	132,107	1.2	29,807	642	2.2	29,165

Nevada	12,640	0.5	3,164	26	0.8	3,138
New Hampshire	41,694	0.2	8,404	27	0.3	8,377
New Jersey	332,671	4.2	71,390	4,863	6.8	66,527
New Mexico	37,011	0.6	8,862	51	0.6	8,811
New York	1,118,035	2.3	253,589	6,193	2.4	247,396
North Carolina	228,459	32.1	58,441	20,082	34.4	38,359
North Dakota	72,902	0.1	18,595	87	0.5	18,508
Ohio	617,001	4.7	138,148	7,861	5.7	130,287
Oklahoma	188,156	7.6	64,941	5,694	8.8	59,247
Oregon	69,520	0.2	16,158	68	0.4	16,090
Pennsylvania	902,469	4.4	201,211	15,392	7.6	185,819
Rhode Island	59,006	2.7	11,176	291	2.6	10,885
South Carolina	144,660	51.3	44,059	25,798	58.6	18,261
South Dakota	65,040	0.2	21,255	62	0.3	21,193
Tennessee	213,409	20.5	59,878	17,774	29.7	42,104
Texas	460,056	18.2	117,395	31,506	26.8	85,889
Utah	46,099	0.4	10,788	77	0.7	10,711
Vermont	30,882	0.2	6,629	22	0.3	6,607
Virginia	206,072	31.2	58,337	23,541	40.4	34,796
Washington	124,125	0.3	28,686	173	0.6	28,513
West Virginia	142,144	9.4	45,355	5,492	12.1	39,863
Wisconsin	266,219	0.3	70,982	224	0.3	70,758
Wyoming	24,892	1.1	7,923	95	1.2	7,828
Alaska			1,962	5	0.3	1,957
Hawaii						5,466
Puerto Rico						15,734

the harvest season reported the alleged "deserters" to the sheriff. At times, draft boards did the same. They deliberately misinformed black men, assuring them that they had been exempted from military service, only to have them arrested on desertion charges. Local sheriffs who delivered "deserters" to camp commanders claimed the $50 reward, which was subsequently deducted from the men's soldier pay, and split it with the white planters or the draft board members who had turned them in.

However, not all black men were inadvertent "slackers," "delinquents," or "deserters." Numerous African Americans made a conscious decision to evade the draft, and a few men even urged draft resistance. The reasons for draft evasion and resistance varied. Some black men simply did not want to leave their families and friends, while others opposed America's involvement in the war, segregation in the armed forces, and the second-class-citizenship status of African Americans. At times, those who sought to avoid military service insisted that they were not of eligible age or they moved and deliberately failed to notify Selective Service administrators of their new addresses. Others, in hopes of failing their physical exam, went on a starvation diet to lower their weight and, in extreme cases, mutilated themselves prior to their appearance before the draft boards. These individual acts of draft evasion were more common than public resistance and open defiance of the Selective Service, because, if detected, black draft dodgers could claim ignorance and hope for leniency. However, government officials soon became aware of this strategy and warned the men that they could no longer claim that they had not received their mail, since draft notices were posted in public places.

To further deter draft resistance, government agents, with the help of patriotic volunteers, organized "slacker raids" and rounded up men suspected of avoiding military service. They systematically searched trains and train stations as well as pool halls, movie theaters, and other entertainment venues in the black neighborhoods. On occasion they stopped draft-age men on the streets, sometimes aiming rifles and bayonets at them, and demanded to see their registration or draft classification cards. Those who failed to produce the documents went to jail until authorities could determine their status. In the North, alleged "slackers" were less likely to spend extensive time in jail, but in the South, many men languished for weeks and sometimes months before federal grand juries examined their cases. Those who made their opposition to the war public or encouraged others to evade the draft also risked arrest. In August of 1918, A. Philip Randolph and Chandler Owen, cofounders of the socialist black newspaper the *Messenger*, appeared at a pacifist rally in Cleveland and urged their audience to oppose the war. Subsequently, U.S.

Department of Justice officials arrested both men and charged them with violation of the Sedition Act. Both men faced potentially long prison sentences. However, after only two days in jail, the judge released Randolph and Owen, claiming that black men lacked the sophistication to adopt a radical socialist position. Other black opponents of the war were not so lucky. When Ben Fletcher, a black labor leader, publicly announced his antiwar position and advocated draft resistance, he was sentenced to ten years in prison as well as a $30,000 fine. The government's effort to suppress any dissent was aided by white vigilante groups who pledged to uphold 100 percent Americanism, which at times led to violent encounters between white vigilantes and African Americans. In South Carolina, a patriotic mob of whites lynched a black minister because he had allegedly opposed the war.

Despite government repression and the risk of attracting the wrath of angry whites, a small number of African Americans offered organized resistance to the draft and some even picked up arms to avoid induction. In Texas, African Americans joined forces with white and Mexican agricultural workers in the Farmers and Laborers Protective Association, which protested America's entry into the war and encouraged its members to resist conscription. In Oklahoma, black and white sharecroppers went a step further, when they launched the Green Corn Rebellion in the summer of 1917. Approximately 2,000 men armed themselves, cut telegraph lines, and headed for Washington, determined to overthrow President Wilson and end the war. Government agents quickly crushed the efforts of both groups. Not surprisingly, most black draft evaders kept a low profile and many neither disclosed their intentions to resist conscription nor their reasons for doing so.

The majority of black men, however, complied with the draft, though it is unclear whether they supported the war or were opposed or indifferent to it. Some black men were enthusiastic about military service, either for personal or patriotic reasons. Others who were too young to qualify for military service but anxious to join the war effort even lied about their age. Eugene B. Bailey, a black draftee from Indiana, was overjoyed when he received his induction notice because "I wanted to be somebody! I wanted to be somebody so bad." While Franklin A. Denison, a member of the Eighth Illinois black National Guard unit proudly proclaimed: "There is no color in patriotism. Patriotism is as deeply rooted under the black skin as under any other." For many though, their loyalty and patriotism was dampened by the persistence of segregation and discrimination. As one black man professed, "I am . . . longing to join body and soul into this war for 'Democracy.' But in the light of present condition I can not see where this much boasted principle is practiced at home."[1]

In October 1917, military authorities ordered the first group of black draftees to report to the training camps. As the men said farewell to their families
and friends, white communities often took little notice of them. While the
majority of cities staged elaborate send-off parades and banquets for white
draftees who were leaving for the training camps, most communities ignored
the mobilization of black soldiers. White crowds did not line the streets and
wave American flags and white mayors did not express their gratitude and ap-
preciation for the black men's service to the nation. Undoubtedly, any publicly
sponsored event honoring African American draftees would have raised black
expectations for racial equality after the war, which was not a message most
whites wanted to convey. However, there were a few exceptions. In some cities
whites joined black residents to cheer on the black draftees. In New Orleans
the mayor reviewed the black conscripts as they marched by city hall, and in
Chicago the mayor and a former governor addressed departing black troops to
bolster their morale. But white support of the black soldiers also met with
white opposition. When whites in Portland, Oregon, hosted a farewell dinner
for black draftees in the municipal auditorium and ran out of desserts, one of
the organizers phoned a friend and asked her to provide additional pies. Initially the woman agreed to do so, but she called back to confirm that the soldiers were white, because "if they are niggers we won't send the pies."[2]

Members of the African American community tried to make up for the
absence of official send-off festivities for the black conscripts. Black churches
and fraternal orders hosted dinner and dance parties to honor the black
draftees and musicians accompanied them and their loved ones to the train
stations. However, many black men left for the training camps without any
public celebrations or display of civilian support. Particularly in the rural
South, African Americans were often apprehensive about staging public
send-offs, because the spectacle of large numbers of black people cheering on
black soldiers who were heading for military training camps was bound to
arouse white hostility that could easily escalate into racial violence.

Once the men arrived at the train stations, black and white Red Cross
volunteers, most of them women, served them refreshments and distributed
candy, cigarettes, sweaters, gloves, and socks. Some of the white women who
worked for the Red Cross provided creature comforts to all men, regardless of
race. However, many others refused to serve them or treated them discourte-
ously. After the men boarded segregated troop transports they went off to
various cantonments. Depending on the men's destination, these trips could
take a few hours to several days. During the journey the men sang songs,
played cards, rolled dice, and ate food prepared by their relatives and friends
or boxed meals handed out by Red Cross canteens.

Photo 4.1 *Many black communities organized send-off parades when the black draftees left for the training camps. After escorting them to the railroad station, these residents of Duluth, Minnesota, are bidding farewell to their men. Source: National Archives. ARC identifier 533530/Local Identifier 165-WW-127(44)*

For many men this was their first time away from home and, since the War Department assigned black soldiers to training camps around the country, for many black Northerners it was also their first encounter with Southern-style racism. Emboldened by their participation in the war, black men from the North openly defied Southern racial etiquette. When a crowd of whites lined the railroad tracks in Jonesboro, Arkansas, black soldiers from Illinois provocatively waved at white women and "threw kisses at the white girls, calling out to them, 'Come over here, baby, give me a kiss!'"[3] After the train stopped, some of the men spotted a "NO NEGROES ALLOWED" sign over the train station doors. Angered by the blatant racism, the men jumped off the train, entered the station, forced two white men sitting in the waiting room to go outside, and ordered them to take down the offending sign. When the white men refused and fled into the station, the black soldiers chased them through the building before boarding their train. As the black men continued their journey, they encountered and challenged other signs of the South's racial order. Many businesses along the troop routes refused to serve the black soldiers, while others catered to them in segregated facilities. In Bostick, Texas, a savvy Chinese grocery store owner, tried to take advantage of the new customers passing through town. As the train arrived, he promptly removed all Jim Crow signs and with equal speed raised his prices. Local black residents came to the aid of the soldiers who did not have enough cash and gave them fruits and sandwiches for the remainder of the trip. However, when another contingent of black troops stopped in Bostick five hours later, the Chinese grocer was not fast enough and failed to take down the Jim Crow signs prior to the arrival of the train. The black men retaliated. They stole his cash register and walked off with cases of canned goods. In other towns they ransacked stores and assaulted proprietors who refused to serve them. Despite these amazing breaches of Southern racial etiquette, local white police authorities made few attempts to pursue or punish the black soldiers. In Tyler, Texas, the local sheriff tried to board and search a troop train, but black soldiers shoved him away with their rifles. Perhaps afraid to face charges of undermining the war effort, they never arrested a single black man.

Upon their arrival in the training camps, the men reported to the base hospitals for thorough health exams. Since large numbers of troops descended on the camps at the same time, this often meant hours of standing in line, before the men finally got to see the doctors. The conscripts stripped

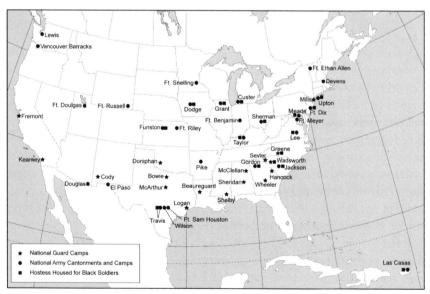

Map 4.1 *U.S. Map of all training camps, YMCA huts, YWCA Hostess Houses. Source: Courtesy of Michael Hradesky, Staff Cartographer, Department of Geography, Ball State University*

down to their waist as Army physicians sounded their hearts and lungs, checked their reflexes, took their blood pressure, tested their vision, and inspected their teeth. Those who passed their physicals received smallpox and typhoid vaccinations. In some cases doctors used white chalk to mark their chests with the letters A.E.F., indicating that they were fit to serve with the American Expeditionary Forces overseas. The men deemed unfit were discharged. Some of them were likely relieved and elated to return home; however, others were disappointed. Royal Christian, a black man from Pennsylvania who was eager to join the Army, was crushed when the doctor at Camp Lee, Virginia, told him that he did not qualify because of the condition of his teeth. The military, the physician informed Christian, accepted only men who had at least two molars on each side of their jaws. This was necessary since the men had to be able to eat a standard staple of the military diet: hardtack, which was a hard biscuit made from flour, water, and salt. More commonly, however, Army physicians rejected men because they had been infected with venereal disease, particularly syphilis. Examinations revealed that venereal disease infection rates ran about seven times higher for black than for white soldiers. Record numbers of diseased men came from South Carolina, Georgia, and Florida, each reporting a 31 percent infection rate among its black troops. Whites, particularly in the South, often saw this as evidence for black men's allegedly insatiable sexual appetite. Many white officers and military physicians shared these racist assumptions, ignoring the fact that the numbers reflected years of neglect by the medical profession as well as a lack of access to social hygiene and sex education.

Following the health exam, the men reported to the segregated sections of the camps. Since each cantonment consisted of up to 2,000 buildings, which could accommodate as many as 40,000 troops, newly arrived black men had to exercise great caution not to wander into the areas occupied by whites. Those who did, faced verbal and physical assaults by white soldiers as well as swift punishment by military commanders, who assigned the violators to clean the camp latrines. The facilities designated for African Americans varied from camp to camp, but in all of them housing, sanitary units, and mess halls were inferior to those provided for whites. Many of the camps had put all of their efforts into the construction of housing for white soldiers and were ill-prepared to accommodate the black troops. Conditions in the Northern camps were usually better than those in the South. At Camp Meade, Maryland, facilities for black soldiers ranked among the best in the South. The men slept in two-story heated wooden barracks, equipped with electric light and furnished with iron cots and straw mattresses. They received linens, towels, and two blankets. Bath houses provided running water and showers and the mess hall served edible food. But even at Camp Meade too many men were crowded into too few barracks. At other camps, conditions were much worse, resembling those of chain gangs. Men slept on straw that had been spread out on barrack or tent floors and took baths in makeshift containers or washed themselves in nearby rivers or streams. Their food, one of them complained, consisted of "half done beans for dinner and concrete pie for supper."[4] At Camp Hill, Virginia, which housed large numbers of black stevedores, the men had to sleep in unheated dirt-floor tents or outside, warming themselves around campfires. They had no sanitary facilities, ate outside, and shared mess kits, and their food was often inadequate. At Camp Alexander, Virginia, conditions were so bad that many men froze to death during the unusually harsh winter of 1917–1918.

In addition to the poor camp facilities, black soldiers also suffered from a lack of suitable clothing. Many of the men who served in labor battalions—all of which were headed by white officers—only received overalls, while others had to wait weeks and sometimes months for their uniforms. Often the uniforms they received were old and used, some of them even cast-offs from the Civil War. Thus, the majority of black men initially worked and drilled in the civilian clothes they had worn the day they left their homes. They lacked proper shoes, socks, sweaters, and coats as well as fresh underwear, which caused severe lice infestations. To rid the men of lice—which the soldiers jokingly dubbed "seam squirrels"—sanitary squads soaked their clothes and blankets in gasoline and scrubbed their bodies with a solution of gasoline, soap, and hot water. Since many of the men had no change of clothing, they had to wait in the nude until their clothes were dry. Not surprisingly, many men became ill. Pneumonia mortality rates among black troops, particularly Southerners who trained in Northern camps, increased dramatically. But those who became ill received little medical attention and were less likely to be hospitalized than white soldiers, since many white officers insisted that African Americans were not sick but merely too lazy to work. A black physician who visited Camp Meade, Maryland, was so appalled by the lack of medical supplies and the poor treatment of sick black soldiers that he shipped a gallon of cough syrup to the camp hospital and volunteered his medical services.

The training of black troops was equally marred by racism. African Americans were usually the last men in the camps to receive their weapons and gas masks, and many of them never got any military equipment. While the Army's regular training program lasted six to seven weeks, the white officers who commanded the vast majority of black soldiers often did little to prepare them for active duty. Most of the black men, they reasoned, had been as-

Photo 4.2   *The sight of black men in arms, like these soldiers in Camp Jackson, South Carolina, frightened many white southerners. Yet, African Americans took great pride in seeing such images. Source: National Archives. ARC identifier 533602/Local Identifier 165-WW-127(110)*

signed to labor units, and any military training—such as the use of rifles, bayonets, machine guns, or hand grenades—would be a waste of time. Indeed, men serving in the labor battalions received no training in arms until October 1918, a month before the war ended. Moreover, many white commanding officers insisted that African Americans were not capable of combat duty because of their inferior intellect.

If white officers needed evidence for their claim, they could point to the Army's intelligence tests, which had revealed a startling high illiteracy rate as well as intellectual deficiencies among the black draftees. Undoubtedly, the poor performance of black soldiers on the military intelligence tests was the product of the second-rate education most of them had endured. But even more so, the results reflected the biased nature of the tests. The Alpha test, administered to literate soldiers, asked the men to identify brand-name products—a difficult task for those who had grown up on sharecropping farms and had no need for bottled cooking oil or were too poor to purchase brand-name toothpaste or soap. The Beta test, given to illiterate and non-English-speaking soldiers, was equally biased. Presented with an incomplete sketch of a tennis court, the men were expected to complete the picture by drawing a net. Black draftees from the rural South were stumped. Based on these flawed pseudo-scientific tests, Army officials claimed that black draftees had the average mental age of ten-year-olds—conclusive evidence that they lacked the intellectual ability necessary for combat training.

In addition to poor military training, inferior housing, and inadequate equipment, black troops suffered verbal and physical abuse at the hands of white soldiers and officers, who routinely referred to black soldiers as "niggers," "darkies," "coons," or "rastus." At least one black soldier, distraught by his treatment, committed suicide. Most of the black men endured the indignities, but they were bitter and grew increasingly restless. They resented the assignment of large numbers of African Americans to noncombat units as well as the substandard living quarters, food, clothing, and sanitary facilities in the camps. They were outraged by military police brutality, racially biased and unusually harsh punishments for military code infractions, and the failure of white soldiers to salute black officers. Furthermore, they complained about the reluctance of white officers to recommend black men for promotion as well as their refusal to give passes to those who asked to go home to be with seriously ill or dying relatives. Finally, they were offended by the discriminatory treatment of black soldiers who visited towns and cities near the camps during their off-duty hours.

Appalled by the camp conditions and the blatant racism of white soldiers and officers, black troops expressed their frustration. Sidney Wilson, a young soldier from Tennessee, made no attempt to conceal his bitterness when he wrote the white chairman of his draft board in no uncertain terms: "you lowdown Mother Fuckers can put a gun in our hands, but who is able to take it out? We may go to France but I want to let you know that it will not be over with untill we straiten up this state."[5] Equally frustrated with the persistence of racism, Des Moines trained George S. Schuyler went AWOL after a bootblack in Philadelphia declined to shine his shoes. In other cases, hungry soldiers stole food from white officers or refused to work until they were fed. Yet others appealed to Emmett J. Scott, the War Department's racial advisor.

Scott, concerned about the declining morale among the black troops, visited several camps shortly after he assumed his post. Eager to avoid an escalation of racial friction, he urged the soldiers to deal with any racially charged situation wisely and temperately. Yet he also alerted Secretary of War Newton D. Baker to the potentially explosive situation. Baker, who worried that racial disorder in the camps would undermine the nation's war effort as well as military efficiency, sought to appease African Americans. Though unwilling to end segregation in the Army, he assured African Americans that he discouraged discrimination. The disproportionate assignment of black troops to labor and service battalions, he explained, was not racially motivated but dictated by military necessity. Indeed, noncombat troops, he insisted, were essential to the war effort, because they provided crucial support and supplies for the men fighting in the trenches. Moreover, Baker announced that he had visited black soldiers in the camps and found no evidence that there is "at this time, any sort of discontent or dissatisfaction."[6] Nonetheless, the Secretary of War promised to investigate the charges in order to prevent simmering racial tensions from exploding.

Baker's public statement did little to defuse the situation, and racial tensions often led to fistfights and even escalated into full-blown riots. In October 1917, black national guardsmen clashed with white soldiers from Alabama and Georgia when some of the black men tore down Jim Crow signs at Camp Mills, New York. In August 1918, rioting started at Camp Meade, Maryland, after a white soldier threw a bottle at a black soldier. In some cases camp commanders took disciplinary actions against whites who had violated military codes of conduct or refused to follow orders. At Camp Meade, Maryland, the commanding officer ordered a white enlisted man who had refused to salute a black officer to do so twenty times in front of his entire company. At the same camp, the bottle-throwing white soldier responsible for inciting the riot was sentenced to three years of hard labor. At Camp Grant, Illinois, the commander reminded white soldiers that "the only color recognized . . . was to be 'O.D.' the olive drab of the Army uniform."[7] And at Camp Upton, New York, the commander threatened white Southern officers that unless they treated black soldiers fairly they would not be dispatched overseas. At Camp Pike, Arkansas, a white officer was court-martialed and dismissed for his refusal to assemble white troops alongside black soldiers.

Racially motivated incidents were not limited to black and white troop encounters inside the camps, but often involved white civilians in communities adjacent to the cantonments. Black soldiers who visited nearby towns while on leave often faced hostile white residents and businesses, particularly in the South. While white restaurant, theater, and grocery store owners welcomed visiting white soldiers, they insisted on maintaining strict segregation and often refused to serve the black troops. Unfamiliar with Southern-style racism, black soldiers from the North were incensed and ready to retaliate. In August 1917 violent clashes between white Houston residents and members of the all-black Twenty-Fourth Infantry had triggered the "Houston Mutiny." Two months later, black troops from New York stationed at Camp Wadsworth, South Carolina, armed themselves and marched into nearby Spartanburg when they heard a rumor that two of their comrades had been lynched at the city's police station. Another hostile encounter between the black troops and white residents of Spartanburg occurred shortly thereafter, when two black soldiers attempted to buy a newspaper inside a hotel lobby. Racial tensions also escalated at Camp Sheridan, Alabama, in November 1917, when black National Guardsmen from Ohio prepared to march into Montgomery to stop the alleged lynching of a black soldier. In the following month, a policeman in Newport News, Virginia, shot a black soldier in the mouth, when the man protested to being searched by the officer. In most cases military authorities intervened and prevented any additional bloodshed. However, in the following year violence erupted in Newport News, Virginia. In September 1918, a hundred black servicemen stationed at Camp Alexander assembled at the city's police station after they heard that local law enforcement officers had arrested and beaten two black soldiers. When the angry men picked up stones and started to throw them at the police, the officers opened fire and wounded seven of the black soldiers.

Only rarely did white soldiers defend their black comrades in arms. In Spartanburg, white soldiers from New York came to the aid of black troops from their home state and threatened to boycott local stores that discriminated against black men in uniform. And, in at least one case, some of the white soldiers started a fistfight with town toughs who had harassed a black soldier. In Charleston, South Carolina, white soldiers intervened when a policeman beat a black stevedore. However, more often than not, white officers instructed black soldiers not to provoke racial disturbances and to stay away from places where their presence was not desired.

Nonetheless, many men continued to visit the towns near the camps during their off-duty hours, which caused military officials considerable headaches. Not only did they worry about the potential for racial conflicts, but they also feared that the men would get drunk, consort with prostitutes, and contract venereal diseases, which threatened to undermine military efficiency. In an attempt to address the problem, the Secretary of War prohibited the sale of liquor to men in uniform and declared prostitute-free zones around each of the training camps. Not surprisingly, neither measure produced the desired result. Banning all soldiers from spending their leisure time in camp communities would have addressed the problem, and some camp commanders decided to issue no passes. However, that did not deter some of the men from leaving the camps. At Camp Stuart, Virginia, Sergeant Ely Green led an entire battalion of disgruntled black soldiers over the camp's barbed wire fence and into a nearby town, where the men partied for several hours. When the soldiers returned to camp, guards arrested Green for mutiny. He got lucky and managed to avoid execution because a white colonel, impressed with Green's gutsiness, intervened on his behalf.

To maintain the men's morale and health as well as military efficiency, the War Department decided that it was best to discourage soldiers from venturing into camp communities by providing them with attractive leisure time programs inside the camps. For that purpose, the War Department created the Commission on Training Camp Activities (CTCA), which recruited several social service organizations to supply the troops with entertainment and recreational activities. The Knights of Columbus and the Young Men's Hebrew Association practiced a racial open door policy, but only few African Americans availed themselves of their services. For African American soldiers, the programs offered by the Young Women's Christian Association (YWCA) and the Young Men's Christian Association (YMCA), though largely segregated, proved to be especially crucial in combating boredom and maintaining morale.

At the core of the YWCA's efforts to assist the troops were its so-called Hostess Houses, which operated in rented or newly constructed buildings near or inside the training camps. The houses provided the women who visited soldiers with restrooms and many of them furnished nurseries as well as makeshift sleeping quarters to accommodate those who had traveled too far to return to their homes on the same day. Moreover, they offered comfortable places where the soldiers could meet with their families, wives, or girlfriends during regular visiting hours. While the YWCA's primary purpose was to safeguard the hundreds of female travelers who visited soldiers in the training camps, the Army hoped that the Hostess Houses would discourage the men from spending their off-duty hours in the red-light districts of adjacent communities.

In June 1917, the YWCA established the first Hostess House for white soldiers at the Officers' Training Camp at Plattsburg, New York. Initially, some of the military commanders were opposed to the presence of women in the camps, however, opposition faded quickly when the houses proved to be useful in conserving camp morale. Stimulated by the popularity of the Plattsburg Hostess House, the Army asked the YWCA to provide similar facilities for all soldiers. Throughout the war, the YWCA operated 124 Hostess Houses in American training camps, seventeen of them for the exclusive use of African Americans. While white Hostess Houses were quickly erected in nearly all of the camps, the majority of those serving African American soldiers did not open their doors until late 1918. The responsibility for organizing and staffing black Hostess Houses fell to the YWCA's "Colored Work Committee," headed by Eva D. Bowles, a black social worker from Columbus, Ohio. Although Bowles was opposed to segregation, she believed that securing separate YWCA services for black female visitors of soldiers was better than providing no services at all.

On November 18, 1917, the YWCA opened its first Hostess House for black soldiers at Camp Upton, New York. Former president Theodore Roosevelt, who had served with black troops during the Spanish-American War, attended the opening ceremony. He was so impressed with the YWCA's work that he donated $4,000 of his Nobel Peace Prize money for the use of black Hostess Houses. After January 1918 the facility at Upton also became the training center for black hostesses. Bowles and Lugenia Burns Hope, wife of John Hope, president of Morehouse College, conducted a four-week course to train black women as Y-secretaries. Eventually, sixty-seven recent black college graduates as well as educated and experienced older women staffed the Hostess Houses. All of the women underwent an intense screening process to ensure that only those with impeccable reputations would serve in the camps. The buildings the women staffed differed in size, ranging from a quickly constructed one-room hut in Kentucky to an eighteen-room mansion in New Jersey. The interior of each house was designed to resemble a middle-class living room that exuded a relaxing homelike atmosphere. Curtains covered the windows, pictures adorned the walls, and comfortable chairs and sofas offered a welcome respite from the drab military furniture in the training camps. Often, residents of adjacent black communities, churches, and women's clubs raised additional funds to equip the houses with pianos, Victrolas, and libraries.

The work of the Hostess Houses was particularly important for African Americans, because many of the training camp communities were ill-equipped to provide the large number of black soldiers and their female visitors with proper accommodation. And, none of the camps had any restrooms set aside for black women. While the houses served primarily as meeting places for black troops and their female visitors, they also catered to the recreational and educational needs of the men. Many soldiers frequented the Hostess Houses to relax for a few hours after military duties. They read books, magazines, and newspapers; wrote letters; played games; listened to music; or talked to other men and the female staff, who lent a sympathetic ear to those who were homesick or had personal problems. In many cases, Y-secretaries, with the help of local communities, organized special events such as musical or theatrical performances. Others offered informal educational classes to teach illiterate soldiers how to write letters to their loved ones. At Camp Taylor, Kentucky, the most urgent need was a cafeteria, because no restaurants in the immediate vicinity were willing to serve black customers. Local women from nearby Louisville volunteered to assist the YWCA and took shifts in serving the men meals.

Although the majority of Hostess Houses were segregated in both Northern and Southern camps, at times, black and white visitors and soldiers used the same facilities. At Camp Dodge, Iowa, for example, black and white women were housed together in the black building during the emergency caused by the Spanish influenza pandemic. In other camps, due to the large number of African Americans troops, only black Hostess Houses served the soldiers and their visitors. At Camp Sherman, Ohio, and Camp Alexander, Virginia, white soldiers and their female visitors had to either use the facilities of the black Hostess Houses or do without. In some cases, if no black Hostess House was available white Y-secretaries let black women use their facilities. At Camp Taylor, white soldiers went a step further and removed the sign that designated the Hostess House as "colored," proclaiming that in "the trenches we will be just Uncle Sam's boy why not the same here?"[8] White challenges to segregation, however, remained the exception.

The Young Men's Christian Association (YMCA) also maintained segregation of its wartime services for soldiers. Jesse E. Moorland, a Howard University graduate who had become one of the nation's highest-ranking black YMCA officials in 1898, supervised the "Colored Work." Black Y-secretaries accompanied the soldiers on their journey to the training camps. Tending to the needs of the men on troop trains, Y-secretaries provided refreshments, distributed envelopes and stationary, wrote letters for illiterate soldiers, and counseled those who were worried about the families they had left behind. After the soldiers' arrival in the training camps, YMCA workers offered a variety of leisure time programs in so-called Y-huts. In a few Northern camps, Y-huts were open to members of both races, which on occasion sparked racial friction. On August 17, 1918, a race riot erupted at Camp Merritt, New Jersey, when white soldiers from Mississippi tried to eject two black men from a Y-hut that was open to white as well as black soldiers. However, the vast majority of Y-huts were strictly segregated, which almost always resulted in inferior facilities and services for black troops. For example, of the nearly 13,000 Y-secretaries who served in the training camps, only 300 were African Americans. Seriously understaffed, they faced the daunting task of catering to the needs of the Army's more than 380,000 black troops in only fifty-five Y-huts. They organized recreational, entertainment, and educational programs to counter a decline in soldier morale caused by boredom, homesickness, and monotony. With the help of the American Library Association, they set up camp libraries that provided the soldiers with books, magazines, and newspapers. They launched athletic and singing contests, organized baseball and boxing matches, conducted church services and Bible study sessions, and recruited professional entertainers and local talent to stage musical and theatrical performances. In addition, Y-huts kept board and card games available, hosted lectures, and showed movies to keep up the spirits of the troops.

Many military officials particularly welcomed the YMCA's educational efforts for soldiers. The draft had revealed that 25 percent of all men tested could not read a newspaper or write an intelligent letter and that a large portion of functionally literate men had deficient schooling. Illiteracy rates among African American troops ran even higher, since 80 percent of the black draftees came from the South, where whites had systematically deprived them of educational opportunities. Some camp commanders reported illiteracy rates of 80 percent and noted that many of the black draftees did not know their date of birth or left from right. This alarming lack of education, the Commissioner of Education observed, hampered military efficiency and posed a serious threat to national security. Illiterate men, he informed Congress, "do not make good soldiers. Modern warfare requires many things impossible for soldiers who can not be depended on to make accurate reports. They can not read signs, orders, or the manual of arms."[9] Thus, the high illiteracy rate among black soldiers became "a menace to the welfare of the whole nation."[10]

Photo 4.3 *YMCA huts, like this one in Camp Travis, Texas, provided recreation, entertainment, and education programs for the soldiers during their off-duty hours. Source: Kautz Family YMCA Archives, University of Minnesota, Minneapolis*

Addressing the problem, the YMCA launched numerous educational programs, ranging from basic English instruction for illiterates to French language courses for soldiers preparing for overseas service. Throughout the war, the YMCA classes served strictly military purposes. Courses for illiterates sought to provide the men with skills necessary to understand, give, and execute military orders, while instructions in French prepared better-educated men for their encounter with allied soldiers and civilians. Although attendance at the classes offered by the Y-secretaries was voluntary, some camp commanders required all illiterate men to attend them. For example, at Camp Dodge, Iowa, where the labor battalions were composed of black draftees from the coal and cotton fields of Alabama, classes for illiterates were mandatory. At least 2,300 men attended the elementary English courses, and within a month 90 percent learned how to sign their names. As Harrison J. Pinkett of the all-black 366th Infantry observed: "This does not mean they can read and write, but it does mean that they will learn."[11] Whether attendance was mandatory or not, reports from other camps indicate that black soldiers enrolled in large numbers in the YMCA classes, even if facilities were inadequate. At Camp Hill, Virginia, two graduates of Hampton Institute conducted classes for 5,000 black stevedores in a tent that served as a temporary Y-hut. And at Camp Shelby, Mississippi, four black Y-secretaries offered classes for illiterates in one of the mess halls. Throughout the war approximately 90,000 black soldiers enrolled each month in the various classes offered at the Y-huts.

Camp commanders supported the YMCA's educational work, hoping that it would improve the fighting efficiency of the troops. But they also saw it as an important tool in maintaining the men's physical strength and health. Until the draft, the federal government had been largely indifferent to the health of the black population. However, the large percentage of black soldiers infected with sexually transmitted diseases made the health of African Americans an issue of national concern. In an effort to reduce the number of sick soldiers, the Army appointed Arthur B. Spingarn, to investigate the reasons for the high venereal disease infection rate among black troops. Arthur, like his brother Joel, had played an active role in the NAACP prior to World War I. He had served as the head of the NAACP's legal committee and upon America's entry into the war joined the U.S. Sanitary Corps as a commissioned officer. Arthur concluded that black soldiers had limited access to clean and decent recreation, since many of the towns near the training camps excluded African Americans from wholesome recreational facilities. Walter Howard Loving, a black military intelligence officer, confirmed Spingarn's findings. Camp communities, he charged, had made little effort to clear out red-light districts in black neighborhoods. In addition, Army offi-cials attributed the diseases' greater incidence among African Americans to a lack of education and a general ignorance of sexual and personal hygiene. To combat venereal disease and foster a healthy lifestyle, Y-secretaries in-vited black physicians to present lectures. In addition, they organized exhib-its, provided instructions in sanitation and personal hygiene, and screened films such as *Damaged Goods*, which illustrated the horrors of venereal dis-ease Even *Soldier's First Book*, a textbook specifically designed for the instruc-tion of illiterate soldiers, reminded the men to bathe frequently, to brush their teeth after each meal, and to avoid drinking liquor, smoking cigarettes, and indulging in vices. As one of the black soldiers recalled, sexually trans-mitted diseases were so prevalent that, "everytime you turned around, you was gettin' a lecture on it."[12]

While many military officials welcomed the YMCA's educational work as a means of maintaining morale and improving the fighting efficiency of the troops, black Y-secretaries often did much more than teach personal hygiene or rudimentary English. Literacy classes not only focused on reading and writing but also included instructions in civics and history. Since all Y-secre-taries used the same government-issued textbooks, ironically, African Amer-ican troops learned about the importance of voting from a *Camp Reader for American Soldiers*. Civics courses, designed to foster patriotism, taught the men to take an interest in politics and government and stressed the right to vote. A less formal but nevertheless important part of education was the emergence of self-help groups. The Y-huts provided a point of contact for African Americans from diverse socioeconomic and geographic backgrounds. Educated men from Howard, Tuskegee, and Hampton encountered men from the rural South, many of whom were illiterate and ignorant even of their own age. Often, the better educated men taught fellow soldiers how to read or write or read books to them. The Y-hut camp libraries also introduced many men to the works of black authors and journalists, which instilled in them a sense of pride and self-esteem. Thus, the government-sanctioned work of the YMCA helped to raise the political awareness of black men and their expec-tations for civil rights after the war.

However, the racism that pervaded every aspect of the wartime mobiliza-tion dampened hopes for gaining equality in exchange for military service. The biased administration of the draft and the discriminatory treatment of black soldiers in the training camps led many black men to question if their military service would garner true democracy for African Americans. While some of the men were disillusioned by the poor camp conditions, the exclu-sion of black laborers from real military training, and the constant racial insults and abuses white officers heaped upon them, others remained hopeful. Once black troops reached France and demonstrated their willingness to die for their country, they predicted that white Americans could no longer deny African Americans full equality.

CHAPTER FIVE

~

Over There

African American Soldiers in France

As the 200,000 black troops made their way across the Atlantic, so too did Jim Crow. Largely relegated to the labor battalions—the so-called Service of Supply—the vast majority of black soldiers were armed not with guns but with shovels, just like they had been in the United States. Only 42,000 black soldiers, those who served with the Ninety-Second and Ninety-Third Divisions, saw combat. Ill prepared for frontline duty, they suffered the consequences of poor training and, like the black laborers in uniform, had to contend with white racist soldiers, officers, and military police. While racism cast a shadow on the black military experience in France, African American troops relished the social interactions with French soldiers and civilians, who treated the men with courtesy and respect and often invited them into their homes and churches. In addition, many black soldiers enjoyed the company of French women, including prostitutes, who were eager to relieve the American troops of their money, regardless of race.

The first black soldiers, approximately 500 stevedores, sailed for France in June 1917. Like all of the men who followed them, they traveled on military transport ships, merchant passenger liners, or German vessels that had been seized by the U.S. government. Departing from Hoboken, New Jersey, or Newport News, Virginia, it was for most of the black soldiers their first glimpse of the sea and for virtually all of them the first trip across the Atlantic. During their journey, which lasted two to three weeks, the men were crammed into tight quarters and many of them suffered from seasickness. Although white and black soldiers and officers traveled on the same ships, sleeping quarters, bathroom facilities, and mess halls were segregated, and certain decks were only open to whites. Much of the men's time was filled with military instruction, life boat drills, and lectures about France. During their spare time, some anxiously watched the sea for German submarines, while others wrote letters to their friends and relatives, sang, played cards, or rolled dice. In addition, Y-secretaries provided for the men's entertainment. They distributed boxing gloves and board games, screened films, and organized musical performances by regimental bands. At dusk, most group activities ceased, as the ships sailed in silence and darkness, to avoid attracting the attention of the enemy.

In the wake of the first stevedores, thousands of other black laborers in uniform soon followed. Preparing for the arrival of American combat troops, the vast majority of the black labor battalions were stationed in French port cities and regional supply and distribution centers that were well behind the front lines. Among the largest camps were those near Brest, which had a permanent black soldier population of 40,000; Bordeaux, which had 10,000; and St. Nazaire, which was home to 9,000 African Americans. At times, due to arrival and departure peaks, these numbers easily doubled. Since the black labor battalions were among the first American soldiers who arrived in France, their living conditions were the worst of any U.S. troops. Initially, there were no cots, and the men slept on the ground in leaky tents or hastily constructed dirt-floor barracks. They ate outside or in primitive mess halls, used crude outhouses, and washed themselves in make-shift bathrooms. Even months after their arrival, housing conditions showed little improvement. By April 1918, the camp in St. Nazaire was still "a typical Hell-Hole" with "No beds no fire, and ground floors in the so called barracks."[1]

The black laborers spent much of their days as well as nights unloading ships, transporting supplies to distribution centers near the front, laying railroad tracks, and constructing barracks and warehouses. In one city alone they erected twenty-eight miles of warehouses. They took care of the Army's horses and mules and moved thousands of tons of cargo, including construction material, equipment, ammunition, fuel, clothes, blankets, medical supplies, mail, and food. Most of the men performed this back-breaking labor without adequate food or proper clothing. Sergeant Ely Green, who served with a stevedore company in St. Nazaire, arrived in France with a pair of pants, one pair of underwear, two pairs of socks, a pair of tan shoes, a shirt, and a raincoat. For the first two months after setting foot on French soil, he and his men waded through knee-deep mud without boots and unloaded shiploads of cold steel and frozen meat without gloves. Those who had spare pairs of socks used them to protect their hands as they worked in constantly pouring rain. To add insult to injury, on their daily march from the camps to the docks, the men passed German prisoners of war who sat under protective tarps and mockingly yelled at them: "You are slaves. We are American prisoners. We don't work in the rain."[2] In addition, the black laborers continued to endure the verbal insults and physical abuses of white soldiers and officers.

Yet, white military personnel were not the only ones who harassed the black labor troops or treated them with contempt. At times, members of the regular black Army units, those who had chosen a career in the military, also tormented the men. Some of them may have had sadistic tendencies and took pleasure in abusing their authority, while others were the product of their military upbringing. The lives of the professional black soldiers had been steeped in military tradition and dominated by strict Army rules and regulations, and their allegiances were with the Army, which had provided them with a career and a steady source of income. These men often despised the draftees, whom they viewed as undisciplined riffraff. And they treated them accordingly. A shocking incident, illustrating the disdain some of the regular black soldiers felt for the draftees, occurred in St. Nazaire. A black sergeant who had previously served with the Tenth Cavalry refused to give food to a draftee who was late for mess. When the man helped himself to a loaf of bread, the sergeant pulled out a pistol and shot him repeatedly in the chest. Ely Green, who witnessed the shooting, watched in horror as the sergeant sat down and casually resumed his conversation with another soldier, "as if he had killed a cock roach." To make sure that all the men who were present understood that there were no bonds of racial brotherhood between the professional soldiers and the draftees, another sergeant announced that "there are several niggers in this company that should have gotten what that nigger got."[3] This was no isolated incident. Months later, Green and his friend Charlie May were standing at a hydrant, when a soldier from the Twenty-Fourth Infantry shot and killed May while he was filling his canteen. Green insisted that the attack was unprovoked and tried to file charges but he found it difficult to challenge members of the regular Army units who had years of seniority.

Suffering verbal and physical abuse and enduring poor living conditions and long dangerous work days, the labor troops had little to look forward to during their off-duty hours. White officers frequently banned the men from visiting nearby towns and cities in an effort to limit alcohol consumption and social contacts between black soldiers and French civilians, particularly women. When black soldiers did receive passes, camp commanders often restricted them to specific areas. For example, the 9,000 black soldiers stationed near St. Nazaire were only permitted to roam in one block of the city, which was home to five dance halls, but offered no other recreational or entertainment venues.

Not surprisingly, morale among those serving in the labor battalions was low. Resentful of their treatment, some black soldiers fought back. When black laborers in St. Nazaire witnessed a white marine bayoneting a black soldier for picking up a piece of candy that had fallen from a broken crate, tensions exploded. The men armed themselves with cargo hooks and started charging the white soldier until two squads of marines arrived on the scene. Using their rifles, the Marines forced the rebellious black troops into a warehouse. Twenty-six of the men were sent to the stockade, where white guards beat them with billy clubs and gun butts and forced them to drink a vile concoction of Epsom salt and castor oil. Those who had not been arrested were outraged by the men's torture and prepared for another confrontation with the white soldiers. Aware that their cargo hooks were no match for the rifles and bayonets of the marines, the men stole the salvaged weapons of fallen soldiers while loading a hospital ship. However, before the men could fire a single shot, the black sergeant in charge of the platoon, fearing for the safety of his men, convinced them to drop the guns off the edge of the wharf.

While racially motivated mutinies did occur, black soldiers were more likely to use subtle forms of resistance. They stole food or cigarettes or slacked off at work. White officers attributed the less-than-stellar work ethic of some of the black laborers to natural laziness, and all-white military courts imposed harsh sentences on slackers. But white commanders also admitted that the men had no incentive to pick up the pace. Acknowledging the poor living and working conditions of the black labor battalions, one white general, obviously ignorant of the cruel treatment of black men in the stockade, observed: "Fining them and putting them in the guard house is very little punishment for them, and to be dishonorably discharged and sent home is just what they desire."[4]

White officers were equally frustrated that black men often ignored their orders not to interact with French civilians as well as the military's ban on alcohol and prostitutes. Under the cover of darkness, many black men slipped away to hoist a few drinks with French villagers and to visit houses of prostitution, even though they were officially off-limits for American soldiers in France. The high venereal disease infection rates and arrests for drunkenness among the black labor battalions in France indicate that these were not isolated incidents. Many white commanders insisted that this was a reflection of the black men's uncontrollable sexual appetite and their inherent weakness for liquor, but failed to recognize that these were often deliberate acts of defiance of white authority. If the military was not going to treat black men fairly, there was no reason for black men to play by military rules.

Unable to stop the men from consuming alcohol or consorting with French prostitutes, the Army mandated vigorous punishment of drunken soldiers and compulsory prophylaxis for all Americans serving in France. In addition, the War Department once again called on the YMCA to provide wholesome leisure time activities for the troops. Like the association's work in American training camps, YMCA services in France remained largely segregated and gravely understaffed. Throughout the war, no more than sixty black Y-secretaries, among them twenty-three women, served the 200,000 black soldiers in France. However, only three of the women—Addie W. Hunton, Kathryn M. Johnson, and Helen Curtis—arrived prior to the armistice. At the Y-huts, which were often no more than tents, black Y-secretaries operated libraries, school rooms, and canteens that served hot chocolate, lemonade, cakes, and ice cream. They screened movies, organized Bible study groups, provided board games, and wrote letters for illiterate soldiers. Limited by a shortage of personnel and overwhelmed by the high demand for leisure time programs, Y-secretaries recruited black men in uniform as well as French civilians to help them. Talented soldiers provided entertainment, athletes organized sporting events, and better-educated men taught reading and writing classes. French teachers and professors offered language courses, led guided tours to historic sites, and presented lectures on French history, culture, and geography. Most of the YMCA's work in France concentrated on providing entertainment, recreation, and educational programs for the vast majority of black troops who served in the labor battalions, as they usually had more time at their disposal than the soldiers on the front. But, when black combat troops started to arrive in France in early 1918, the YMCA also assigned three field secretaries to organize recreational activities among the men fighting in the trenches.

The first black combat units that sailed for France were the four infantry regiments of the Ninety-Third Provisional Division. The 369th, formerly the Fifteenth New York Volunteer Infantry, was under the command of white New Yorker Colonel William Hayward and his staff of mostly white officers. The 370th, originally the Eighth Illinois National Guard, was the only regiment led by a full quota of black officers, including its commander, Colonel Franklin A. Dennison, eight medical officers, and two dentists. The 371st, composed of Southern draftees who were initially intended to serve as laborers, had all-white officers. And the 372nd, made up of black National Guard units as well as draftees from the North, was commanded by a majority of

Photo 5.1 *YMCA huts in France were popular destinations for the black troops, particularly the labor battalions who were not serving in the line of fire. Source: Kautz Family YMCA Archives, University of Minnesota, Minneapolis*

white officers, many of whom were Southerners. The four regiments of the Ninety-Third Provisional Division reached France between January 1 and June 10. Shortly thereafter, they were joined by the Ninety-Second Division, which arrived between June 18 and July 12. Headed by General Charles C. Ballou, the Ninety-Second consisted largely of black draftees and lower-ranking Des Moines-trained black officers, while white officers held all of the senior positions.

The 369th was the first black combat regiment that arrived in France. The regiment, which had trained at Camp Wadsworth, South Carolina, had been quickly dispatched overseas after racial tensions had escalated between black soldiers and white residents of Spartanburg in the fall of 1917. However, the men's journey to France was anything but quick. Following their departure from Spartanburg on October 24, 1917, they reached New York City, where they were quartered in several armories and tents set up in a city park. On November 11, the 369th received orders to board the transport ship *Pocahontas*. But only one day into the journey, the ship had to return to port due to engine problems. The men disembarked and reported to Camp Merritt, New Jersey, where they remained for the next three weeks until their ship was repaired. On December 2, they boarded the *Pocahontas* once again, but a fire on the ship kept the troops in port for eleven days. On December 13, when the men made their third attempt to sail to France, their ship collided with a British oil tanker. This time, however, military officials decided to let the soldiers repair the ship en route and the regiment finally left the United States the following day.

The 369th landed in France on January 1, 1918. Upon the regiment's arrival, the men were assigned to perform labor duties and to guard a German prisoner of war camp. Since the War Department had assured the black soldiers that they would serve in arms at the front, troop morale began to crumble. Embarrassed by their work detail, some of the men fabricated elaborate stories of their battle participation in the letters they wrote home. However, morale picked up when the men learned of their assignment to the front. In March 1918, General John J. Pershing, commander of the American Expeditionary Force (AEF) in Europe, responded to French requests for troop reinforcements and transferred the 369th to the French Army. Some contemporaries speculated that Pershing's decision was the product of political pressure, rather than racism. After all, Pershing had a long history of working and serving with African Americans. Following his graduation from high school in 1878, Pershing had taught at a black school in his hometown Laclede, Missouri. But by 1882 he had discovered a penchant for the military and left Missouri to enroll in the U.S. Military Academy at West Point, New York. After four years of studies, he graduated and the Army assigned him to cavalry service in the West. In 1896 Pershing took charge of the all-black Tenth Cavalry, the so-called Buffalo Soldiers, which earned him the nickname "Nigger Jack" in military circles. Reporters changed the offensive nickname to the moniker "Black Jack" when Pershing led the Tenth Cavalry into battle during the Spanish-American War. In 1916, the Tenth Cavalry once again served with Pershing when the Buffalo Soldiers participated in the punitive expedition to Mexico, where another West Pointer, Charles Young, attracted Pershing's attention. Impressed with Young's distinguished performance in Mexico, Pershing supported his promotion to the rank of lieutenant colonel, making him the highest-ranking black officer in the United States Army. Pershing's service with black soldiers and his support of Young's promotion prior to World War I seem to indicate that the general's decision to transfer black combat soldiers to the French Army was not motivated by racism. Nonetheless, assigning African American soldiers to serve with the French, clearly rid Pershing of potential racial problems. Regardless of his motive, the 369th was placed under the command of the French, as were the remaining three regiments of the Ninety-Third Provisional Division.

Throughout the war, the men of the Ninety-Third Division were the only American troops who served under French command. They retained their American uniforms, but were otherwise fully integrated into the French Army. They received French gear, French weapons, and French rations, all of which created challenging problems for the black soldiers. The men had to surrender their modern American Springfield rifles in exchange for inaccurate and anti-quated French rifles, which held only three cartridges at a time and with which they had no familiarity. They had to contend with new gas masks and ill-fitting helmets, which had been designed for the slighter physique of the average French man. Moreover, only few of the black soldiers had any French language skills, and reliance on interpreters made communication difficult. In addition, there were cultural differences. The French Army ration consisted of two meals per day, often soups or stews, rather than the three meat-based meals provided by the American Army, and it included a daily allotment of a quart of wine. Although white American officers instructed the French not to issue wine to the black troops, French commanders apparently ignored the request. In addition, French soldiers often shared their wine rations as well as other alcoholic beverages with their black comrades in arms. Ralph D. Taylor, who served with the 372nd and kept a diary throughout 1918, frequently noted that wine, champagne, and cognac were flowing like water.[5]

The black soldiers were delighted with the French troops' willingness to treat them as brothers-in-arms. Some racially enlightened white commanders of black soldiers welcomed the fraternization, hoping it would foster *esprit de corps* and lead to better performance in battle. For example, Colonel Hayward of the 369th was quite pleased that his men not only marched and fought, but also ate, drank, sang, laughed, and danced together with the French soldiers. However, most white American military officials were troubled by close personal contacts between the black combat troops and the French soldiers. They feared that if African Americans experienced a sense of equality in the French Army, they might expect the same treatment in the American Army.

Even more alarming to American military leaders were the frequent social interactions between the black combat troops and French civilians, particularly women. Unlike the black labor troops, the black combat soldiers were less likely to consort with prostitutes, since most of the women who engaged in the sex trade stayed near the base camps where large numbers of men provided a permanent pool of customers. This was indicated by the small number of men who sought treatment for sexually transmitted diseases. Indeed, the combat soldiers of the Ninety-Second Division had the lowest venereal disease infection rate of any American troops serving in France.

Most of the combat soldiers sought friendships, romantic liaisons, and other meaningful relationships with French civilians, which irked American military officials. Opportunities to meet French women arose frequently, since the combat soldiers were not assigned to permanent camps but moved along the front. As a result they were often billeted in French towns and lived in the homes or barns of French people. After learning a few French words, black soldiers courted local women. Rayford W. Logan, for example, had several girlfriends while serving with the 372nd in France. Logan, who would after the war became one of the foremost black scholars of the twentieth century, took great pleasure in escorting them around town, much to the consternation of Southern white soldiers. In a number of cases romance led to marriage and some black soldiers brought French wives back to the United States.

Indeed, French civilians often favored personal contacts with black American soldiers rather than whites. At times this preference was due to the arrogant attitude and behavior of many white Americans, who exhibited little tact in their interaction with the local population. An additional source of friction between white American soldiers and French civilians were the doughboy's inexhaustible funds. Wherever the soldiers went, French business proprietors raised their prices, much to the objection of the local

Photo 5.2 *French civilians, including these children, often interacted with the black troops. The experience revealed to the men the possibility of racial equality.*
Source: Kautz Family YMCA Archives, University of Minnesota, Minneapolis

population. Black soldiers, on the other hand, had less money, and racism in the United States had conditioned them to display respectful demeanor in their interaction with whites, especially women. Ely Green recalled that when he and his men went to one of the dance halls in St. Nazaire, the men were initially too shy to approach the French women.

White American soldiers were concerned about the frequent personal contacts between French civilians, particularly women, and the black troops and tried to prevent any interaction between them. Often white soldiers informed the French in advance about the arrival of African Americans, claiming that they were ignorant, dangerous, and diseased and had only recently "been caught in the American forests, and only been tamed enough to work under the white American's direction."[6] One black soldier remembered that French children often lifted the men's "overcoats to see if they had tails like a monkey."[7] In addition, some white commanders of black troops instructed military police to prevent the men from talking to or even addressing French women, however, with little success. Frustrated by the continued friendly interaction between black soldiers and French civilians, the French mission of the U.S. Army headquarters in Paris issued a secret memorandum. It advised French officers, soldiers, and civilians to avoid any friendly or intimate contact with black troops and urged them not to spoil the men with equality. Some white commanders went a step further and warned French civilians to carry arms and to remain indoors and not let black soldiers into their homes. However, the efforts to curb friendly relations between black troops and French soldiers and civilians did not produce the desired result, and many men made lasting friendships. Ralph D. Taylor, for example, befriended Joseph Le Blanc, with whom he was billeted, and continued to correspond with his family for several decades after the war.

Ironically, American military officials in France inadvertently contributed to the friendly relations between the black troops and French civilians. In February 1918, shortly after the arrival of the 369th in France, AEF headquarters dispatched its regimental band to entertain American troops serving overseas. Legendary bandleader and composer Jim Reese Europe, whose band had been the first African American band to play at Carnegie Hall in 1912, embarked with his forty-four musicians on a 2,000-mile train tour. During their thirty-seven-day journey through France, Europe and his band stopped in more than twenty-five French cities and towns where the musicians performed for American soldiers as well as French civilians. Wherever the band set up its instruments, large crowds of French people greeted them with enthusiasm, particularly when the band played a jazzy version of "La Marseillaise," the French national anthem.

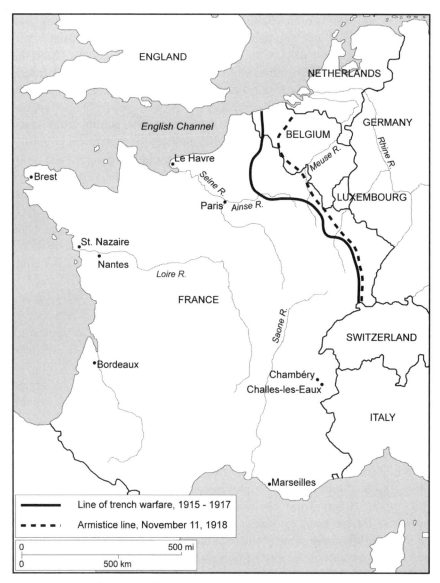

Map 5.1 *Map of France and Western Front indicating American ports of debarkation and cities with large black soldier populations. Source: Courtesy of Michael Hradesky, Staff Cartographer, Department of Geography, Ball State University*

The cordial interaction with the French, which was neither tainted by race prejudice nor restricted by Jim Crow laws, was a welcome respite for the men, particularly the combat troops who spent a lot of time at the front. In the trenches, the men faced the unspeakable horrors of modern war. Surrounded by barbed-wire entanglements they were exposed to constant shelling, machine gun and artillery fire as well as gas and sniper attacks. Often the men stood in knee deep water, which produced the much dreaded trench foot, a condition characterized by open sores, fungal infections, and gangrene and, if left untreated, required amputation of the foot. Even more horrendous was the effect of mustard gas. Exposure to the gas caused painful skin blisters; inflammation of the nose, throat, and respiratory system; fever, vomiting, and diarrhea; and irritation of the eyes, which could lead to blindness.

While fending off enemy attacks as well as battle fatigue, many men slept for weeks in wet soiled clothes in damp cold dugouts that were teeming with rats. Other constant companions of the men in the trenches were lice, which were impossible to get rid of because of poor sanitary condition. Equally bad was the food. Most of the time, the men ate their meager rations while standing in the rain. On occasion rolling kitchens provided warm meals, but often the soldiers lived off canned corned beef—which the men called Corned or Tinned Willie—hard tack, chocolate, or a piece of soggy bread. In many cases, they went without food for several days. In the winter the water in their canteens froze and in the summer they could smell the overpowering stench of their own excrement as well as of dead soldiers who were rotting in no-man's land, the area between the opposing trenches. Ralph D. Taylor, who spent 105 consecutive days in the trenches, recalled that a German sniper shot one of his comrades as he was making his way over the top of the trench. The man fell in no-man's land and his body was impaled on the remnants of a small tree, while his feet were still sticking into the trench. Unable to move the body, the soldiers watched the dead man decompose.

While trench warfare was exhausting and dangerous for all combat soldiers, it took an especially heavy physical and psychological toll on the black men of the Ninety-Third Division. Assigned to the French, they had to overcome foreign language barriers and adjust quickly to new weapons and equipment. Moreover, none of the men had received sufficient training. The average American soldier trained for about six months in the United States and an additional two months overseas before going into battle. But most black troops had no more than a few weeks of military training. In addition, white officers who considered themselves to be racial liberals often led the troops into unnecessarily dangerous missions in an effort to prove that black men were indeed good soldiers. Arthur W. Little, a white captain with the 369th regiment, felt remorse after an especially deadly encounter with the enemy. Throughout the war, the Ninety-Third suffered 3,534 battle casualties, a rate of 32 percent, which was in part due to the Army's decision to fill the depleted ranks of the division with inexperienced draftees, many of whom had never loaded a gun until they reached the frontline trenches.

Unwilling to concede that the black troops faced severe disadvantages—caused by poor training, unfamiliar foreign weapons, high-risk combat ventures, and the large-scale infusion of ill-prepared draftees—some whites blamed black officers for the heavy losses. The black officers, they claimed, were inefficient and had no business commanding troops in battle. The first to go was Colonel Franklin A. Dennison of the 370th Infantry Regiment, the former Eighth Illinois National Guard. Dennison had been the only black man commanding a combat regiment until he was relieved of his duty on medical grounds. Many of the men under his command remembered the forced retirement of Colonel Young and suspected that racism was responsible for Dennison's removal. In the 372nd, Herschel Tupes, the white commander, sought to eliminate all black officers in his regiment. He insisted that the men lacked initiative and were incompetent and negligent in the performance of their duties. Tupes asked Pershing to transfer his black officers to other units and not to assign any new black officers to his regiment. Pershing responded to the request and authorized Tupes to initiate efficiency hearings. A board composed of white officers sat in judgment over black officers and recommended the removal of seventy-seven men, earning it the nickname "Court of Elimination." A disgruntled Ralph D. Taylor noted in his diary: "The dirty dogs have thrown out almost all the Colored officers."[8] The other regiments also lost their black officers. The 369th, which had sailed for France with five black commissioned officers had only its bandleader, Lieutenant Jim Reese Europe, left by the end of the war.

The Germans, aware of the racial problems, tried to capitalize on the dissatisfaction of African Americans. German planes dropped propaganda leaflets behind allied lines, urging black soldiers to put down their weapons and desert the U.S. military. While none of the men accepted the German invitation, troop morale reached a nadir, and white military police were dispatched to maintain order and prevent a possible insurrection.

Some of the white officers of the Ninety-Third Division were painfully aware of the extraordinary obstacles black soldiers had to overcome and were sympathetic to the plight of the black troops under their command. Both Colonel Hayward and Captain Arthur W. Little of the 369th Infantry Regiment took great pride in the heroic exploits of the black soldiers and saw to it that they received proper press attention. Hayward, for example, made sure that white reporters from New York City, who were visiting the front, learned about the accomplishment of Sergeant Henry Johnson, a red cap from Albany, and Private Needham Roberts, a seventeen-year-old volunteer from

New Jersey. Though severely injured, Johnson and Roberts had killed four Germans, wounded thirty-two, and seized a significant number of enemy weapons and supplies. Hayward also took time to write a personal letter to the wife of Henry Johnson, informing her in great detail of her husband's courageous hand-to-hand combat encounter with the enemy. Moreover, both Hayward and Little took every opportunity to stress that the "Harlem Hellfighters"—as the men of the 369th came to be known—spent 191 consecutive days under fire, longer than any other American regiment. But regardless of their praise, even Hayward and Little were often condescending and patronizing. Hayward, for example, referred to the black men in his charge as his "singing, laughing, black, brave children" and "Les Enfants Perdus" (the lost children), while Little called them "my black babies."9

The black combat soldiers of the Ninety-Second Division faced even more blatant racism than those who served with the Ninety-Third Division. The Ninety-Second, under the command of General Charles C. Ballou and lower-ranking Des Moines-trained black officers, arrived in France between June and July 1918. Most of the regular troops were recent draftees, who had received only rudimentary training and lacked proper equipment. The Ninety-Second had trained in the United States for only fifty-seven days and had been dispersed to seven different camps. Its artillery regiments had never fired a single shell before arriving in France, and the men did not receive all of their equipment until after the end of hostilities. Ill prepared for battle, the Ninety-Second Division was attached to General Robert Lee Bullard's Second American Army. Alabama-born Bullard initially believed that black soldiers might perform well in combat, especially if they were led by capable white officers, particularly Southerners like him, who had allegedly experience in handling African Americans. Indeed, black men, he claimed, shared certain characteristics that made them ideal soldiers. They were, Bullard insisted, accustomed to defer to whites and therefore more easily disciplined. Moreover, years of poverty had prepared them for the austere living conditions in the military. However, when the poorly prepared black troops did not meet Bullard's expectations, he changed his tune and insisted that the men be assigned to labor details. The white officers serving under Bullard shared many of his racist beliefs and started to circulate rumors that black soldiers had raped French women.

Demoralized by racist allegations, poor white leadership, lack of preparation, and insufficient equipment— the men had no maps, grenade launchers, wire cutters, or signal flares—the soldiers of the Ninety-Second Division moved to the front. Not surprisingly, the men did not perform well and suffered 1,647 battle casualties. Bullard was quick to condemn the entire division as a failure. The black officers and the black men under their command, he insisted, were not only inefficient but cowardly. Courts-martial found several men guilty of cowardice and sentenced them to death, though a War Department investigation later exonerated them. Looking for a scapegoat, Bullard turned on Ballou, the commanding general of the Ninety-Second Division, and requested his removal. Ballou, who had in the past often praised the ability of the black soldiers under his command, was disappointed in their combat performance. He criticized the War Department for assigning incompetent officers to the division, but also started to view the black troops as a liability in the advancement of his own military career. He blamed lower-ranking black officers for not controlling the men and started to replace many of them with whites.

Despite the seemingly insurmountable odds that the black combat soldiers faced during their service in France, many of the men performed heroically in battle. The French recognized their distinguished acts of bravery and decorated more than 500 hundred African Americans with the Croix de Guerre. Among the recipients were Henry Johnson, who became the first American soldier to receive the coveted medal, as well as Sergeant Jack Mason, who had been wounded in action 350 times, prompting his comrades to nickname him "the human sieve."[10] In addition, the French honored several African Americans with the Médailles Militaires, one of the rarest French decorations bestowed on foreigners. Even the U.S. government recognized the extraordinary heroism of black soldiers and awarded nearly a hundred of them the American Distinguished Service Cross. However, no African American soldier received the Congressional Medal of Honor, the highest American military award, even though the commanding officer of the 371st Infantry Regiment had recommended Corporal Freddie Stowers for the medal. Apparently his recommendation had been mysteriously misplaced. It was not until April 1991 that Stowers's sister accepted the medal for her deceased brother.

When the war ended on November 11, 1918, some racial barriers between black and white soldiers broke down, however briefly. Overjoyed by the armistice, regimental and camp commanders lifted all restrictions on passes and black and white soldiers flocked into French towns. There they joined French soldiers and civilians for impromptu exuberant victory parties and parades, and some of the white American soldiers celebrated Germany's surrender with their black comrades. Ely Green recalled that a white man from Mississippi even hugged him. But the victory celebrations were short lived. In the aftermath of the armistice, as the men reported to French port cities in preparation for their journey home, black men continued to face segregation and discrimination, dreadful living and working conditions, and the prospect of spending another miserable Thanksgiving and Christmas without their families.

While awaiting their ship assignments, the men were deloused and kept busy with endless hikes and meaningless drill exercises. And once again, black combat soldiers traded their rifles for shovels. They dismantled military installations, salvaged equipment and materials, and loaded ships bound for America. As thousands of troops descended upon the embarkation camps, housing, sanitary, and recreational facilities deteriorated quickly. The men slept in tents surrounded by knee-deep mud, they had no access to proper toilets, and YMCA huts were hopelessly overcrowded. At Camp Pontanezen near Brest only one Y-secretary served the 40,000 black troops, and he did not arrive until the spring of 1919. Conditions in the camps were so bad that one black officer compared them to penal institutions. Many men got sick and others feigned illnesses in hopes of being sent to the hospital ward and out of the mud. In addition, the men faced the constant abuse of white soldiers, particularly military police, who were determined to prevent African American men from socializing with French civilians and to crush any black demands for equal rights. When black soldiers dared to complain, white commanders punished them. They assigned them to the dirtiest, most dangerous, and repulsive jobs; withheld their monthly pay; or threatened to place them at the bottom of the sailing list.

The situation went from bad to worse, when General Erwin, a white man from Georgia, replaced Ballou as commander of the Ninety-Second Division less than two weeks after the end of the war. On November 22, 1918, Ballou bid farewell to the black men under his command, much to the elation of many. Corporal Reuel M. Jordan, hoping that a new general might improve conditions for the soldiers, proclaimed that "our sighs of relief must have been heard in America for we knew that worse could never come."[11] But it did. Within a month after taking charge of the Ninety-Second Division, Erwin issued a long list of orders that mandated two general roll calls and six hours of drilling daily as well as weekly inspections, reviews, and long marches with fifty-pound gear packs. In addition, Erwin ordered military police to prevent enlisted men from talking to French women. Most of Erwin's subordinates implemented his orders with an iron fist and arrested those who were caught in the company of women. Some went even a step further and tried to convince French policemen to arrest all women who associated with black soldiers on charges of prostitution.

Not surprisingly, demoralization threatened to undermine the period of demobilization. Secretary of War Newton D. Baker, who toured the camps in

France shortly after the armistice, tried to appease the men. He assured them that the nation appreciated their services and that all Americans, black and white, were proud of their performance. However, Baker's efforts to boost morale among the black soldiers was not sufficient and the War Department asked Robert Russa Moton, successor of Booker T. Washington as principal of Tuskegee Institute, to visit the black troops who were awaiting their embarkation orders in Europe. Moton, who arrived in France shortly after the armistice, went on a 1,000-mile cross-country automobile trip to calm down the disgruntled soldiers. A devout accommodationist, Moton urged them not to expect significant racial changes. It was more important, he insisted, that they took pride in their personal achievement. He assured the soldiers that the white and black public would cordially welcome them home, but he cautioned the men to exercise self-restraint and to return with a manly, yet unassuming and modest, attitude. To the black men who had just risked their lives to make the world safe for democracy, Moton's admonition must have felt like a slap in the face. Ralph W. Tyler Sr., the only accredited black war correspondent in France, noted with bitterness "'modestly and unassumingly' which translated means, as Moton would have it 'come back with your tails between your legs.'"[12] Ely Green was likewise incensed by Moton's message and heckled him while he was addressing black troops. "Say, Moton," he yelled, "why in the hell did President Wilson send you over here to tell us how he honors the Negro? . . . go back to the States and teach that S.O.B. to the Halleluia Negro that don't know any better."[13] Military police quickly removed the troublemaker.

Moton, however, was not the only race leader who toured the American camps in France. W. E. B. Du Bois, the editor of the NAACP's *Crisis* magazine, who had sailed with Moton and even shared a cabin with him, also visited the black troops following the armistice. Unlike Moton, who had gone to France at the request of Emmett J. Scott, the War Department's special racial advisor, Du Bois traveled without the approval of the State Department. Securing passage as an accredited member of the United States Press Delegation, Du Bois went on a fact-finding mission to gather information for a book about African American soldiers. Troubled by the presence of Du Bois, whom the Army considered a radical, the War Department offered him no assistance and military intelligence officers closely monitored his speaking engagements. Du Bois was appalled by the conditions of the black soldiers in France. Using the pages of the *Crisis* he lashed out at Moton and Scott. He criticized Moton for his accommodationist stance and blamed Scott for his failure to address the miserable treatment of the black troops. "Did you know the treatment which black troops were receiving in France?

. . . if you DID know, what did you do about it?" he asked Scott.[14] But despite Du Bois's outrage, the conditions of the black soldiers in France showed little signs of improvement, and racial tensions continued to simmer in the weeks following the armistice.

Major Walter H. Loving, a black agent with the Military Intelligence Branch, warned military authorities that a race war was imminent. Loving predicted that black troops, with the help of sympathetic French soldiers, would rise against their white American oppressors. Loving was right; however, it was not the black American men who rose, but the French. Returning from the front, French soldiers became increasingly impatient with white Americans who had taken over their towns and in many cases their wives or girlfriends. Tensions exploded in St. Nazaire when white American troops attempted to evict colonial French African soldiers from a café. Violence erupted and soon French men throughout the city were hunting down white Americans. Ironically, Ely Green, who was light skinned, nearly became a victim of the angry mob. To make his way back to camp safely, Green stuck close to a fellow soldier who was darker skinned than he was. Nonetheless, French men charged Green, until his friend shouted that he was not white. Rayford W. Logan had a similar encounter. Disgruntled French sailors, mistaking Logan for a white American soldier, began to beat him and only stopped when he identified himself as an African American by rubbing his assailants' hands over his head. Logan's curly hair was sufficient evidence for the sailors. They released him, apologized for the attack, and continued their pursuit of white Americans. To prevent a potential alliance between the black soldiers and the French, who became increasingly resentful of the continued presence of their American allies, Loving urged his superiors to ship all black troops home as quickly as possible. The War Department, at least in part, did heed Loving's advice. By February 1919 all of the black combat soldiers had sailed for the United States.

However, large numbers of African Americans continued to stay in France for several weeks or even months. Among them were those who were too weak to travel. These included soldiers who had been wounded in battle, labor troops who had been injured while performing dangerous tasks, and men stricken with the deadly flu virus. These men remained in base hospitals until they were strong and healthy enough to make the journey home. But even in the hospitals, Jim Crow reared his ugly head. Although the military did not segregate its hospital wards in France, white staff usually confined black patients to one area and forced black officers to share rooms with rank-and-file soldiers, even though military policy stipulated that they were entitled to private rooms. At times, white nurses moved black patients from hospital beds onto military cots to make the more comfortable beds available to white soldiers. And in some cases, black soldiers received medical attention only after white doctors and nurses had tended to the needs of white patients, including German prisoners of war. As a result, some black men were not treated for several days. In some wards, black men were crammed into areas with no heat and had to wait for food until after all whites had been served. One soldier recalled that an especially cruel nurse ordered a black soldier to make his own bed and when it was not done to her satisfaction berated the man until he was driven to tears. When the black soldiers were finally healthy enough to be transported to the United States, they usually had to wait until white convalescents boarded the hospital ships.

The last African Americans who left for the United States were the labor troops. Many of them stayed in France until the summer of 1919. They salvaged equipment from the battlefields, cleared the land of barbed wire, filled in the trenches, removed unexploded shells, and helped construct the Pershing Stadium near Paris, which hosted the Inter-Allied games between June 22 and July 6. In addition, black labor troops were charged with the gruesome task of collecting and reburying the decomposed bodies of thousands of fallen soldiers.

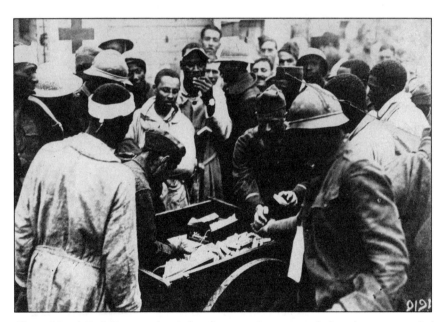

Photo 5.3 *A Red Cross worker is handing out cigarettes and chocolate to wounded black soldiers. Despite the organization's policy of nondiscrimination, many white workers refused to serve black men. Source: National Archives. ARC identifier 533572/ Local Identifier 165-WW-127(81)*

As they exhumed the corpses, they also found the remains of mutilated bodies of black soldiers, some still with nooses around their necks. Not surprisingly, rumors of lynchings spread quickly, and the Senate appointed a special committee to investigate the allegations. After interviewing numerous black veterans and compiling a 1,000-page report, the committee concluded that there had been no executions without trial or court-martial. However, given the racial climate, nothing could have convinced the black labor troops of that.

The only relief for those who were left behind to clean up the debris of the war was a seven-day furlough every four months, which the men spent in holiday resorts run by the YMCA. French resort towns, which had ample entertainment and recreational facilities and whose hotel rooms stood empty as a result of the war, were eager to collaborate with the YMCA. The first of the so-called leave areas opened in Aix-Les-Bains on February 15, 1918. Eventually the YMCA operated nineteen leave areas in France. Initially, soldiers eligible for leave had to pay their own travel and accommodation expenses, which virtually excluded black labor troops from the resorts. But

Photo 5.4 *Following the end of the war, many of the black troops still in France were assigned to rebury the decomposed bodies of the men killed in battle. Source: U.S. Army Military History Institute, Carlisles Barracks, Pennsylvania*

within a month, the Army assumed financial responsibility and special trains started to transport the men to the resort towns, where YMCA secretaries met them and assigned them to hotels in the vicinity. During the hostilities, the leave area at Aix-les-Bains catered to both white and black soldiers, but the number of black vacationers remained small. Only after the armistice did they arrive by trainloads.

When the number of vacationing black soldiers increased, white soldiers on leave and white YMCA secretaries working in the resorts started to object to the presence of African Americans. Unwilling to tolerate racial discrimination during their furlough, a group of 1,200 black troops vacationing in Aix-les-Bains appealed to the YMCA and requested a leave area for the exclusive use of African Americans. John Hope, President of Morehouse College, who supervised the work of the black Y-secretaries in France initially opposed the creation of separate leave areas. Accepting the long-standing segregation of African Americans in the military was a necessary evil, but initiating segregation where it did not exist was unacceptable, he believed. However, when Hope received reports about racial incidents that threatened the safety of black soldiers, he reluctantly approved the establishment of segregated vacation resorts staffed by black Y-secretaries.

In December 1918 the YMCA set aside the leave areas at Chambéry and Challes-les-Eaux for African Americans. By the summer of 1919 nearly 20,000 black soldiers had spent their week-long military leaves there, enjoying fine food, comfortable beds, and a host of leisure time activities. Black YMCA secretaries organized canteens, libraries, games, indoor and outdoor sports events, musical shows, movies, hiking trips, sightseeing excursions, and educational classes, while local teachers presented lectures on French society. The leave areas offered the men not only rest and entertainment but also an escape from the daily military routine as well as the racial abuses of white officers and soldiers. And, once again, the men had ample opportunity to socialize with French women. Arthur B. Spingarn, who investigated the spread of venereal disease in the leave areas, noted considerable sexual intercourse between the troops and the female hotel employees, as well as the large numbers of prostitutes who not only followed the men to the resorts but accompanied them on the trains. Yet the black soldiers also enjoyed the affection of the respectable white residents who organized weekly dances for the men. Whether the men solicited the services of prostitutes, enjoyed the company of other French civilians, or merely relaxed in the luxurious surroundings that most of them would have been unable to afford in the United States, all of them must had dreaded returning to the embarkation camps. After a week-long break from the military routine and the racial insults and

Photo 5.5 *Black soldiers on leave. Addie W. Hunton, seated in the front row, was one of a handful of black women who staffed the two segregated YMCA resorts in France. Source: Kautz Family YMCA Archives, University of Minnesota, Minneapolis*

harassments of white officers, the men returned to the embarkation camps for the last time before sailing for the United States in the summer of 1919.

For the majority of African American soldiers, their service in France had been a bittersweet experience. Whether armed with shovels or with guns, the men had not only fought the German enemy but also racism within the American Army. Black labor troops had endured atrocious working conditions; deplorable housing and sanitary facilities; limited leave time; and ill-equipped, understaffed, and overcrowded Y-huts. Black combat soldiers had suffered the consequences of poor training and concerted white American efforts to discredit their military proficiency. And all of them had been subjected to racial abuses, insults, and harassments. Yet despite the racism that had tainted their overseas service, the black soldiers also got a taste of freedom and democracy as a result of their interaction with the French, who treated them with respect, gratitude, and genuine affection. Exposure to French culture and society, without the limiting restraints of Jim Crow, radicalized many of the men. As Du Bois observed, "they were filled with a bitter, dogged determination never to give up the fight for . . . equality in America."[15] The war certainly radicalized Ely Green, who insisted that his discharge papers identify him not as a black man, but as an American citizen.

CHAPTER SIX

~

Closing Ranks?

African Americans on the Home Front

The majority of African Americans did not join the military, but experienced the war at home. Many took advantage of enhanced economic opportunities triggered by defense production and continued to move to industrial centers in the North. Those who remained in the South benefitted from an increase in cotton prices and labor shortages created by the draft as well as the large number of migrants who left the region. Whether they moved to the North or stayed in the South, many African Americans supported the war. They worked in defense industry plants and agriculture and helped produce weapons, food, clothing, and other supplies for America and its Allies. In addition, they donated money, provided relief for the men in uniform and their dependents, staged patriotic rallies and parades, and served as volunteers in various government agencies and private organizations. Nonetheless, African Americans also continued to challenge Jim Crow. Race leaders constantly reminded Americans that the nation could not hope to make the world safe for democracy without establishing racial equality in the United States. Black newspaper editors and the National Association for the Advancement of Colored People (NAACP) in particular urged President Wilson to end segregation, discrimination, and disfranchisement and to protect African Americans from lynch mobs.

Black protest against racial injustices generated suspicion that German agents were exploiting racial discontent and conducting subversive activities among African Americans. Uncertain about black loyalty, the Wilson administration spied on African Americans and harassed outspoken critics of

Jim Crow. However, the federal government also began to address some of the grievances of African Americans. In 1918, in response to reports about growing racial unrest, Wilson publicly condemned lynching and appointed several black men and women as racial advisors to various government agencies. But perhaps more importantly, in June of that year the federal government invited black newspaper editors and other race leaders to Washington to discuss their concerns. Many African Americans considered the highly publicized conference a significant sign of racial progress. For the first time, the Wilson administration appeared to acknowledge the importance of African Americans in sustaining the nation's war effort. In the aftermath of the conference, W. E. B. Du Bois urged African Americans to "forget our special grievances and close our ranks."[1]

Indeed, most African Americans, seemed to have closed ranks, despite the persistence of Jim Crow and the surge in racial violence—thirty-nine African Americans had died during the East St. Louis race riot and the number of lynchings rose from thirty-eight in 1917 to sixty-three in 1918. However, it is impossible to assess why African Americans supported the war. They may have done so in hopes of winning civil rights, to deflect charges of disloyalty, or to avoid prison sentences for seditious and subversive activities. Yet others may have been coerced by whites. For example, in Shreveport, Louisiana, whites forced black residents to buy United War Savings Stamps, and in Vicksburg, Mississippi, whites, with the help of local police, tarred and feathered a black dentist who refused to buy $1,000 worth of stamps. However, white coercion was the exception, rather than the rule. Many African Americans likely supported the war for very personal reasons. They had relatives and friends who served in the Army and closed ranks to hasten America's victory and help bring the black soldiers home quickly.

Regardless of their motives, African Americans donated money, time, and other resources to support the war effort. They purchased more than $250 million worth of bonds and stamps during the five National Liberty Loan campaigns and numerous United War Savings Stamps drives. Moreover, they contributed money to the Young Men's Christian Association, the Young Women's Christian Association, the Red Cross, and other public welfare organizations and charities that provided relief for the troops. In addition, black civilians organized recreation and entertainment programs for the soldiers and helped to raise funds to aid the black men in uniform and their dependent families. Black residents of Philadelphia launched the Crispus Attucks Circle, named after an African American who was the first man to die during the Revolutionary War; black Bostonians initiated the Soldiers Comfort Unit; and African Americans in Washington, D.C., established the

National Colored Soldiers' Comfort Committee. In New York, African Americans, in collaboration with concerned whites, founded the Circle for Negro War Relief, which eventually set up local branches in communities around the country. These organizations as well as many other local groups in conjunction with black churches, fraternal organizations, women's clubs, and schools, collected money to buy Victrolas, records, magazines, books, Christmas trees, cigarettes, chewing gum, and other items for the men in the camps. In addition, black civilians set up canteens for soldiers in transit and social clubs for those on leave. They brought the men in the camps homemade meals, hosted dinners and dances, wrote letters, and visited those who were hospitalized.

Despite black civilian support of the war effort, many whites questioned the patriotism and loyalty of African Americans. Indeed, black morale had been severely tested since the start of the war. Throughout 1917, black enthusiasm for the war was dampened by military segregation, the racially biased implementation of the draft, the Army's decision to assign the majority

Photo 6.1 In many cities, African American civilians raised funds to organize social clubs for black soldiers in transit and on leave. Source: National Archives. ARC identifier 533535/ Local Identifier 165-WW-127(49)

of black soldiers to labor units, the forced retirement of Charles Young, the president's failure to condemn lynchings or the atrocities committed during the East St. Louis race riot, and the treatment of black men in American training camps as well as those charged with the Houston Mutiny. Concerns about the detrimental impact of poor racial conditions on the war effort sparked fears among whites that African Americans would be especially susceptible to German propaganda.

Rumors of subversive German activities in the black community spread quickly during the first months of the war, particularly in the South. White Southerners, worried about losing their black workforce, claimed that German undercover agents attempted to weaken Southern agriculture by encouraging African Americans to migrate to Mexico or the North. Yet others asserted that German spies were not only urging black men to resist the draft, but secretly organizing disgruntled African Americans to revolt. One of the most notorious and widely circulated rumors about a German-inspired black insurrection was the so-called Plan of San Diego, which allegedly called on African Americans to collaborate with Mexicans and seize Texas to establish an independent black republic. Many whites also insisted that German agents tried to instill racial unrest by encouraging black uppity behavior. African American demands for higher wages, enhanced job opportunities, and equal rights, they argued, were evidence of systematic German propaganda endeavors among the black population.

The federal government, which viewed any challenges to patriotism and loyalty as a threat to home-front unity and national security, investigated the charges. Agents of the Justice Department's Bureau of Investigation (which became the Federal Bureau of Investigation in 1935), the Military Intelligence Branch (which became the Military Intelligence Division on August 26, 1918), the Post Office Department, and the State Department, in collaboration with local and state officials as well as the volunteer-based American Protective League, closely monitored the black community. The Military Intelligence Branch (MIB) kept an eye on African Americans with the help of Major Walter H. Loving, a black intelligence agent. Loving was a retired regimental bandmaster who, upon the suggestion of the governor general of the Philippines, William Howard Taft, had helped to establish the Philippine Constabulary Band in 1902. When Taft became president four years later, he invited Loving and the band to escort him from the White House to the Capitol for his inauguration—an honor traditionally reserved for the U.S. Marine Band. In 1916, poor health forced Loving to retire from the military; however, his retirement was short-lived. In September of 1917, the MIB requested his services and assigned him to probe black subversive activities and to develop counterpropaganda to lift the morale of African Americans.

Throughout the war, Loving investigated the loyalty of black civilians and soldiers, often with the help of black informants, including Hallie E. Queen, a Howard University graduate who taught at Washington's prestigious Dunbar High School, as well as Tuskegee's principal, Robert Russa Moton. Loving, focusing much of his attention on those who advocated racial reform, supplied the MIB with reports about suspicious activities in the black community and German propaganda efforts among African Americans. But while Loving spied on black activists, he was also sympathetic to their cause. Having suffered the indignities of racism himself, Loving impressed upon his superiors that not German agents but appalling racial conditions were responsible for undermining black morale. At times, he even tried to shield African Americans who had aroused government suspicion from legal repercussions. He informed several race leaders that they were the subject of an MIB investigation and urged them to adopt a moderate tone in order to avoid prosecution.

Although government agents found no evidence that alleged enemy activities aimed at African Americans succeeded in provoking black disloyalty, they continued to be troubled by those who challenged the racial status quo. In an effort to silence civil rights advocates, they harassed African Americans who demanded an end to Jim Crow. Armed with the 1917 Espionage Act and the 1918 Sedition Act, which authorized the federal government to impose prison sentences of up to twenty years as well as stiff fines on individuals who criticized Wilson's administration or the armed forces, agents sought to stifle dissent and intimidate those who advocated racial equality.

Government agents paid special attention to the black press, particularly editors who opposed the war or those who questioned Jim Crow. The most notorious cases involved G. W. Bouldin of the *San Antonio Inquirer* and A. Philip Randolph and Chandler Owen, editors of the socialist *Messenger*. Bouldin was sentenced to a two-year prison term for printing an article that praised the Houston mutineers, while government agents ransacked the offices of the *Messenger* and briefly jailed Randolph and Owen. In addition, agents harassed many black editors and kept secret surveillance files on those who linked black support of the war to demands for racial reform. Among the most famous were *Crisis* editor Du Bois, Robert S. Abbott of the *Chicago Defender*, William Monroe Trotter of the *Boston Guardian*, and antilynching advocate Ida B. Wells-Barnett. Using the threat of censorship, government agents reminded black editors that the Espionage and Sedition Acts authorized the postmaster general to exclude from the mails any publications that were critical of the government. Since both laws placed unprecedented limits on freedom of speech, black editors had to tread lightly if they wanted to keep their papers in circulation. Aware that charges of treason or sedition would result in a loss of their mailing privileges, but equally concerned about advancing civil rights, they performed a delicate balancing act. On the one hand, they assured the government of the unquestionable loyalty of the black population and encouraged their readers to support the nation's war effort. On the other, they continued to demand racial equality and pointed out that lynching, discrimination, and segregation played into the hands of the German enemy and were inconsistent with the nation's goal to make the world safe for democracy.

A case in point was the controversy that erupted in the spring of 1918, when the black press published General Charles C. Ballou's infamous Bulletin No. 35. Ballou, who had been in charge of the Des Moines officers training camp until it closed in the fall of 1917, had subsequently assumed command of the all-black Ninety-Second combat division. Stationed at Camp Funston, Kansas, the black soldiers serving under Ballou became the center of black media attention when a black sergeant purchased a movie theater ticket in nearby Manhattan and the white manager assigned him to a segregated seating area. The soldier reported the incident to Ballou, who ordered an investigation, which revealed that the theater owner had violated state laws that prohibited segregation. Ballou requested the proprietor's prosecution and eventually the man was convicted and sentenced to pay a $10 fine. However, Ballou's effort to prosecute the white theater owner did not earn him the praise of African Americans. Instead, his handling of the case generated widespread outrage among black soldiers and civilians when the black press published a bulletin that Ballou had released in response to the incident. In Bulletin No. 35, the general admonished black soldiers to avoid racial friction and "to refrain from going where their presence will be resented."[2] The bulletin did not come as a surprise for the men who had served under Ballou at Des Moines, where he had similarly reprimanded black officer candidates. However, this time, the black press got a hold of Ballou's order. Black editors vehemently condemned the bulletin as an insult to all members of the race, who, they insisted, had been loyal and patriotic supporters of the war.

Afraid of racial unrest, Emmett J. Scott, special racial advisor in the War Department, asked Ballou to provide him with a public statement that would not only clarify the general's position but also appease African Americans and counter declining black morale. Unfortunately, Ballou's open letter made matters worse. The general was surprised by the negative black reaction to Bulletin No. 35 and insisted that he had worked tirelessly to promote ra-cial harmony. He cautioned African Americans that the War Department viewed the training of black combat soldiers merely as an experiment, which would last only as long as the black troops did not cause any disorder. Ballou's assessment, while unpopular among African Americans, was accurate. In late 1917, when Newton D. Baker had created the two black combat divisions, he had reminded black troops that military service was "an opportunity to serve and not an occasion for creating discord or trouble."[3]

Initially, many race leaders had adopted a conciliatory tone and applauded Baker's decision to train black men in arms, despite segregation. However, by the time Ballou issued his controversial order, the mood of the African American community had changed. In the spring of 1918, black soldiers were sacrificing their lives in the trenches of France, and news coverage of the heroic combat performance of Henry Johnson and Needham Roberts filled the front pages of black newspapers. African Americans, who took great pride in their soldiers, were outraged when they learned of Ballou's or-der. Already incensed by reports about poor conditions in the training camps as well as overseas, African Americans grew increasingly restless. Demands for equal rights grew louder and black home-front morale reached a nadir. Indeed, Scott feared the situation was "little short of dangerous."[4]

In response to the mounting discontent among African American civil-ians, which had the potential of triggering racial unrest and disrupting de-fense industry production, the federal government made a deliberate effort to reach out to the black community. This was a significant departure from the first year of the war, when the Wilson administration had done little to in-corporate African Americans into the civilian war effort. Throughout 1917, no government agency—with the exception of the War Department, where Scott represented black interests—had any special racial advisors or divisions specifically in charge of mobilizing African Americans. However, this changed in the aftermath of the public outcry generated by Ballou's order.

The Department of Labor became the first government agency that made a special effort to rally African Americans behind the nation's war effort. It created a Division of Negro Economics to address the concerns of black workers, many of whom had entered war industries as a result of the Great Migration. The Division was the brainchild of Secretary of Labor William B. Wilson, a self-proclaimed advocate of the working class, and Assistant Sec-retary of Labor Louis F. Post, a racial liberal who had cofounded the National Negro Conference, a forerunner of the NAACP. Concerned about securing the necessary manpower for wartime production, Wilson and Post launched two separate investigations of the impact of the Great Migration. They recruited two black investigators, Charles E. Hall and William Jennifer, to conduct the first study. After touring the South in the summer of 1916, Hall and Jennifer concluded that the mass exodus of African Americans neither harmed Southern agricultural production nor threatened to disrupt Northern industries. However, since the number of those leaving the South appeared to increase dramatically, they recommended an in-depth study of the causes and effects of the migration. In the following year, Post asked Dr. James H. Dillard, the white manager of the Jeanes-Slater Funds for Negro Education, to supervise another investigation of the migration.

While Dillard was compiling the data for his report titled *Negro Migration in 1916–17*, Department of Labor officials met with race leaders, including Scott as well as NAACP and National Urban League representatives. The black representatives urged the Secretary of Labor to appoint George E. Haynes to head the Division of Negro Economics. Haynes, a professor of sociology and economics at Nashville's Fisk University, was preeminently qualified for the job. He had earned his MA at Yale in 1904 and eight years later became the first African American to receive a PhD from Columbia University. He was a cofounder of the National Urban League and its first executive secretary and had a long history of working to expand employment opportunities for African Americans. On May 1, 1918, Haynes assumed his post and became director of the Division of Negro Economics in the Department of Labor.

Throughout the war, Haynes focused on helping African Americans find jobs and maintaining their morale to reduce turnover rates, which had the potential of undermining defense production. For this purpose, Haynes established state branches, which, with the help of interracial local volunteer advisory committees, set up employment bureaus for black workers. While the government was mainly concerned about ensuring efficient wartime production, Haynes was interested in improving the conditions of black workers by combating racial discrimination. Thus, his division monitored racism in the work place, investigated wage disparities, and collaborated with business and community leaders to provide adequate housing for black workers. Moreover, Haynes launched educational efforts to improve race relations. He recruited speakers who traveled the country to foster racial harmony, and the Division distributed pamphlets and posters that stressed the importance of black workers for the war effort. In the South, the Division intervened when whites used compulsory work laws to prevent African Americans from leaving the region. These so-called work or fight laws stipulated that all able-bodied men had to be employed in war-related jobs; otherwise they could face conscription into the military or jail terms. White planters, claiming that agricultural production was crucial to the war effort, often invoked the "work or fight" laws to keep African Americans bound to the land. Division representatives countered attempts at forced labor and organized job fairs, which sought to provide white Southerners with a sufficient number of workers and workers with competitive wages. In the North, the Division urged white employers and workers to treat African Americans fairly, insisting that racism in the workplace was unpatriotic because it lowered the morale of black laborers and subsequently their productivity. The detrimental impact of racism on wartime production was evident throughout the country. For example, in Pittsburgh black defense workers walked off the job when the manager of an engine company failed to remove an offensive Jim Crow sign from the factory's bathroom.

Although government officials proclaimed that incidents like these posed a threat to national security, the Wilson administration failed to grant Haynes any real power. He had no legal means to compel industries to treat black workers fairly, but had to rely on voluntary cooperation. Aware of the limits of his position, Haynes tried to bully employers who discriminated against Afri-

Photo 6.2 *Northern industries, facing labor shortages caused by the war, used this kind of propaganda to attract black workers. Source: Warshaw Collection of Business Americana, Archives Center, National Museum of American History, Behring Center, Smithsonian Institution, Washington, D.C.*

can Americans by threatening them with the withdrawal of government contracts. However, it is unclear if his strategy helped to improve the conditions
of African American workers. Indeed, many race leaders who had applauded
Haynes's appointment doubted his effectiveness. Nonetheless, they acknowledged that his appointment reflected a significant change in the government's
attitude toward African Americans during the second year of the war.

Indeed, throughout 1918, the Wilson administration took a growing interest in mobilizing African American civilians for the nation's war effort.
Particularly the MIB and the Committee on Public Information (CPI)
launched patriotic propaganda campaigns aimed at lifting the morale of African Americans. Loving, the MIB's black intelligence agent, recruited
Booker T. Washington's nephew Roscoe Conkling Simmons, a well-known
orator, to go on a nationwide tour speaking on the topic: "My Country and
My Flag." Simmons, a former journalist who had been instrumental in increasing the *Defender*'s circulation throughout the South, had a reputation
for captivating his audiences, despite the fact that he tended to speak for
several hours. Armed with outlines provided by Loving, Simmons addressed
thousands of blacks and whites both in the North and in the South. Meanwhile, the CPI also tried to fan the flames of race loyalty. The agency specifically designed pamphlets for African Americans, including "To Make the
World Free," as well as press releases, traveling exhibits, posters, and films,
such as the morale booster *Colored Man No Slacker*. But perhaps the most
famous government produced propaganda films targeting African American
audiences were *Our Colored Fighters* and *The Training of Colored Troops*. Both
films depicted the enlistment of African American troops and their training
in the camps, and *Our Colored Fighters* even showed their combat experience
overseas. Although *The Training of Colored Troops* reflected some of the
prevalent racist stereotypes, such as the portrayal of dancing and watermelon-
eating black soldiers, it also treated African Americans with an unprecedented degree of dignity, showing the men marching competently in formation and drilling with weapons. In addition to distributing propaganda
material, the CPI dispatched "Four Minute Men" speakers, who gave pep
talks at black schools, churches, clubs, and fraternal lodges. Finally, the CPI,
at the suggestion of Scott, organized the Committee of One Hundred, which
consisted of famous black educators, politicians, religious leaders, newspaper
editors, and civil rights activists who staged public rallies to drum up support
for the war effort among African Americans.

Although government-sponsored propaganda campaigns among African
Americans reached new heights in the spring of 1918, black morale remained
low in the wake of Ballou's bulletin. Concerned about the deterioration of

race relations, Joel E. Spingarn, the NAACP's white chairman who had been an early advocate of the black officers training camp, hatched several ambitious plans. In May of 1918, the MIB appointed Spingarn to its counterespionage division and put him in charge of black subversion. His appointment seems peculiar, since he was affiliated with a black protest organization that was under government scrutiny for subversive activities. However, Spingarn's involvement in the NAACP, which provided him with connections in the black community, was precisely what made him attractive to the MIB. Spingarn used his position not only to boost black morale and refute allegations of black disloyalty, but also to advance racial reform. Like Loving had done before him, he appealed to race leaders to tone down their criticism of the Wilson administration. Yet at the same time, he tried to convince the government that Jim Crow and not German subversive activities among African Americans were responsible for growing black discontent.

Addressing black demands for racial justice, Spingarn urged President Wilson to speak out against lynchings and asked General Pershing to rebut rumors that black troops were used as cannon fodder in France. Wilson ignored Spingarn's request, but Pershing responded with a detailed statement, countering allegations that the Army had used African Americans as shock troops and assigned them only to the most dangerous military missions in order to save the lives of white soldiers. Finally, Spingarn proposed to Scott a joint conference of government officials and race leaders, particularly black newspaper editors. The conference, he hoped, would lift black morale and allow participants to "let off steam."[5] Scott presented Spingarn's proposal to George Creel, the CPI's chairman, who agreed to pay for the traveling costs of conference participants. Creel, concerned about German subversive activities among African Americans, then approached President Wilson and urged him to address the group. A few inspirational words from the president, Creel believed, would serve as an antidote to black discontent. Not surprisingly, Wilson declined. Ever since his meetings with *Boston Guardian* editor William Monroe Trotter, the president's relationship with African Americans had been strained. Wary of potentially explosive encounters with race leaders, Wilson did what he had done since his first term in office: avoid racially charged confrontations. Despite the president's refusal to meet with race leaders, Creel went ahead and made plans for the conference.

The CPI invited forty-seven prominent black men, the vast majority of them editors of black newspapers, to attend the three-day government-sponsored conference in the nation's capital. Forty-four of them showed up when the meeting convened at the Department of the Interior building between June 19 and 21, 1918. The roster of participants read like a veritable who's who of race leaders. Among those attending were Scott; Haynes; Tuskegee principal Moton; the assistant superintendent of Washington's public schools, Roscoe Conkling Bruce; former governor of Louisiana P. B. S. Pinchback; the president of the NAACP's Washington branch, Archibald H. Grimké; District of Columbia Municipal Court judge Robert H. Terrell; representatives of the Baptist and Methodist churches; as well as the publishers and editors of the most influential black newspapers, including Du Bois of the *Crisis*, Robert S. Abbott of the *Chicago Defender*, Calvin Chase of the *Washington Bee*, Robert L. Vann of the *Pittsburgh Courier*, John H. Murphy of the *Baltimore Afro-American*, Ralph W. Tyler of the *Cleveland Advocate*, and Henry Allen Boyd of the *Nashville Globe*. Conspicuously absent was Trotter, who had been invited but had decided not to attend. Recalling earlier encounters with the president, Trotter had lost all faith in the Wilson administration and suspected that the conference was merely the government's attempt to silence black critics. In addition to notable race leaders, several high-ranking American government and French military officials attended the conference, including its sponsor, CPI chairman Creel; Secretary of War Newton D. Baker; Assistant Secretary of the Navy Franklin D. Roosevelt; the chairman of the U.S. Shipping Board, Edward N. Hurley; the military attaché of the French embassy; and two representatives of the French High Commission, as well as Spingarn.

Although Spingarn had initiated the conference, it was Scott who organized the meeting and who presided at all of the sessions. Scott compiled the list of participants, invited the men, and assured them that the gathering would serve as a forum to discuss the attitude of African Americans toward the war. However, when the participants arrived in Washington, Scott reminded them that their purpose was to discuss the mobilization of the black community and not race problems. He instructed attendants that "Our first duty is to fight, and to continue to fight until this war is won. Then we can adjust the problems that remain in the life of the colored men."[6] Participants listened to the speeches of various American government officials, who praised the performance of black soldiers and warned about the dangers of venereal diseases. In addition, French military representatives highlighted the contributions of African colonial troops. Nonetheless, black attendants also aired their grievances, insisting that lynchings and not German propaganda were responsible for the growing discontent among African Americans.

At the end of the conference the black participants adopted a series of resolutions that reflected the approach the black press had taken since the start of the war. The resolutions, drafted by Du Bois, assured the administration of the unwavering loyalty and patriotism of African Americans. At the

Photo 6.3 *In June 1918, high-ranking government officials met with race leaders to discuss ways of reversing declining black morale. This was the first time the federal government sought the advice of African Americans on any public issue. In the front row are Emmett J. Scott (third from left), Robert R. Moton (fifth from left), W. E. B. Du Bois (fourth from right), and Joel Spingarn (third from right). In the second row is Robert S. Abbott (fifth from right). Source: Special Collections and Archives, W. E. B. Du Bois Library, University of Massachusetts, Amherst*

same time, conferees cautioned the government "that justifiable grievances of the colored people are producing . . . an amount of unrest and bitterness which even the best efforts of their leaders may not be able always to guide."[7] To defuse the potentially explosive situation, the black representatives urged the federal government to address some of the most pressing complaints of African Americans. They asked the president to issue a statement condemning lynchings and called on Congress to pass a federal antilynching law. Furthermore, they demanded an end to discrimination in the civil service, in the Navy, and in the recruitment of Red Cross nurses. Finally, they insisted that the government, which controlled the railroads as a result of the wartime mobilization, use its war powers to end segregation on trains. Moreover, conference participants drafted a "Bill of Particulars" that listed fourteen specific demands, emulating Wilson's Fourteen Points. In addition to those already stated in the conference resolutions, the "Bill of Particulars" called for the training of additional black officers, the recruitment of black physicians for military service, the proportionate assignment of black and white soldiers to labor battalions, the systematic dissemination of news about the conditions of blacks troops, and clemency for the Houston mutineers. Another demand was the reinstatement of Colonel Charles Young, who was heading for the nation's capital at the time of the conference. In early June, Young had embarked on his 497-mile horseback trip from his home in Ohio to demonstrate that he was physically fit for active duty. As Young arrived in Washington and the conference came to a close, African Americans were cautiously optimistic. For the first time, the Wilson administration had consulted with race leaders and appeared to pay attention to black grievances. The government, some hoped, might address at least some of the concerns of African Americans.

While the majority of black newspapers praised the conference, claiming that it was as an important step toward racial progress, others doubted the sincerity of the government. The administration, they argued, was not interested in improving racial conditions, but merely sought to quell black protest. Among the most vocal critics of the conference was *Boston Guardian* editor Trotter, who convened a National Liberty Congress in Washington, D.C., only three days after the government sponsored conference adjourned. Trotter had made plans for his congress long before the Wilson administration had invited race leaders to the nation's capital. When Spingarn learned of the plans, he asked MIB intelligence officers to convince Trotter to postpone the congress, fearing that it would distract from the conference he had helped to organize. But Trotter was adamant and not about to defer to a white man, much less a Jew.

Trotter's group, which consisted of 115 black representatives from around the country, gathered in Washington between June 24 and 29. Delegates to the National Liberty Congress represented the radical element of the black population, and intelligence agents, including Loving, closely monitored the proceedings. Unlike the race leaders who had attended the black editors' conference a few days earlier, they were less willing to cooperate with a government that continued to condone Jim Crow and failed to condemn lynchings and race riots. No members of the Wilson administration attended the meeting, and only two whites—congressmen Martin B. Madden of Chicago and Leonidas C. Dyer of St. Louis, both representing large black constituencies—addressed the group. The resolutions of the National Liberty Congress lacked unconditional assurances of black loyalty and patriotism, but mirrored many of the demands of the black editors' conference. In addition, Trotter's group petitioned the administration to prohibit segregation and discrimination in federal offices, to provide equal pay to federal employees, to integrate the armed forces, and to enforce the Thirteenth, Fourteenth, and Fifteenth amendments.

While the tone of the government-sponsored editors' conference had been "sober and statesmanlike," congress delegates attacked Wilson and lashed out against Scott and Spingarn, charging them with kowtowing to the government.[8] Du Bois in particular attracted Trotter's wrath when he published his "Close Ranks" editorial in the month following the conference. In the editorial, Du Bois, who had always opposed accommodation, called on African Americans to support the war and forgo the struggle for equal rights for the duration of the war. Since the editorial appeared shortly after the black editors' conference, Trotter concluded that Du Bois had sold out to the Wilson administration and betrayed his race. Other African Americans were equally disturbed by Du Bois's uncharacteristic endorsement of Booker T. Washington's racial advancement strategy, and most of the black newspapers attacked the *Crisis* editor.

Criticism of Du Bois further escalated, when the black press discovered that he had applied for an Army commission in the same week his "Close Ranks" editorial appeared in the *Crisis*. Du Bois's decision to join the Army was largely the product of Spingarn's lobbying efforts. In early June, Spingarn had convinced Du Bois to apply for a commission as an intelligence officer to work with him in the MIB's "Negro Subversion" unit. Spingarn believed that Du Bois could play a crucial role in shaping black public opinion as well as changing the government's policy toward African Americans. Indeed, Du Bois had taken a military entrance exam at Washington's Army Medical School just prior to the editors' conference; however, he had failed the physical fitness test, largely due to the removal of one his kidneys in the previous year. Spingarn, who was eager to collaborate with Du Bois, successfully intervened, and the Army decided to consider his application. On June 24, only three days after the closing of the editors' conference, Du Bois submitted his application for a captaincy in the U.S. Army

When the news of Du Bois's military aspirations surfaced, African Americans were shocked. Many suspected that the conciliatory and accommodationist tone of his "Close Ranks" editorial was evidence of a corrupt bargain. Du Bois, they charged, was a Benedict Arnold who had betrayed the race and sold his integrity for a captaincy in the Army. Others expressed disappointment in the man they had come to identify with the struggle for equal rights. What made matters worse was that Du Bois wanted to retain general oversight of the *Crisis*. In early July, in the midst of the protest generated by his "Close Ranks" editorial, Du Bois informed the NAACP Board of Directors that he was interested in accepting a captaincy. However, he also wanted to continue to serve as editor of the *Crisis* and asked the NAACP to supplement his captain's pay, which was $1,000 less than his current annual salary. When the board of directors rejected Du Bois's proposal, insisting that the *Crisis* needed a full-time editor, Spingarn threatened to resign from the organization he had helped to create. As Du Bois was weighing his options, he continued to face severe criticism from the black press, which not only attacked him for his endorsement of accommodation but now also ridiculed him because he had asked the NAACP to supplement his income. By the end of July, the government made the decision for Du Bois, when it rejected his application for an Army commission. However by then the damage to Du Bois's reputation was done.

While the controversy sparked by Du Bois's "Close Ranks" editorial and his application for an Army commission overshadowed much of the summer of 1918, African Americans had some reason to rejoice. On July 26, President Wilson, in a widely circulated statement, publicly condemned lynching as a disgrace to the nation. Reiterating the concerns of the editors' conference, Wilson proclaimed that mob violence was contrary to America's war aims and urged all Americans to eradicate the lawless practice, which cost the lives of sixty-three African Americans in 1918. It is not clear to what degree black protest influenced Wilson's decision to speak out against lynching, but the president was certainly aware of the rumors of German subversive activities among African Americans. Indeed, Secretary of War Baker and CPI chairman Creel repeatedly warned Wilson about the dangers of ignoring black discontent, which had the potential of erupting into racial unrest, undermining the war effort, and threatening national security. Wilson also knew that Congress was considering several antilynching bills. In the spring of 1918, two Republicans, Leonidas C. Dyer of Missouri and Merrill Moores of Indiana, had introduced antilynching legislation, and in early June Spingarn had presented a bill to the House Judiciary Committee. Spingarn, in particular, argued that a federal antilynching law was necessary to counter German subversive activities among African Americans. However, none of the bills passed, largely due to Southern opposition as well as Wilson's failure to support them. Southern Congressmen objected to federal antilynching legislation, arguing that it was an infringement of state rights, while Wilson believed that only time, not legislation, could overcome Jim Crow.

Nonetheless, the federal government took several promising steps to address black grievances in the months following the black editors' conference. In July, the War Department announced its plan to establish Student Army Training Corps at all colleges. By the fall, young black men prepared for careers in the military at ten black universities, including Howard, Atlanta, Morehouse, Fisk, Hampton, and Tuskegee. In August, shortly after publicly condemning lynchings, President Wilson commuted the death sentences of ten of the Houston mutineers to prison terms. The decision, he explained, was a sign of his respect for the loyalty and patriotism African Americans had displayed since the start of the war. Moreover, the administration appointed three African Americans to serve on the Committee on Public Information (CPI), the Council of National Defense (CND), and the Food Administration.

In September, in direct response to the demands of the black editors' conference, the CPI accredited Ralph W. Tyler as its only black war correspondent. Tyler, a native of Columbus, Ohio, had been auditor of the Navy between 1907 and 1913, an organizer of Booker T. Washington's National Negro Business League, and national secretary of the Washington-based Colored Soldier's Comfort Committee. Moreover, he was one of only a few black journalists employed by a white-owned newspaper. In addition to his work for the *Columbus Dispatch*, Tyler was a frequent contributor to various black newspapers, including the *Chicago Defender* and the *New York Age*. Tyler, whose three sons served at the front, arrived in France in late September and immediately started to send reports about the black troops to the CPI, which then forwarded them to Scott, who edited and distributed them to the black press. Since government censors eliminated all controversial information about the treatment of black troops, Tyler could do little else than provide glowing accounts of the gallant and heroic performance of African American soldiers in France. Despite Tyler's one-sided reports, which made no references to segregation and discrimination, black newspaper editors praised his appointment as an important government concession to African Americans.

The Wilson administration also started to pay greater attention to black women. In the summer of 1918, the Council of National Defense (CND)— the agency in charge of coordinating the mobilization of the nation's resources and industries—appointed Alice Dunbar-Nelson to organize black women's volunteer efforts in the South. Dunbar-Nelson, the widow of famous black poet Paul Laurence Dunbar, was an accomplished author and a well-known activist in the black women's club and women's suffrage movements. Like Du Bois, she was an adamant opponent of Jim Crow, but like the *Crisis* editor, she placed patriotic duty ahead of the struggle for racial justice. Indeed, in her 1918 play, *Mine Eyes Have Seen the Glory*, Dunbar-Nelson promoted black support of the war, despite the persistence of segregation and discrimination. However, Dunbar-Nelson owed her appointment not to her

public display of patriotism, but to Scott, with whom she had a romantic liaison and who recommended her to the CND

As a field representative of the CND's Woman's Committee, Dunbar-
Nelson went on a six-week speaking tour throughout the South to drum up
support for the war among black women and to assess to what degree State
Councils of Defense incorporated them into their programs. Dunbar-Nelson
discovered that the Southern State Councils of Defense—with the exception
of Florida—largely ignored or even discouraged black women's volunteer efforts, despite the fact that the CND had instructed its state affiliates that the
mobilization of African Americans behind the nation's war effort was of
"vital importance."[9] Dunbar-Nelson tried to rectify the situation and urged
white councils to utilize black women's talents, skills, and resources. However, since Dunbar-Nelson only served in an advisory capacity, she had to
rely on voluntary cooperation, which meant that whites usually disregarded
her appeals. Nonetheless, Nelson-Dunbar's appointment signaled the Wilson
administration's unprecedented interest in black women's war work.

Although black women were frustrated with their exclusion from the
work of the Southern State Councils, it did not dampen their patriotism.
Instead of working through government agencies, they often launched their
own organizations, which sought to mobilize the resources of the black community. Black women sent clothing and other items to the men in the training camps as well as those serving overseas and provided the troops with
comfort kits filled with cigarettes, chocolate, chewing gum, magazines, and
Bibles. They volunteered for work in the black Hostess Houses in American
training camps, wrote letters to the men in uniform to boost their morale,
rolled bandages, organized knitting and sewing clubs, and hosted dances,
concerts, and dinners for soldiers on leave.

While many black women found an outlet for their patriotism in volunteer work, their morale was dampened by the Army's and the Red Cross's
failure to utilize them as nurses. Despite a severe shortage of nurses, military
and Red Cross officials insisted that the wartime emergency did not allow for
the additional construction of segregated housing quarters and other facilities
necessary to accommodate black women. It was not until the fall of 1918,
when the influenza pandemic killed 500,000 Americans, that the Army and
the Red Cross relented. In September of that year, the Red Cross accepted
2,000 black nurses, and two months later the Army Nurses Corps admitted
18 black women and assigned them to serve in various base hospitals and
camps, virtually all of them in the North. Following the armistice, an additional 16 black nurses arrived in France to assist sick and wounded black
soldiers during the demobilization period.

Photo 6.4 *Although the Red Cross excluded black nurses, African American women nonetheless volunteered their services. These women roll bandages at a surgical dressing unit in St. Paul, Minnesota. Source: Minnesota Historical Society*

Black women also played an important role in the nation's food supply. Not only were they in charge of the preparation and consumption of meals in their own households, but many of them worked as domestic servants or cooks for whites. Thus, most black women handled proportionately more food than white women. The Food Administration, under the leadership of Herbert Hoover, initially tried to use black newspapers to educate black women about the nation's wartime needs. Articles in the black press admonished their readers to eat and waste less; to save surplus food by canning, drying, pickling, and preserving; and to eliminate scarce items from their diet. Furthermore, they reminded black women to prepare wheatless meals on Mondays and Wednesdays, for both their own families as well as those of their white employers. The Food Administration's Negro Press Section, headed by Arthur U. Craig, a black teacher at Washington's Dunbar High School and an occasional MIB informant, did apparently little else than disseminate the agency's press releases. However, by the fall of 1918, severe food shortages and the futility of Craig's approach—many black women, particularly in the South, lacked the reading skills necessary to benefit from the government's press releases—led the Food Administration to establish a Negro Activities division. In September, the agency appointed Ernest T. Atwell, a Tuskegee business professor, to impress upon black women the importance of increased production, conservation, and substitution of scarce food, particularly wheat, sugar, and pork. While Atwell continued to use the black press, he also helped to create a system of black state directors who gave lectures, screened films, and organized public cooking demonstrations as well as food and canning clubs. Many black women participated in the food conservation drives, planted victory gardens, and exchanged recipes for meals that used food substitutes.

It is unclear to what degree black home-front support of the war was the direct result of the work of racial advisors such as Haynes, Tyler, Dunbar-Nelson, and Atwell, especially since none of them exercised any real power. Most of the time, government officials listened to their complaints, but did nothing to address racial grievances. Nonetheless, their appointments signaled the administration's recognition that black morale was crucial to the war effort. Although the government did not meet all of the wartime demands of race leaders, the administration's concern about the negative impact of racial unrest on home-front unity and national security, did generate some concrete results. These included the president's public condemnation of lynching, his decision to grant clemency to ten of the Houston mutineers, the Red Cross's and Army's recruitment of black nurses, the War Department's creation of the Student Army Training Corps at black colleges, and the reinstatement of Charles Young in late 1918. Though these may have been only small victories, they raised the hopes and expectations of many African Americans for democratic rights after the war.

~

Epilogue

Returning to Racism

When World War I ended, many African Americans expected civil rights as a just reward for their military service and their home-front support of the war. After all, black soldiers had fought "to make the world safe for democracy" and black civilians had done their share to secure America's victory abroad. John R. Williams, who had served in France, articulated what many black soldiers must have thought. Every man, he explained, who had "fought on the side of the Allies supported a noble cause and deserves at least to enjoy that for which he dedicated his life—DEMOCRACY."[1] Many black civilians, who had worked in defense industries, donated money, volunteered time, and made countless other sacrifices for the war, shared these sentiments. Black physician W. Harry Barnes expressed his frustration in an open letter to the *Philadelphia Tribune*: "I have bought Liberty Bond and War Savings Stamps. I have given my home over to the Red Cross for campaigns. I have laid aside my wife, aged parents and little children. What more can I do?"[2]

Although the Wilson administration had never promised African Americans civil rights in exchange for support of the war, it contributed to the heightened expectations for racial equality. The draft itself, which had conscripted American men regardless of race, NAACP leaders claimed, was "prima facie evidence of citizenship."[3] Military officials had indirectly affirmed that claim, when they issued camp readers for the instruction of soldiers that emphasized the link between military service and citizenship. African American expectations for civil rights had received another boost when the War Department, despite its insistence on segregation, had agreed

Photo E.1 *Joyous black soldiers coming home from France, determined to return fighting. Source: National Archives. NWDNS-165-WW-127 (12)*

to train black officers and combat soldiers. Secretary of War Newton D. Baker had further raised black hopes when he assured African Americans that once they supported the war they would be "entitled to the gratitude of the country."[4] In addition, high-ranking Army officials, including General John J. Pershing, had praised the performance of black troops, using language that suggested that racial changes were forthcoming. Likewise, the government's propaganda machinery had praised the performance of black soldiers and had acknowledged the contributions of black industrial workers, calling them the second line of defense. And there were other promising signs that seemed to suggest that the administration not only acknowledged the importance of African Americans for the nation's war effort, but was also willing to address some of their grievances. These included the government sponsored conference with race leaders, President Wilson's condemnation of lynching, his decision to grant clemency to ten of the Houston mutineers, and his appointment of black racial advisors to several highly visible posts in the federal government, as well as the Army's admission of black nurses, the launching of the Student Army Training Corps at black colleges, and the reinstatement of Colonel Charles Young. Even the white public appeared to be genuinely appreciative of the wartime support of African Americans. On February 17, 1919, tens of thousands of Americans, both black and white, had given a warm welcome to the 2,900 men of the 369th Infantry Regiment, the old New York Fifteenth National Guard. Led by Jim Reese Europe's marching band, the regiment had paraded down New York's Fifth Avenue savoring the applause of whites and blacks. Other cities, including Buffalo, Chicago, and St. Louis, staged equally elaborate parades. Not surprisingly, many African Americans were hopeful that the end of the war would ring in a new era of racial equality.

The Wilson administration was aware that African American aspirations had changed as a result of the war. Military officials warned that the black man "returning from France will not be the same sort of negro he was before donning the uniform" and urged the government to prepare for the reintegration of black soldiers into civilian society.[5] Military leaders, they suggested, should collaborate with state governors and black clergymen to dampen black expectations, which were sure to clash with racial realities and lead to bloodshed. The Army took the lead. When military commanders discharged the black soldiers they handed them the pamphlet, "A Greeting to our Colored Soldiers," which counseled the men to be patient and to have faith in their country. "Then—not all at once, perhaps but slowly and surely—a better day will dawn for you and your children."[6] Some Southern whites, sharing the Army's concern about potential unrest resulting from the heightened expectations of returning black soldiers, took steps to foster racial harmony. In early 1919, they launched the Commission on Interracial Cooperation, which provided African Americans and liberal white Southerners with a platform to discuss race relations. In many Southern communities, black and white commission members, though they gathered in separate locations, exchanged ideas about improving racial conditions. Although the commission did not challenge Jim Crow, but merely sought to make separate-but-equal truly equal, it initiated an interracial dialogue, which led some white Southerners to explore the ramifications of segregation and discrimination. However, most white Southerners had no interest in addressing black grievances. According to them, African Americans should expect nothing in return for their wartime services. "This is strictly a white man's country," Mississippi Governor Theodore Bilbo proclaimed, "and any dream on the part of the Negro Race to share social and political equality will be shattered in the end."[7]

Indeed, black hopes for racial reform were quickly dashed in the months following the war. After the victory celebrations ended African Americans once again faced racial violence and an impenetrable color line. The Ku

Photo E.2 *Thousands of black and white civilians cheered the 369th Infantry Regiment as it marched down Fifth Avenue in New York City on February 17, 1919. The Harlem Hellfighters spent 191 consecutive days in battle, more than any other American unit. Source: National Archives. ARC Identifier 533495/Local Identifier 165-WW-127 (11)*

Klux Klan, which had reemerged in 1915, attracted more than 100,000 members who pledged to uphold white supremacy. Both in the South and North, Klansmen and other white vigilantes terrorized African Americans to suppress any black claims for civil rights. From Maine to Georgia, white mobs, intent on maintaining Jim Crow, tarred, feathered, and lynched African Americans, including ten black veterans who were still wearing their Army uniforms. Nationwide, the number of lynchings increased from sixty-three in 1918 to seventy-seven in 1919. In addition, more than twenty-six race riots erupted in the first summer following the war. The racial unrest that swept across the country resulted in so much bloodshed that the NAACP's field secretary, James Weldon Johnson, called it the "Red Summer." The most serious of the riots occurred in Chicago, where white residents threw stones at seventeen-year-old Eugene Williams who, while swimming in Lake Michigan, had inadvertently drifted into the white section of the lake. When Williams drowned, fistfights between black and white bathers ensued. Given the tense racial climate caused by the continuing influx of black migrants as well as returning black and white soldiers who were competing for jobs and housing, the unrest quickly spread from the beach into the city. The violence sparked the worst race riot in U.S. history. When the rioting died down after thirteen days, 15 whites and 23 African Americans lay dead and more than 500 were injured. In addition, the racial unrest led to the destruction of over a million dollars worth of property and left more than 1,000 families homeless, most of them black. Riots in other cities followed a similar pattern.

African Americans, who had in the previous two years helped to "make the world safe for democracy," were dismayed by the escalation of racial violence in the aftermath of the war. They noted with bitter irony that black men had been safer in the trenches of France than after their return to the United States. Even Emmett J. Scott, who had adopted a conciliatory tone during the hostilities, admitted that he felt "personally a deep sense of disappointment, of poignant pain, that a great country in time of need should promise so much and afterwards perform so little."[8]

Photo E.3 *Among those celebrating the return of the 369th Infantry Regiment were these women and children, who extended a royal welcome to their husbands and fathers. Source: National Archives. ARC Identifier 533508/Local Identifier165-WW-127 (24)*

As heightened expectations for racial reform gave way to disillusionment, some African Americans turned inward and sought refuge in churches, fraternal lodges, and other black-run community organizations. Following the war, membership in the two largest black denominations—the Methodist and Baptist churches—continued to grow. But more importantly, a host of new religious groups appealed to black worshipers, particularly in the cities that had attracted large numbers of migrants during the war. Many of these so-called storefront churches catered to small local congregations, providing parishioners with religious fellowship as well as faith-based community institutions that shielded them from the racial humiliations they faced in mainstream American society. While many disillusioned African Americans found comfort and a safe haven in the black churches, others flocked to Marcus Garvey's Universal Negro Improvement Association (UNIA). Garvey expressed the desperation of African Americans who faced an increasingly hostile environment after the war. Rather than seeking to advance civil rights in the United States, he extolled the virtues of racial solidarity and self-help and advocated a return to Africa. Embittered by the broken promises of the war and the lack of racial progress, hundreds of thousands of African Americans joined the UNIA.

Although the postwar disillusionment generated bitterness and despair among many African Americans, it emboldened others and strengthened their resolve to fight racism, not only in the United States, but globally. Following the war, W. E. B. Du Bois helped organize several Pan-African Congresses, which sought to raise international awareness of the plight of people of color throughout the world. Moreover, Du Bois, who had advised African Americans to close ranks during the war, now called on them to continue their fight for racial democracy in the United States. Reflecting the militant mood of the "New Negro"— a term used to describe the proud, assertive, and racially conscious African American born on the battlefields of Europe—Du Bois declared that "we Soldiers of Democracy . . . return from fighting. We return fighting."⁹

While Du Bois envisioned a fight for civil rights based on political lobbying and public protest, Jamaican-born poet Claude McKay encouraged African Americans to take up arms. Shocked by the atrocities committed during the Chicago race riot, McKay wrote his famous poem "If We Must Die," which advocated black armed resistance in response to white violence. Some black veterans adopted McKay's militant rhetoric and proclaimed that they were "ready to declare war any minute."¹⁰ Indeed, many black veterans violated Army policy and brought back weapons and ammunition they had seized from German soldiers, including rifles, automatic revolvers, and machine guns. However, many more African Americans used nonviolent means to pressure the federal government for civil rights and antilynching legislation. Following World War I, large numbers of disaffected African Americans joined the NAACP, increasing its membership from 10,000 in 1917 to 90,000 in 1919. The NAACP, which emerged from the war as the foremost civil rights organization, used legislative and legal efforts to promote equality and curb racial violence. The association's steady growth in the postwar decades was a clear sign that African Americans were no longer willing to accept Jim Crow.

Another indication was the steady flow of black migrants who protested with their feet and left the rural South in the years following World War I. The ongoing migration resulted in a significant growth of the black population in the urban North as well as a shift from agricultural labor and domestic service to industrial employment. Entering the industrial workforce in unprecedented numbers, African Americans joined a growing urban consumer society, which contributed to a dramatic increase of black-owned businesses and an expansion of the black middle class. Black grocery stores, restaurants, movie theaters, barber shops, and beauty parlors—including the numerous franchises of legendary Madame C. J. Walker—flourished in the 1920s. The concentration of the black urban population in the North also increased the political power of African Americans in that region. In 1928, Oscar De Priest, Chicago's first black alderman was elected to the U.S. House of Representative— the first African American to serve in Congress in nearly thirty years.

Despite economic advances and modest political gains, African Americans who had helped to make "the world safe for Democracy" did not achieve democracy for themselves. Segregation, discrimination, lynchings, and race riots remained a painful reality in the years following World War I. Nonetheless, the war did generate an important change. African Americans who had served in the military and supported the war on the home front would remember the broken promises of World War I. In 1941, when the nation mobilized for World War II, they were not about to close ranks and forget their racial grievances. Instead, they adopted the "Double V" slogan and insisted on a victory for democracy overseas as well as at home. The militant rhetoric of African Americans in World War II was, at least in part, responsible for the desegregation of the armed forces in 1948 as well as the emergence of the modern civil rights movement.

Appendix
Documents

Living and Working Conditions in the South

Prior to World War I, the majority of African Americans lived in the South, where they barely eked out a living. The following document, a U.S. Department of Labor investigation, illustrates the hardships of black sharecroppers, who rented land from whites and in lieu of money paid with a share of their crop. Struggling to survive, rural black Southerners faced poor nutrition, lack of sanitation, limited access to health care, and inferior schools for their children. African Americans who lived in the cities of the South often did not fare much better than the black rural population. The account of a black nursemaid from Georgia details the long working hours, the low pay, and the constant threat of sexual harassment by white male employers that characterized the working conditions of many domestic servants.

Living Conditions in the Rural South

Living conditions among all classes of tenants in the black-belt counties are in need of great improvement. The houses in which the vast majority of Negroes live contain no modern conveniences and are little better than rudely constructed shanties. Large Families quite commonly live in one small room, in which there is little window space. Too often the houses have been placed in a bleak spot of ground which is barren of grass or trees, and the environment of the home is such that cleanliness and sanitation are impossible of attainment. Except in isolated instances, the schools must be characterized as wholly inadequate. In the rural districts many communities have no schools whatever.

In many others the buildings have been improvised from vacated Negro dwelling houses which consist of a single room. That the school term is of short duration, that the houses are poorly equipped and the attendance irregular, that the teachers are incompetent, and that there is an absence of interest and spirit which are necessary for a healthy school system are facts. . . .

Source: U.S. Department of Labor, Division of Negro Economics, *Negro Migration in 1916–1917* (Washington, DC: U.S. Government Printing Office, 1919; reprinted New York: Negro Universities Press, 1969), 68.

A Black Woman Recalls Working Conditions in the Urban South

. . . more than two-thirds of the negroes of the town where I live are menial servants of one kind or another, and besides that more than two-thirds of the negro women here, whether married or single, are compelled to work for a living,—as nurses, cooks, washerwomen, chambermaids, seamstresses, hucksters, janitresses, and the like . . . the condition of this vast host of poor colored people is just as bad as, if not worse than, it was during the days of slavery. . . .

I frequently work from fourteen to sixteen hours a day. I am compelled by my contract, which is oral only, to sleep in the house. I am allowed to go home to my own children . . . only once in two weeks. . . . I not only have to nurse a little white child . . . but I have to act as playmate . . . to three other children in the home. . . . You might as well say that I'm on duty all the time—from sunrise to sunrise, every day in the week I am the slave, body and soul, of this family. And what do I get for this work—this lifetime bondage? The pitiful sum of ten dollars a month! And what am I expected to do with these ten dollars? With this money I'm expected to pay my house rent, which is four dollars per month, for a little house of two rooms, just big enough to turn round in; and I'm expected, also, to feed and clothe myself and three children. . . .

Perhaps some might say, if the poor pay is the only thing about which we have to complain, then the slavery in which we daily toil and struggle is not so bad after all. But the poor pay isn't all—not by any means. . . . I believe nearly all white men take, and expect to take, undue liberties with their colored female servants—not only the fathers, but in many cases the sons also. Those servants who rebel against such familiarity must either leave or expect a mighty hard time, if they stay. . . .

No white person . . . at the South ever thinks of addressing any negro man or woman as Mr., or Mrs., or Miss. . . . In many cases our white employers refer to us, and in our presence, too, as their "niggers." No matter what they call us—no matter what they teach their children to call us—we must tamely submit, and answer when we are called; we must enter no protest; if we did object, we should be driven out without the least ceremony. . . .

Another thing. Sometimes I have gone on the street cars or the railroad trains with the white children, and, so long as I was in charge of the children, I could sit anywhere. . . . If a white man happened to ask some other white man, "What is that nigger doing in here?" and was told, "Oh, she's the nurse of those white children in front of her!" immediately there was the hush of peace. Everything was all right, so long as I was in the white man's part of the street car or in the white man's coach as a servant—a slave—but as soon as I did not present myself as a menial, and the relationship of master and servant was abolished by my not having the white children with me, I would be forthwith assigned to the "nigger" seats or the "colored people's coach." . . .

Source: "More Slavery at the South," *Independent* 72, 25 January 1912, 196–200.

Letters from Southern Migrants

When World War I started and demands for workers in the industrial centers of the North increased, many black Southerners were eager to leave the South. The following letters, addressed to Robert S. Abbott, editor of the most widely circulated black newspaper, the Chicago Defender, *illustrate the desperation of many black Southerners who were hovering on the verge of starvation. In the North they hoped to earn decent wages, provide their children with the opportunity to attend good schools, and live in a less racially oppressive climate. Fearful that white Southerners might prevent them from leaving the South, they asked Abbott not to print their names in the* Defender.

Ellisville, Mississippi, May 1, 1917

Kind Sir: I have been takeing the Defender 4 months I injoy reading it very much I don't think that there could be a grander paper printed for the race, then the defender. Dear Editor I am thinking of leaving for Some good place in the North or West one I dont Know just which I learn that Nebraska was a very good climate for the people of the South. I wont you to give me some ideas on it, Or Some good farming country. I have been public working for 10 year. I am tired of that, And want to get out on a good farm. I have a wife and 5 children and we all wont to get our from town a place an try to buy a good home near good Schools good Churchs. I am going to leave here as soon as I get able to work. Some are talking of a free train May 15. But I don't know anything of that. So I will go to work an then I will be sure, of my leaving Of course if it run I will go but I am not depending on it Wages here are so low can scarcely live We can buy enough to eat we only buy enough to Keep up alive I mean the greater part of the Race. Women wages are from 1.25$ Some time as high as $2.50. just some time for a whole week.

Hoping Dear Editor that I will get a hearing from you through return mail, giving me Some ideas and Some Sketches on the different Climate suitable for our health.

P.S. You can place my letter at Some of the Defender Colums but done use my name in print, for it might get back down here.

Source: Emmett J. Scott, "Letters of Negro Migrants of 1916–1918," *Journal of Negro History* 4, no. 3 (July 1919), 305–6.

Newbern, Alabama, April 7, 1917

Dear Sir . . .

Doubtless you have learned of the great exodus of our people to the north and west from this and other southern states. I wish to say that we are forced to go when one things of a grown man wages is only fifty to seventy five cents per day for all grades of work. He is compelled to go where there is better wages and sociable conditions, believe me. When I say that many places here in this state the only thing that the black man gets is a peck of meal and from three to four lbs. of bacon per week, and he is treated as a slave. As leaders we are powerless for we dare not resent such or to show even the slightest disapproval. Only a few days ago more than 1000 people left here for the north and west. They cannot stay here. The white man is saying that you must not go but they are not doing anything by way of assisting the black man to stay. As a minister of the Methodist Episcopal Church (north) I am on the verge of starvation simply because of the above conditions. I shall be glad to know if there is any possible way by which I could be of real service to you as director of your society. Thanking you in advance for an early reply, and for any suggestions that you may be able to offer.

With best wishes for your success, I remain,

Very sincerely yours.

Source: Emmett J. Scott, "Additional Letters of Negro Migrants of 1916–1918," *Journal of Negro History* 4, no. 4 (October 1919), 419–20.

Wartime Labor Contract

When World War I triggered a growing demand for defense industry products and a simultaneous decline of the immigrant workforce, Northern industries used labor agents to recruit black workers in the South. The agents, armed with labor contracts like the one below, often had to work secretly and with the help of black as-

sistants who disguised themselves as traveling salesmen in order to avoid attracting the attention of hostile whites. As the number of black migrants increased, white Southerners feared losing their black workforce and tried to stop the labor agents. In some cases they used legal means, but often they relied on intimidation and violence to prevent African Americans from leaving the South.

It is hereby understood that I am to work for the above-named company as _____, the rate of pay to be _____. The _____ Railroad agrees to furnish transportation and food to destination. I agree to work on any part of the _____ Railroad where I may be assigned. I further agree to reimburse the _____Railroad for the cost of my railroad transportation, in addition to which I agree to pay _____ to cover the cost of meals and other expenses incidental to my employment.

I authorize the company to deduct from my wages money to pay for the above expenses.

In consideration of the _____ Railroad paying my car fare, board, and other expenses, I agree to remain in the service of aforesaid company until such time as I reimburse them for the expense of my transportation, food, etc.

It is agreed upon the part of the railroad company that if I shall remain in the service for one year the _____ Railroad agrees to return to me the amount of car fare from point of shipment to _____. By continuous service for one year is meant that I shall not absent myself from duty any time during the period without the consent of my superior officer.

It is understood that the _____ Railroad will not grant me free transportation to the point where I was employed.

I am not less than 21 or more than 45 years of age, and have no venereal disease. If my statement in this respect is found to be incorrect this contract becomes void.

_____ _____.

Laborers name.

Source: U.S. Department of Labor, Division of Negro Economics, *Negro Migration in 1916–1917* (Washington, DC: U.S. Government Printing Office, 1919; reprinted New York: Negro Universities Press, 1969), 120.

Housing Camps for Single Male Migrants in the North

The first black migrants were almost exclusively single males between the ages of twenty-one and forty-five. Brought North by railroad companies and steel mills, they often moved into quickly constructed camps that consisted of wooden sheds packed with cots or bunk beds. Sanitary conditions were good in some camps, where the workers enjoyed access to clean showers, bathrooms, and flush toilets. However, in others, sleeping quarters were so crammed and conditions so appalling that one scholar compared them to slave ships. The quality of food also varied greatly. Some camps had well-staffed and clean kitchens that offered inexpensive nutritious meals or packed lunches, while others were filthy, teeming with flies and reeking with stench. Only a few of the camps had any kind of recreational facilities, consisting at best of a few pool tables and a couple of checkerboards.

The outstanding fact of the Negro migration from the South is that the movement is preponderately one of single men. Certainly 70 or 80 per cent of the migrants are without family ties in the North. A large number, particularly of those employed by the railroads and in the steel industry, are housed in camps.

The Pennsylvania Railroad has developed the most extensive camp system, especially on the lines East. In the fall of 1916 a more or less uniform system of camp construction was inaugurated at considerable expense. These camps are wooden sheds, covered with tar paper and steam heated and equipped with sanitary cots, often placed in tiers. There are separate sheds furnished with flush toilets, wash rooms, and shower baths, and a separate eating room. The commissary is organized by the company and charges for board have varied from $4 to $7 a week. A nominal charge of $1 or $2 a month is charged for lodging.

As many as 35 camps, each housing more than 40 men, the majority of whom are Negroes, were reported in July 1917, distributed over the eastern Pennsylvania, western Pennsylvania, New York, Maryland, and Delaware divisions of the Pennsylvania Railroad.

Almost 2,000 Negro laborers were reported to be so housed in August, 1917. A typical large camp is at Girard Point in South Philadelphia. Here there were 170 men on August 10. The camp had a capacity of 360, and the construction was of the usual sort—eight houses, with two-tier beds, a clean kitchen and mess room. The camp was located in a hot, dusty place between railroad tracks.

The Curtain Street Pennsylvania Railroad camp in Harrisburg housed 25 Negroes in a reconstructed building. The kitchen, dining room, and the rest room downstairs were in model condition, but the upper floor, fitted up as a dormitory, with single cots and wooden lockers, was congested, as a space 20 by 40 feet was filled with 30 cots, and there were but three windows. The commissary, with four cooks, served very good meals and packed lunches at 20 cents a meal. The men paid $1 a month for lodging. . . .

Many smaller concerns through Pennsylvania, Ohio, and New Jersey operate camps and bunk houses of varying sizes. One of the worst of the camps visited was on a construction operation at Essington, Pa. Here about 400 Negroes were housed in 10 rough shacks, 10 by 30 feet in size. Wooden bunks were built closely, in tiers of three and four, housing about 35 men in a shack. One larger shack of 40 by 40 feet, of similar bunk construction, housed 45. Mattresses were filthy and verminous; old clothes, cans, and whisky bottles were thrown about and the shacks had not been cleaned for some days. The toilets and wash room were open sheds, and no sanitary plumbing facilities were provided. The commissary privilege was let to an Italian commission firm of South Philadelphia. There were three men in the store and three Italian policemen on duty when the camp was visited at lunch time. The commissary was run like a company store, selling goods at current city prices. No mess hall was provided, but in the store there were a few crowded tables. The stench and flies made it impossible to stay in the room. The men were paying $1 a month for lodging, and food at the commissary cost from $6 to $8 a week. The condition of this camp was reported to the State department of labor and industry, and it was later materially improved.

Source: U.S. Department of Labor, Division of Negro Economics, *Negro Migration in 1916–1917* (New York: Negro Universities Press, 1919; Reprinted, 1969), 145–46, 148.

Black and White Responses to the Great Migration

Not all Americans welcomed the black mass exodus. Southern whites, afraid of losing their workforce, tried to deter African Americans from migrating north. They circulated stories of disillusioned blacks who returned to the South and intimidated, harassed, and arrested labor agents and black migrants. Nonetheless, the migration continued, largely due to the availability of jobs in Northern industries. While the war created unprecedented economic opportunities for African Americans, employment and housing competition often led to racial violence. Some African Americans urged potential migrants to stay in the South. The black editor of the New Orleans Southwestern Christian Advocate, *discouraged those who had no employment contract from leaving the South and implored others to prepare for the move by contacting pastors in Northern cities where they planned to live. African Americans who had made the move north admitted that they missed their families and friends and at times complained about living conditions. However, the majority of letters migrants wrote to those who stayed in the South, praised the North's well-paying jobs, the relative absence of racism, and the enhanced educational opportunities for their children.*

A Southern Black Newspaper Cautions Black Migrants about Conditions in the North

The great mistake that some of our people are making in their moving to the North is their going without any definite place to go and with no definite employment in sight. There is enough risk when there is a bona fide offer of good positions in the North of the work that is congenial and work which our people can do, but it is a little less than foolhardy because some of our people are moving north for others to go in a harem scarem way. Those who go without definite employment are making trouble. Going into the cities of the North they have been forced to go into temporary camps, there having been no provision made for them, housing facilities being inadequate and no immediate employment to be had.

These facts lead us to say: In no case should our people attempt to go north until they know where they are going, to what they are going and whether the firms that offer employment are reliable. They must not forget that there are labor agents who get so much per head for men who go North but these labor agents cannot guarantee employment for the shiftless, worth-less laborer whether he is in the South or in the North.

There is another thing to which attention should be called, in per-fect frankness. Our people who move North should not expect to find everything rosy. There will be considerable disappointment if they think they will not encounter prejudice in the North. There is less prejudice there of a kind. There are better opportunities for education, and there is better protection, but there is the more intense prejudice on the part of the Labor Unions against skilled workmen who are Ne-groes. We give a warning note to our people against this foolhardy pull-ing up and moving into the complications of city life without knowing definitely what awaits them.

Moreover, the city with its allurements is no place for our people who are not accustomed to city life. Many Negro boys and girls who have otherwise been innocent in the South will be victims of all sorts of schemes and pitfalls and influences for degradation in the cities. It is well, therefore, when our people contemplate moving North, before they start, that they get in touch with some of the pastors of the churches of whatever denominations in the city where they expect to go. . . .

Source: *Southwestern Christian Advocate*, 5 April 1917.

Black Migrants Praise Life in the Urban North
Philadelphia, Pennsylvania, October 7, 1917

Dear Sir: . . . with the aid of God I am making very good I make $75 per month. I am carrying enough insurance to pay me $20 per week if I am not able to be on duty. I don't have to work hard. Don't have to mister every little white boy who comes along I havent heard a white man call a colored a nigger you no now—since I been in the state of Pa. I can ride in the electric street and steam cars any where I gt a seat. I don't care to mix with white . . . but if I have to pay the dsame fare I have learn to want the same acomidation. And if you are first in a place here shopping you don't have to wait until th white folks get thro tradeing yet amid all this I shall ever love the good old South and I am praying that God give every well wisher a chance to be a man regardless of his color, and if my going to the front would bring about such conditions I am ready any day. . . .

Source: Emmett J. Scott, "Additional Letters of Negro Migrants of 1916–1918," *Journal of Negro History* 4, no. 4 (October 1919), 461.

Chicago, Illinois, November 13, 1917

Dear M——: . . . I am all fixed now and living well. . . . I was promoted on the first of the month I was made first assistant to the head carpenter when he is out of the place I take everything in charge and was raised to $95. A month. . . . I should have been here 20 years ago. I just begin to feel like a man. It's a great deal of pleasure in knowing that you have got some privilege. My children are going to the same school with the whites and I don't have to umble to no one. I have registered—Will vote the next election and there isnt any "yes sir" and no sire . . .

Source: Emmett J. Scott, "Additional Letters of Negro Migrants of 1916–1918," *Journal of Negro History* 4, no. 4 (October 1919), 458–59.

The National Urban League Responds to the Great Migration

Founded in 1911, the National Urban League collaborated with social service and welfare agencies, philanthropic institutions, civic groups, churches, and municipal officials to help Southern rural migrants adjust to Northern urban industrial life. The League received much of its funding from white philanthropists, but its membership was largely composed of members of the educated professional black middle class. They became concerned when the wartime migration triggered a dramatic black population explosion in the cities of the North, causing housing shortages, overcrowding, and sanitation and health problems as well as a lack of recreational facilities. These conditions, they feared, would result in heightened racial tensions and dis-

crimination. Thus, the League asked black newspapers to urge prospective migrants to prepare for their journey to the North and avoid becoming "a burden to the northern communities." Once the migrants arrived in the North, League members met the newcomers at the railroad stations and directed them toward the League's branches, which provided employment bureau services, housing registers, temporary shelter, day care facilities, and health care, educational, and recreational programs.

The National Urban League Appeals to Black Newspaper Editors, 1916
Dear Editor:

We write this letter for publication in your next issue because we feel that it touches upon a situation of vital importance to every member of the race.

Negroes in large numbers are leaving the south for the north. Many are securing good positions. Those that are sober and responsible and know how to give an honest days toil are holding their positions. The indolent inefficient men, however, are soon discharged, become a burden to the northern communities and bring reproach and humiliation to thrifty Colored citizens in communities where white people have not hitherto considered Negroes undesirables.

The National League on Urban Conditions among Negroes urges the right thinking Negroes of the south and everywhere to discourage the wholesale migration of shiftless people between any two points, be they north or south. The league also warns Negroes against fraudulent agents who are collecting employment fees and who disappear soon afterwards.

Negro labor is in demand. Use that fact to improve the efficiency of that labor by demanding: First, better wages where the wages of Colored men are below the current wage; second, better working conditions so that your health will not be impaired by the work you do; third, better living conditions both for yourself and family, so that your efficiency as a worker will not be impaired by living conditions which prevent proper rest and recreation to fit you for the day's labor, and base these demands on the facts that all these things will make your work more valuable to yourself and your employer and make for better feeling between the races.

The National Urban League urges Negroes everywhere to take advantage of this great industrial opportunity to work in co-operation with their local neighbors, whether north or south, for the improvement of conditions which will affect both races.

Very truly yours,

Eugene Kinckle Jones,

Executive Secretary

We are in hearty accord with the sentiments of the letter—The Editor.

Sources: "The National Urban League Discusses 'Migration' Question," *Cleveland Advocate*, 9 December 1916, 1.

Chicago Urban League Aids Migrants, 1917

Organized four months ago, the league has concentrated the forces available for service to the Negro emigrant. Organizations comprising more than 1,200 persons and more than 30 smaller organizations have been enlisted to cooperate through an executive board associated with the league. Departments for travelers' aid, factory investigation, and employment have been formed. In addition a block system of visiting has been devised and sections have been assigned to organizations and clubs. Under direction, it is planned for visitors to go to the homes of the newcomers and establish friendly contact as a basis for assistance and instruction. An outline of topics—including care of health, cleanliness, deportment in public places, care of children, dress efficiency, high rents, over crowding—has been made. Along these lines the visitor will give advice and suggestions and will emphasize the importance of their observance in establishing new residence. This service rendered by the resident people to their own race will be invaluable in giving social anchorage.

The league, which maintains an employment bureau, reports that the demand for common laborers exceeds the supply. Wages received regularly for steady work are the basis of family advancement. The small number of unemployed were strangers who did not know of the facilities of the league until the visitor called.

Conditions for the employment of women are not so favorable. The league is unable to place the women applying for work owing to scarcity of jobs and unfitness in domestic training. To remedy this club women are meeting applicants at league rooms to instruct them in the requirements and methods in use in northern homes. Efforts are also being made to secure suitable factory work for girls and women.

In cooperation with the league are the churches which number the largest membership among Negroes. Only 4 families were without church affiliations. . . . Establishing church connections is of inestimable value in making social contact. Visitors extend invitations and emphasize the benefit from immediate identification with a religious organization.

The visitor . . . found in nearly every family need for friendly service or counsel. With special knowledge of organized social agencies, she acted as the link connecting those in need of services and the supply. Little children who had not been enrolled in school in Chicago were accompanied by her on the difficult "first day." Illness in need of attention was found in several families and the visiting nurse was called in. In other cases cards were given to dispensaries. To restless boys she suggested the YMCA for companionship and recreation. Better methods in housekeeping were suggested. Directions in regard to employment were given. Her interest and help extended through the entire family, its work and play and other interests.

Source: U.S. Department of Labor Division of Negro Economics, *Negro Migration in 1916–1917* (Washington, DC: U.S. Government Printing Office, 1919; reprinted New York: Negro Universities Press, 1969), 23–24.

Etiquette Manual for Migrants

Many black middle-class residents of Northern cities were troubled by the appearances and public conduct of the Southern migrants, which they considered to be unrefined, unsophisticated, and uncivilized. They were appalled by the migrants' choice of clothing, their lack of education, their Southern drawl, their unrefined tastes for "down-home cooking," their crude backward ways, and their inability to maintain middle-class standards of hygiene and cleanliness. Black middle-class contempt for the migrants' behavior was linked to fears that the newcomers' demeanor would reflect poorly on all members of the race and contribute to a deterioration of race relations. In response, the Chicago Defender *published numerous etiquette manuals that admonished the migrants not to discredit their race.*

The *Chicago Defender* Lists Do's and Don'ts, 1918

All our thoughts must not be directed against the real and fancied wrongs brought on us by those of the other Race. . . . If public attention is called to our frailties, then let it be accepted in the proper spirit and all work together, and we will get somewhere. . . . The place to begin is in the home. . . . Here are some Don'ts and Do's. Read them, think over them, talk about them, everywhere, reprint them, and use them for the good of all:

> Don't let your property run down . . .
> Don't forget to cut the grass.
> Don't fail to keep all trash and garbage in proper receptacles.
> Don't neglect washing your windows often . . .
> Don't sit around in the yard and on the porch barefoot and unkempt.
> Don't talk so loud, we're not all deaf . . .
> Don't wear handkerchiefs on your head . . .
> Don't let your window curtains get black with dirt.
> Don't be a damphool and say this is none of our business. It is.

Do These Things
Do plant flowers in your yard.

Do be courteous to strangers.

Do, gentlemen, tip your hat to the ladies.

Do give the ladies a seat in the street cars, especially those with babes.

Do have music in the home.

Do have good newspapers and books.

Do have pictures of our own leaders and work of our artists.

Do buy from our businesses men when you can.

Do dress neat and clean, but not gaudy.

Do have becoming table manners, in public and private.

Do sweep the house and scrub the kitchen every day, if needed.

Do try to make your home the prettiest and most comfortable in town.

Do take an interest in the civic life of our community.

Do start a bank account and buy Thrift Stamps . . .

Do take a part in everything that will bring victory in the war.

Do stand up for your rights, but respect the other fellow's.

Do be a patriotic and justice loving American Citizen.

Do understand that you are 100 per cent American.

Source: "A Few Do and Dont's," *Chicago Defender*, 13 July 1918, 16.

The East St. Louis Race Riot, 1917

The 1917 East St. Louis race riot erupted when unscrupulous politicians exploited white fears that black Southern migrants were willing to serve as strikebreakers and work for lower wages than whites. Beginning in May, hostilities escalated as whites harassed and beat African Americans and set several black homes on fire. When black residents armed themselves to protect their families and their neighborhoods, a full-scale riot started. On July 2, white mobs roamed the streets, burning, hanging, shooting, and stoning to death every black man and woman in sight. Uncontrollable white rage and the failure of police and National Guards to protect African Americans produced a bloodbath of unprecedented proportions: thirty-nine blacks were killed, hundreds wounded, thousands fled town, and entire city blocks were smoldering or lay in ashes.

African Americans were shocked, since the riot occurred only a few months after the United States had entered World War I "to make the world safe for democracy." Appalled by the violence and President Woodrow Wilson's refusal to condemn it, the National Association for the Advancement of Colored People, the nation's leading civil rights group, organized the first black protest march in the history of the United States. On July 28, 10,000 black men, women, and children marched silently through Harlem, carrying banners that reminded the president to make America safe for democracy. Kelly Miller, Dean of Howard University's College of Arts and Sciences and one of the nation's leading black intellectuals, appealed to Wilson and urged him to speak out against the atrocities, however, the president remained silent.

Eyewitness Account of the East St. Louis Riot

For an hour and a half last evening I saw the massacre of helpless negroes at Broadway and Fourth Street, in downtown East St. Louis, where a black skin was a death warrant.

I saw man after man, with hands raised, pleading for his life, surrounded by groups of men—men who had never seen him before and knew nothing about him except that he was black—and saw them administer the historic sentence of intolerance, death by stoning. I saw one of these men, almost dead from a savage shower of stones, hanged with a clothesline. Within a few paces of the pole from which he was suspended, four other negroes lay dead or dying, another having been removed, dead, a short time before. I saw the pockets of two of these negroes searched, without the finding of any weapon.

I saw one of these men, covered with blood and half conscious, raise himself on his elbow and look feebly about, when a young man, standing directly behind him, lifted a flat stone in both hands and hurled it upon his neck. I saw negro women begging for mercy and pleading that they had harmed no one, set upon by white women of the baser sort, who laughed and answered the coarse sallies of men as they beat the negresses' faces and breasts with fists, stones, and sticks. I saw one of these furies fling herself at a militiaman who was trying to protect a negress, and wrestle with him for his bayoneted gun, while other women attacked the refugee. . . .

"Get a nigger," was the slogan, and it was varied by the recurrent cry, "Get another!" It was like nothing so much as the holiday crowd, with thumbs turned down in the Roman Coliseum, except that here the shouters were their own gladiators, and their own wild beasts. . . .

The sheds in the rear of negroes' houses on Fourth Street had been ignited to drive out the negro occupants of the houses. And the slayers were waiting for them to come out.

It was stay in and be roasted, or come out and be slaughtered. A moment before I arrived, one negro had taken the desperate chance of coming out, and the rattle of revolver shots, which I heard as I approached the corner, was followed by the cry, "They've got him!" . . .

As I turned back toward Broadway, there was a shout at the alley and a negro ran out, apparently hoping to find protection. He paid no attention to missiles thrown from behind, none of which had hurt him much, but he was stopped in the middle of the street by a smashing blow in the jaw, struck by a man he had not seen.

"Don't do that," he appealed. "I haven't hurt nobody." The answer was a blow from one side, a piece of curbstone from the other side, and a push which sent him back on the brick pavement. He did not rise again, and the battering and kicking of his skull continued until he lay still, his blood flowing half way across the street. Before he had been booted to the opposite curb, another negro appeared and the same deeds were repeated. . . .

The butchering of the fire-trapped negroes went on so rapidly that, when I walked back to the alley a few minutes later, one was lying dead in the alley on the west side of Fourth Street and another on the east side.

And now women began to appear. One frightened black girl, probably 20 years old, got as far as Broadway with no worse treatment than jeers and thrusts. At Broadway, in view of militiamen, the white women, several of whom had been watching the massacre of negro men, pounced on the negroes. . . .

Right here I saw the most sickening incident of the evening. To put the rope around the negro's neck, one of the lynchers stuck his fingers inside the gaping scalp and lifted the negro's head by it, literally bathing his hand in the man's blood. "Get hold, and pull for East St. Louis," called a man with a black coat and a new straw hat, as he seized the other end of the rope. The rope was long, but not too long for the number of hands that grasped it, and this time the negro was lifted to a height of about seven feet from the ground. The body was left hanging there.

Source: *St. Louis Post-Dispatch*, 3 July 1917.

Leaflet Distributed during the Silent Parade

We march because by the grace of God and the force of truth the dangerous, hampering walls of prejudice and inhuman injustices must fall.

We march because we want to make impossible a repetition of Waco, Memphis, and East St. Louis by arousing the conscience of the country, and to bring the murderers of our brothers, sisters and innocent children to justice.

We march because we deem it a crime to be silent in the face of such barbaric acts.

We march because we are thoroughly opposed to him Jim Crow cars, etc., segregation, discrimination, disfranchisement, lynching, and the host of evils that are forced on us. It is time that the spirit of Christ should be manifested in the making and execution of laws.

We march because we want our children to live in a better land and enjoy fairer conditions than have fallen to our lot.

We march in memory of our butchered dead, the massacre of honest toilers who were removing the reproach of laziness and thriftlessness hurled at the entire race. They died to prove our worthiness to live. We live in spite of death shadowing us and ours. We prosper in the face of the most unwarranted and illegal oppression.

We march because the growing consciousness and solidarity of race, coupled with sorrow and discrimination, have made us one; a union that may never be dissolved in spite of shallow-brained agitators, scheming pundits and political tricksters who secure a fleeting popularity and uncertain financial support by promoting the discussion of a people who ought to consider themselves as one.

Source: "A Negro's March with Muffled Drums," *Survey*, 4 August 1917, 405–6.

The Disgrace of Democracy, 1917
4 August, 1917
Hon. Woodrow Wilson, President of the United States,
The White House, Washington, D.C.

Mr. President:

I am taking the liberty of intruding this letter upon you because I feel that the issues involved are as important as any questions now pressing upon your busy attention. The whole civilized world has been shocked at the recent occurrences in Memphis and East St. Louis. . . .

These periodic outbreaks of lawlessness are but the outgrowth of the disfavor and despite in which the race is held by public opinion. The evil is so widespread that the remedy lies in the hands of the national government. . . .

What the nation needs is not investigation of obvious fact, but the determination and avowed declaration on the part of the President speaking for the people of the United States to put an end to lawlessness wherever it raises its hideous head. . . .

The evil is indeed national in its range and scope, and the nation must provide the remedy. Striking indeed is the analogy between the spread of lawlessness today and the extension of the institution of slavery two generations ago. Like slavery, lawlessness cannot be localized. As the nation could not exist half slave and half free under Abraham Lincoln, so it cannot continue half law-abiding and half lawless under Woodrow Wilson. . . . If the

Negro is allowed to be lynched in the South with impunity, he will soon be lynched in the North, so easy is the communicability of evil suggestion. . . .

So general and widespread has become the practice that lynching may well be characterized as a national institution, to the eternal disgrace of American democracy. . . .

Mr. President, you are commander-in-chief of the Army and Navy. You express the voice of the American people in the great world conflict which involves practically the entire human race. You are the accepted spokesman of the world democracy. You have sounded forth the trumpet of democratization of the nations, which shall never call retreat. But, Mr. President, a chain is not stronger than its weakest link. A doctrine that breaks down at home is not fit to be propagated abroad. . . . Why democratize the nations of the earth if it leads them to delight in the burning of human beings after the manner of Springfield, Waco, Memphis, and East St. Louis while the nation looks helplessly on? You add nothing to the civilization of the world nor to the culture of the human spirit by the technical changes in forms of government. . . .

If democracy cannot control lawlessness, then democracy must be pronounced a failure. The nations of the world have a right to demand of us the workings of the institutions at home before they are promulgated abroad. The German press will, doubtless, gloat with ghoulish glee over American atrocities against the Negro. . . .

The nation must be responsible for what it permits. Sins of permission are as reprehensible as sins of commission. . . . Every high-minded American must be touched with a tinge of shame when he contemplates that his rallying cry for the liberation of humanity is made a delusion and a snare by these racial barbarities. . . .

Mr. President, the American conscience has been touched and quickened by the East St. Louis outbreak as it has never been before. . . . By some fatuous delusion they seem to hope that the atrocities of Springfield, Wilmington, Waco, Atlanta, Memphis and a thousand other places of evil report would never be repeated, nor the memory rise up to condemn the nation. But silence and neglect merely result in compounding atrocities. . . . Reproach is cast upon your contention for the democratization of the world, in the face of its lamentable failure at home. . . .

When you speak of democratization of the world and the liberation of mankind, you are setting up a standard to which the whole world must rise in the ages to come, despite its attitude at the present time. It may be far from the purpose of our present-day statesmen to admit the Negro into this democracy on terms of equality with the rest. But in spite of the purpose of this statesmanship, this must be the ultimate goal of human democracy. . . .

The Negro's patriotism is vicarious and altruistic. It seems to be an anomaly of fate that the Negro, the man of all men who is held in despite, should stand out in conspicuous relief at every crisis of our national history. His blood offering is not for himself or for his race, but for his country. . . .

In the midst of the world war for the democratization of mankind the Negro will do his full share. . . . The Negro, Mr. President, in this emergency, will stand by you and the nation. Will you and the nation stand by the Negro? . . .

The time has come to make lawlessness a national issue, as a war measure if not from any higher consideration. As a patriotic and military necessity, I suggest that you ask the Congress of the United States to invest you with the power to prevent lynching and to quell lawlessness and violence in all parts of the country during the continuance of the war. . . .

Mr. President, ten million of your fellow citizens are looking to you and to the God whom you serve to grant them relief in this hour of their deepest distress. All moral reforms grow out of the people who suffer and stand in need of them. The Negro's helpless position may yet bring America to a realizing sense that righteousness exalteth a nation, but sin is reproach to any people.

Source: Kelly Miller, *Kelly Miller's History of The World War for Human Rights: Being an Intensely Human and Brilliant Account of the World War and Why and for What Purpose America and the Allies Are Fighting and the Important Part Taken by the Negro. Including: The Horrors and Wonders of Modern Warfare, the New and Strange Devices, etc.* (New York: Negro Universities Press, 1919; reprinted 1969), 481–95.

The Black Officers Training Camp in Des Moines, Iowa, 1917

When the United States entered World War I, many African Americans hoped that black military service would bring about full equality. However, the Army was segregated and many African Americans feared that the military would relegate black soldiers to menial labor tasks. Equally troublesome was the exclusion of black men from the nation's fourteen officers training camps. Determined to secure a leading role for black men in the military, African Americans faced a dilemma. Since the Army did not provide officer training for black men, should African Americans forgo higher-ranking military positions or should they push for a separate black officers camp? Joel E. Spingarn, the white chairman of the NAACP's board of directors, was confident that a separate camp, while not ideal, was better than no camp at all. Lobbying for a black officers training camp, Spingarn gained the support of his friend W. E. B. Du Bois, editor of the NAACP's Crisis magazine; Lieutenant Colonel Charles Young, the highest-ranking black officer in the U.S. Army; and the students and faculty of black colleges and universities. However, many African Americans, particularly editors of black newspapers opposed the campaign for a "Jim Crow" camp. "If we are good enough to fight," Robert S. Abbott of the Chicago Defender *proclaimed, "we are good enough to receive the same preparatory training our white brothers receive." Opposition to military segregation did not die during the war, but it faded when the War Department agreed to open a black officers training camp in Des Moines, Iowa, in the summer of 1917.*

W. E. B. Du Bois Supports Black Officers Training Camp

We Negroes ever face it. We cannot escape it. We must continually choose between insult and injury; no schools or separate schools; no travel or "Jim Crow" travel; homes with disdainful neighbors or homes in slums.

We continually submit to segregated schools, "Jim Crow" cars, and isolation, because it would be suicide to go uneducated, stay at home, and live in the "tenderloin."

Yet, when a new alternative of such choice faces us it comes with a shock and almost without thinking we rail at the one who advises the lesser of two evils.

Thus it was with many hasty editors in the case of the training camp for Negro officers which Dr. J. E. Spingarn is seeking to establish.

Does Dr. Spingarn believe in a "Jim Crow" training camp? Certainly not, and he has done all he could to induce the government to admit Negroes to all training camps.

The government has so far courteously refused.

But war is imminent.

If war comes to-morrow Negroes will be compelled to enlist under white officers because (save a very few cases) no Negroes have had the requisite training.

We must choose then between the insult of a separate camp and irreparable injury of strengthening the present custom of putting no black men in positions of authority.

Our choice is as clear as noonday.

Give us the camp.

Let not 200, but 2,000, volunteer.

We did not make the damnable dilemma.

Our enemies made that.

We must make the choice else we play into their very claws.

It is a case of camp or no officers.

Give us the officers.

Give us the camp.

A word to those who object:

1. The army does not wish this camp. It wishes the project to fail. General Wood refuses to name date or place until 200 apply. The reason is obvious. Up to March 8, sixty-nine men have applied.

2. The camp is a temporary measure lasting four weeks and designed to FIGHT, not encourage discrimination in the army. . . . We want trained colored officers. This camp will help furnish them.

3. The South does not want the Negro to receive military training of any sort. For that reason the general staff reduced its estimate from 900,000 to 500,000 soldiers—they expect to EXCLUDE Negroes!

4. If war comes, conscription will follow. All pretty talk about not volunteering will become entirely academic. This is the mistake made by the Baltimore AFRO-AMERICAN, the Chicago DEFENDER, the New York NEWS. And the Cleveland GAZETTE. They assume a choice between volunteering and not volunteering. The choice will be between conscription and rebellion.

Can the reader conceive of the possibility of choice? The leaders of the colored race who advise them to add treason and rebellion to the other grounds on which the South urges discrimination against them would hardly be doing a service to those whom they profess to love. No, there is only one thing to do now, and that is to organize the colored people for leadership and service, if war should come. A thousand commissioned officers of colored blood is something to work for.

Give us the camp!

Source: *Crisis* (April 1917), 270–71.

"Jim Crow" Training Camps—No!

The theory that half a loaf is better than no loaf at all has long since been exploded. . . . We have put up with the crumbs that have fallen from the white man's table as our portion so long we are considered ungrateful if we even dare to hint it is about time we were eating at the first table. The fact that we are paying for cake and ice cream and getting skimmed milk and hardtack should strike the average mind as being a trifle unjust. There are many good people who believe we should continue to take what is handed to us without complaint, in the hopes of getting more and better things in the future. . . .

Dr. Spingarn and some other estimable gentlemen are advocating the establishment of a "Colored Officers' Training Camp," and put forth arguments in its favor that are worthy of consideration only because these gentlemen are sincere, friendly, and believe they are aiding us to take a step forward. . . .

To ask for permission to fight with a class of people who absolutely need and cannot do without our service in the event of war, is a huge joke from every point of view. White men have no objections to Colored regiments, if they can officer them. . . . A half loaf isn't always better than no loaf at all; better that we have no regiments than have them officered by white men. Prejudice is a barrier that cannot be broken down in a day, but the effort must come to break it, and there is no better time than the present to begin. When our country needs men to defend its honor, the black man shoulders his gun without a murmur, and the white man, through the kindness of his heart, gives him a prominent place in the front ranks where the bullets are the thickest. . . . Though it might seem too idealistic to have mixed regiments, that is what Uncle Sam will be compelled to do, if we are to have a united country.

No one denies that we sorely need efficient military training for officers, privates and every citizen, but we do not want it, nor will we take it in a "Jim Crow" way, if we never get it. . . . If we are good enough to fight, we are good enough to receive the same preparatory training our white brothers receive.

Source: "'Jim Crow' Training Camps—No!" *Chicago Defender*, 28 April 1917, 3.

Resolutions of the Washington Conference, 1917

Seven hundred representatives from the NAACP; black newspapers, businesses, schools, and churches; as well as civic and social welfare organizations met in May 1917 at Howard University in Washington, D.C., to discuss the role of African Americans in the war. Conference participants pledged to support the war effort, despite the military's Jim Crow policy, but also vowed to continue their fight for racial justice and equality. They assured the nation of black loyalty and patriotism, yet they also demanded that the government provide combat and officer training for black troops. A victory for world democracy, they reminded the government, had to include democratic rights for African Americans. The black representatives adopted a list of resolutions that illustrated their determination to reconcile their accommodationist recommendations with their integrationist aspirations.

We . . . earnestly urge our colored fellow citizens to join heartily in this fight for eventual world liberty; we urge them to enlist in the army; to join in the pressing work of providing food supplies; to labor in all ways by hand and thought in increasing the efficiency of our county. We urge this despite our deep sympathy with the reasonable and deep-seated feeling of revolt among Negroes at the persistent insult and discrimination to which they are subject and will be subject even when they do their patriotic duty.

Let us, however, never forget that this country belongs to us even more than to those who lynch, disfranchise, and segregate. As our country it rightly demands our whole-hearted defense. . . .

Absolute loyalty in arms and in civil duties need not for a moment lead us to abate our just complaints and just demands. . . . [W]e demand and of right ought to demand:

1. The right to serve our country on the battlefield and to receive training for such service;
2. The right of our best men to lead troops of their own race in battle, and to receive officers' training in preparation for such leadership;
3. The immediate stoppage of lynching;
4. The right to vote for both men and women;
5. Universal and free common school training;
6. The abolition of Jim Crow cars;
7. The repeal of segregation ordinances;
8. Equal civil rights in all public institutions and movements.

These are not minor matters. They are not matters that can wait. They are the least that self-respecting, free, modern men can have and live.

Source: *Crisis* (June 1917), 59–60.

The Houston Mutiny: An NAACP Investigation

On the evening of August 23, 1917, approximately 100 black soldiers of the Twenty-fourth Infantry marched from Camp Logan into nearby Houston, Texas. Retaliating for white civilian harassment and police brutality, the black soldiers opened fire. During the ensuing shooting spree, eighteen whites and two black soldiers died. The so-called Houston Mutiny resulted in the largest court martial in U.S. history. In three separate trials 118 defendants were charged with mutiny and premeditated murder. The courts acquitted seven of the men and sentenced twenty-eight to death and forty to life in prison. Others received sentences for lesser crimes, including desertion. None of the white officers in charge of the black troops were held accountable. The following report, prepared by Martha Gruening, a white NAACP investigator, explores the underlying causes of the mutiny.

The primary cause of the Houston riot was the habitual brutality of the white police officers of Houston in their treatment of colored people. Contributing causes were (1) the mistake made in not arming members of the colored provost guard or military police, (2) lax discipline at Camp Logan which permitted promiscuous visiting at the camp and made drinking and immorality possible among the soldiers.

Houston is a hustling and progressive southern city . . . and, as southern cities go, a fairly liberal one. Its population before the Negro exodus, which has doubtless decreased it by many thousands, was estimated at 150,000. Harris County, in which it is situated, has never had a lynching, and there are other indications, such as the comparative restraint and self-control of the white citizens after the riot, that the colored people perhaps enjoy a greater degree of freedom with less danger than in many parts of the South. It is, however, a southern city, and the presence of the Negro troops inevitably stirred its Negrophobe element to protest. There was some feeling against the troops being there at all, but I could not find that it was universal. Most of the white people seem to have wanted the financial advantages to be derived from having the camp in the neighborhood. The sentiment I heard expressed most frequently by them was that they were willing to endure the colored soldiers if they could be "controlled." I was frequently told that Negroes in uniform were inevitably "insolent" and that members of the military police in particular were frequently "insolent" to the white police of Houston. It was almost universally conceded, however, that the members of the white police force habitually cursed, struck, and otherwise maltreated colored prisoners. One of the important results of the riot has been an attempt on the part of the Mayor and the Chief of Police of Houston to put a stop to this custom.

In deference to the southern feeling against the arming of Negroes and because of the expected co-operation of the city Police Department, members of the provost guard were not armed, thus creating a situation without precedent in the history of this guard. A few carried clubs, but none of them had guns, and most of them were without weapons of any kind. They were supposed to call on white police officers to make arrests. The feeling is strong among the colored people of Houston that this was the real cause of the riot. . . .

On the afternoon of August 23, two policemen, Lee Sparks and Rufe Daniels—the former known to the colored people as a brutal bully—entered the house of a respectable colored woman in an alleged search for a colored fugitive accused of crap-shooting. Failing to find him, they arrested the woman, striking and cursing her and forcing her out into the street only partly clad. While they were waiting for the patrol wagon a crowd gathered about the weeping woman who had become hysterical and was begging to know why she was being arrested. In this crowd was a colored soldier, Private Edwards. Edwards seems to have questioned the police officers or remonstrated with them. Accounts differ on this point, but they all agree that the officers immediately set upon him and beat him to the ground with the butts of their six-shooters, continuing to beat and kick him while he was on the ground, and arrested him. In the words of Sparks himself: "I beat that nigger until his heart got right. He was a good nigger when I got through with him."

Later Corporal Baltimore, a member of the military police, approached the officers and inquired for Edwards, as it was his duty to do. Sparks immediately opened fire, and Baltimore, being unarmed, fled with the two policemen in pursuit shooting as they ran. Baltimore entered a house in the neighborhood and hid under a bed. They followed, dragged him out, beat him up and arrested him. It was this outrage which infuriated the men of the 24th Infantry to the point of revolt. . . .

Police brutality and bad discipline among the soldiers led up to the riot, which cost the city of Houston eighteen lives. . . .

The Houston *Post* and the white people generally explained it as another illustration of the well-known fact that "the South is the Negro's best friend"; that race riot and bloodshed are really indigenous to northern soil; and that the relations between black and white in the South are highly cordial. The colored people of Houston, however, are migrating north, and to this more than to any element in the case I attribute the new restraint in the attitude of white Houstonians. While I was in Houston, 130 colored people left in one day. In June one labor agent exported more than nine hundred Negroes to points along the Pennsylvania Railroad. The Houston Chamber of Commerce became so alarmed over the Negro exodus that it telegraphed to the head of the railroad asking that this exportation be discontinued. The railroad complied with this request, but the colored people continued to leave. Colored men and women in every walk of life are still selling their homes and household goods at a loss and leaving because, as one of them, a physician, put it to me, "Having a home is all right, but not when you never know when you leave it in the morning if you will really be able to get back to it that night." . . .

Source: *Crisis* (November 1917), 14–19.

Black Troops Traveling from the North to the South, 1917

This excerpt from the "Diary of a Soldier" relates the journey of the black Eighth Illinois National Guard unit from Chicago to Camp Logan, Texas. It illustrates not only the racism black soldiers encountered in the South, but also the glee with which the men from the North challenged it. Unlike the black draftees, the men attached to the Eighth Illinois had a long and illustrious history. Organized prior to the Spanish-American War, the volunteer unit had served in Cuba between August 1898 and May 1899 and along the Mexican border in 1916. During World War I, the Eighth was reorganized as the 370th regiment and became part of the Ninety-Third Combat Division, which served under French command in Europe

At 2:30 we pulled into Pine Bluff. We detrained and went through some calisthenics while the band played every piece it knew and nine others. We weren't allowed to leave the station but there happened to be a large restaurant right at the train. Of course, our people weren't served there, and if any of our fellows didn't know it 'twas because they couldn't read. Anyhow, one look at the place just before the train pulled out was sufficient to convince one that a restaurant had been bombed, burned out, and then swept by a hurricane and flood. . . . Away back at Jonesboro this morning some poor cracker became angry and cussed out one of the Eighth boys. . . . That man's relatives will remember the Eight regiment until the 73d of Juvember, 2001 1/7. . . .

First thing this morning we pulled into Tyler, Tex. Everyone with any money got off to buy something to eat. Opposite the station was the chief grocery store, kept by a Chinaman. . . . surrounded by numerous lunch rooms. Possibly the people saw us coming; this fact was evinced by the raising of prices and the removal of signs. When we pulled in no signs were in sight and we walked right in the main entrances and bought out very place in town. After we had all spent as much dough as we thought necessary we beat it for the train, to be followed by numerous young ladies who gave the boys oranges, apples, and sandwiches and other good eats.

Source: "The Diary of a Soldier," *Chicago Defender*, 17 November 1917, 8.

Life at Camp Meade, 1917

The following black newspaper article illustrates the experience of black troops in the training camps. While military instruction and drills filled much of the men's day, the soldiers also had considerable leisure time. The War Department, concerned that the men would spend their off-duty hours in the red-light districts of adjacent cities, asked the Young Men's Christian Association to provide wholesome entertainment and recreation inside the camps. Underfunded, the segregated Y-huts were often ill equipped and had to rely on donations from the black community.

Camp Meade's diversified population which includes a little over 6,000 colored men chosen through the selective draft, are learning war tactics with a rapidity that is astonishing to some. . . .

Men who are to fight for world democracy, but who have been denied equal rights at home; men whose anxiety to get into the thickest of the fray against the Germans is indicated by the lustiness with which they sing, "We're Going to Get the Kaiser," are here in profusion.

An idea of the stupendous task that is entailed upon those seeking to "lick" these raw recruits into shape may be had when one knows that quite a number of them are illiterate and come from the environments that do not easily shape one to be a soldier. The illiterates for the most part came from Tennessee and some from the rural sections of Maryland . . . where school facilities for colored youth are poor. . . . Their lack of education is a sad commentary on the white South for curtailing greatly the educational opportunities of the Negro. . . .

The drafted men are carried through numerous drills daily and given other instruction pertaining to army life. . . .

Physical examinations are in progress, and it is expected that a number of men will be sent back home at the end of the month. Drafting boards, it appears, certified a larger percentage of colored men than whites, and many are not up to army standards physically. . . .

The Y.M.C.A. buildings are not large, however, for all of the social diversions needed. The men need pianos and pool tables for their barracks, and would be thankful if their friends outside would raise sufficient funds to purchase the same. . . .

Many of the soldiers are without funds and need money for tobacco and stamps. They would be grateful if their friends back home would send those little things that add to the joy of their life. They are thankful for the sweaters that they have received within the past week, but will still more so when other little necessaries arrive.

The drafted men say that they would like to see more of their friends on the visiting days—Wednesday, Saturday and Sunday—as they feel somewhat lonely when the folks "back home" seemingly forget them.

On Sundays hundreds of visitors come. On Wednesdays the crowds are not so large, and the drafted men amuse themselves in various ways. . . . A visit to the commissary is an interesting sight. There men will be seen buying cake, candy and soft drinks. Strong drink is tabooed. . . .

Source: "With the Boys at Camp Meade," *Baltimore Afro-American*, 19 November 1917, 1, 4.

Black Resentment of Military Discrimination, 1918

The War Department, afraid that growing black resentment of discrimination in the Army would spark racial unrest, ordered the Military Intelligence Branch (MIB) to investigate black troop morale. The MIB recruited Major Walter H. Loving, a retired black regimental bandmaster, to probe subversive activities among African Americans and to develop counterpropaganda to lift black morale. The following military intelligence report illustrates the numerous complaints of black soldiers about their treatment in the Army.

Various charges and allegations of unfair treatment have been made by colored officers and enlisted men, and by their civilian friends, both colored and white. These all have their origin in the conviction that colored soldiers do not invariably receive the same treatment as the white soldiers. It has been alleged, specifically, that colored officer-material has not been recommended on a basis of merit for officers' training schools; that colored men capable of becoming competent non-commissioned officers have been discriminated against; that there is discrimination against colored officers in the matter of promotion; that white officers handling colored draftees, in their efforts to enforce discipline, have used methods contrary to army regulations; that officers in command of colored soldiers have referred to their men as "niggers," . . . that many colored service battalion have received no military training at all; that the same precautions are not taken to guard the morals and health of the negroes as are taken for the whites; that negroes are allowed to enter districts of a kind from which the white soldier is barred; that white doctors have in many cases neglected the negro venereals; that competent colored doctors, holding commission in the Medical Reserve Corps, have not been called into service and assigned to duty with the colored soldiers who were in need of better medical care; that qualified colored dentists have been kept on duty as privates in labor battalions, without proper use being made of their professional qualifications; that the non-military agencies, authorized to carry on work for the soldiers, have not always provided the same facilities for the negroes as they have for the whites; that the colored troops have not had adequate Y.M.C.A. facilities; that in matters of recreation, dance halls, visiting privileges for friends, hostess houses, and classes to remove illiteracy, the negroes have been less well cared for than have the whites.

Source: Memorandum for the Director, Military Intelligence Division and Chief, Morale Branch, Executive Division, General Staff, December 23, 1918, in National Archives and Records Administration, Washington, DC, RG 165 War Department: General and Special Staffs—Military Intelligence Division, Casefile 10218-279.

Secret Information Concerning Black American Troops, 1918

African American soldiers were among the first U.S. troops to arrive in France. Exhausted from years of warfare, French soldiers and civilians welcomed the black men in arms. However, the fraternization of black soldiers with the French, particularly women, troubled white American military commanders. Hoping to dis-

courage any friendly or intimate contact between the French population and black troops, the American Expeditionary Forces distributed the following memorandum to French officers. In it, the American Army warned the French that any familiar contacts with African American soldiers were "matters of grievous concern to the Americans." When the document reached the French National Assembly, French politicians were outraged and passed a resolution that condemned racial prejudice.

French Military Mission Stationed with the American Army
August 7, 1918

Secret Information Concerning Black American Troops
1. It is important for French officers who have been called upon to exercise command over black American troops, or to live in close contact with them, to have an exact idea of the position occupied by Negroes in the United States. . . .

2. The American attitude upon the Negro question may seem a matter for discussion to many French minds. But we French are not in our province if we undertake to discuss what some call "prejudice." American opinion is unanimous on the "color question" and does not admit of any discussion.

The increasing number of Negroes in the United States (about 15,000,000) would create for the white race in the Republic a menace of degeneracy were it not that an impassable gulf has been made between them.

As this danger does not exist for the French race, the French public has become accustomed to treating the Negro with familiarity and indulgence.

This indulgence and this familiarity are matters of grievous concern to the Americans. They consider them an affront to their national policy. They are afraid that contact with the French will inspire in black Americans aspirations which to them [the whites] appear intolerable. It is of the utmost importance that every effort be made to avoid profoundly estranging American opinion.

Although a citizen of the United States, the black man is regarded by the white American as an inferior being with whom relations of business or service only are possible. The black is constantly being censured for his want of intelligence and discretion, his lack of civic and professional conscience and for his tendency toward undue familiarity.

The vices of the Negro are a constant menace to the American who has to repress them sternly. For instance, the black American troops in France have, by themselves, given rise to as many complaints for attempted rape as all the rest of the army. And yet the [black American] soldiers sent us have been the choicest with respect to physique and morals, for the number of disqualified at the time of mobilization was enormous.

Conclusion

1. We must prevent the rise of any pronounced degree of intimacy between French officers and black officers. We may be courteous and amiable with these last, but we cannot deal with them on the same plane as with the white American officers without deeply wounding the latter. We must not eat with them, must not shake hands or seek to talk or meet with them outside of the requirements of military service.

2. We must not commend too highly the black American troops, particularly in the presence of [white] Americans. It is all right to recognize their good qualities and their services, but only in moderate terms, strictly in keeping with the truth.

3. Make a point of keeping the native cantonment population from "spoiling" the Negroes. [White] Americans become greatly incensed at any public expression of intimacy between white women with black men.

Source: W. E. B Du Bois, "Documents of the War," *Crisis* (May 1919), 16–17.

German Propaganda Leaflet "To the Colored Soldiers of the United States Army"

Propaganda leaflets dropped by German airplanes behind American lines tried to capitalize on low troop morale among the black soldiers. As this leaflet indicates, the Germans were well informed about racial conditions in the United States. Exploiting the existence of segregation and discrimination in America, the Germans tried to entice black soldiers to put down their weapons and desert the U.S. Army, however, without any success.

Hello boys, what are you doing over here? Fighting the Germans? Why? Have they ever done you any harm? Of course, some white folks and the lying English-American papers told you that the Germans ought to be wiped out for the sake of humanity and Democracy. What is Democracy? Personal Freedom; all citizens enjoying the same rights socially and before the law. Do you enjoy the same rights as the white people do in America, the land of freedom and Democracy, or are you not rather treated over there as second class citizens?

Can you get into a restaurant where white people dine? Can you get a seat in a theatre where white people sit? Can you get a seat or a berth in a railroad car, or can you even ride in the South in the same street car with the white people?

And how about the law? Is lynching and the most horrible crimes connected therewith, a lawful proceeding in a Democratic country? Now, all this is entirely different in Germany, where they do like colored people; where they treat them as gentlemen and as white men, and quite a number of colored people have fine positions in business in Berlin and other German cities. Why, then, fight the Germans only for the benefit of the Wall Street robbers, and to protect the millions that they have loaned to the English, French, and Italians?

You have been made the tool of the egotistic and rapacious rich in America, and there is nothing in the whole game for you but broken bones, horrible wounds, spoiled health, or death. No satisfaction whatever will you get out of this unjust war. You have never seen Germany, so you are fools if you allow people to make you hate us. Come over to see for yourself. Let those do the fighting who make the profit out of this war. Don't allow them to use you as cannon fodder.

To carry a gun in this service is not an honor but a shame. Throw it away and come over to the German lines. You will find friends who will help you.

Source: Addie W. Hunton and Kathryn M. Johnson, *Two Colored Women with the American Expeditionary Forces* (Brooklyn, NY: Brooklyn Eagle Press, 1920), 53–54.

Letter from a Black Officer to an American Friend, 1919

Following the end of hostilities on November 11, 1918, black soldiers serving in France remained in Europe until they received orders to board troop ships bound for the United States. While waiting for their return passage, the men dismantled military installations, salvaged equipment and materials from the battlefields, removed unexploded shells, and reburied the decomposed bodies of fallen American soldiers. The following letter from a black officer depicts the horrible living conditions in a camp in France, comparing it to "a penal institution." Inadequate housing, poor sanitation, and health problems contributed to low troop morale, which worsened when white camp commanders placed those who complained about the conditions "at the bottom of the sailing list."

This Camp is practically a penal institution and prejudice against us is very strong. Some day there is likely to be some grave disturbance here. The conditions are simply awful: mud everywhere, leaky tents and barracks and lack of sufficient and proper toilets. The men are worked quite hard, some at night and others in the day, rain or shine. As a consequence there are quite a number of sick men in our organization. Since our arrival there the roads have been improved quite a bit (due to the work of the 92nd div) and you do not have to wade in ankle deep mud. Board walks here to nearly all the tents and barracks. There is so much talk about the rotten conditions that the Camp Officials are making feverish efforts to be ready for the proposed inquiry.

The work of each organization is graded by the Camp Officer in Charge of details and if not satisfactory, the organization may be placed at the bottom of the sailing list or removed temporarily. Commanding Officers of separate units or regiments are practically helpless and if they complain too much against the treatment accorded them, are kept here until the Commanding General sees fit to let them go.

I am beginning to wonder whether it will ever be possible for me to see an American (white) without wishing that he were in his Satanic Majesty's private domain. I must pray long and earnestly that hatred of my fellow man be removed from my heart and that I can truthfully lay claim to being a Christian.

Source: W. E. B. Du Bois, "Documents of the War," *Crisis* (May 1919), 20.

Robert Russa Moton, Head of Tuskegee Institute, Visits Black Troops in France, 1919

In 1915, Robert Russa Moton succeeded Booker T. Washington as principal of Tuskegee Institute, Alabama, one the nation's leading black colleges. Like his predecessor, Moton exhorted African Americans not to challenge segregation but to accommodate to Jim Crow. In 1919, the War Department sent Moton to France to prepare the black soldiers for their return to the United States. Moton urged the men to bask in the glory of their personal achievements rather than to expect significant changes to the racial status quo. While many of the soldiers welcomed Moton, Sergeant Ely Green was incensed by his message and heckled him.

Head of Tuskegee Sees Colored Units
Dr. Moton Addresses Many of 250,000 Negroes in A.E.F.
During the past two weeks many of the 250,000 colored soldiers in the A.E.F have been visited by Dr. Robert B. Moton, successor to the late Booker T. Washington as principal of Tuskegee Institute, who has come to France at the instance of President Wilson and Secretary Baker as an advisor on African matters to the American Peace Mission. Dr. Moton, in the course of a 1,000 mile automobile trip from Laon down through Lorraine and Alsace, met and talked with the men of the 92nd Division, and the 369th, 370th, 371st, and 372nd Infantry Regiments, which have been brigaded with French troops for a long period.

At Brest, where he landed, he spoke before an assembly of colored officers. His trip also included stops at St. Nazaire, Bordeaux and Gilvres. Everywhere he has been, he says, he has found colored soldiers in good health and spirits.

Must Be Manly Yet Modest

In his talks to the men, Dr. Moton, after complimenting them on their record and their willingness to work, has assured them that white and colored Americans alike will cordially welcome them upon their return home. Above all, he has stressed the Importance of the colored soldier's going back to the United States in a manly, yet modest, unassuming manner.

"In war," said Dr. Moton, at one point, "you have met the test and won, but a far greater test and a much more doubtful victory awaits you now than you faced during the past year and a half. It is a greater test and much more severe and important battle than you ever fought before. It is a battle not against Germans, but against black Americans. This battle is against the men into whose faces I now look. It is your individual, personal battle—a battle of self-control, against laziness, shiftlessness and willfulness. The best time to begin to show self control is right here in France. Leave such a reputation here as will constrain our Allies, who have watched as with interest, to say forever that the American negro will always be welcome not only because of his courage but because of his character."

Source: "Head of Tuskegee Sees Colored Units," *Stars and Stripes* 1, no. 48 (Paris, France) 3 January 1919.

Sergeant Ely Green Heckles Moton

[T]he regiment was being given a half day to honor our new Negro leader Doctor Moton who was to speak at ten oclock at the Y.M.C A. grounds. I made it over to the Y. All of the regiment assembled to hear.

He stood in a truck and delivered his speech. I interrupted him and was escorted away by the guards. His address began saying that President Wilson had sent him to France to tell you Negros how proud the Govt. of the United States and the American white people are of their Negros. You Negros have made history in Washinton. . . .

. . . I was so bitter hearing him talk about the slave name Negro like all of our suppose to be leaders has preached Negro for the last fifty years. . . .

Before Moton could resume his address . . . I yelled out: Say, Moton, why in the hell did President Wilson send you over here to tell us how he honors the Negro? . . . We are represented as men to France. So go back to the States and teach that S.O.B. to the Halleluia Negro that don't know any better.

By the time the guards was pushing me away. I was seized by the arms and ushered from the grounds. . . .

Source: Ely Green, *Ely: Too Black, Too White* (Amherst: University of Massachusetts Press, 1970), 391.

Military Intelligence Recommends That Black Troops Be Returned to the United States with the Least Possible Delay, November 18, 1918

After the war ended, American soldiers in France enjoyed an increase in leisure time, which alarmed military officials. Many black men, they feared, would socialize with French women during their off-duty hours, which was bound to offend white soldiers. To prevent an escalation of racial friction, black military intelligence agent Walter H. Loving advocated a quick return of the black troops to the United States.

Now that the war is over, I would like to point out . . . some of the impending dangers which will undoubtedly confront the military authorities should negro troops be kept in France for any great length of time. . . . [T]he negro soldiers who fought bravely and courageously . . . to bring complete victory to the Allies, will naturally look forward to enjoying . . . special passes and furloughs. You will agree with me that he is due these privileges, but what might be the final consequences? The American white man is not unmindful of the fighting value of the negro soldiers, and will fight with them in trenches and on battlefields, but when it comes to meeting the negro at social functions and other paces of amusements where the latter comes in contact with white women . . . the man draws the line. Colored soldiers, like any other soldiers, will seek diversion when the fighting tension . . . is relaxed, and with them diversion and women are synonymous. No American white man, whether he comes from the north or from the south, wants to see colored men mingling with white women in sporting houses and other questionable places. . . . If colored and white soldiers meet under the circumstances above mentioned, I cannot see anything but an American race war in France. Such a catastrophe would be disastrous and disgraceful before the whole civilized world. . . .The brave French soldier who welcomed the American negro on French soil and fought side by side with him . . . might not look with favor on the viewpoint of the American white soldiers, and sympathy for them . . . might draw a few of the French soldiers on the American negro's side. . . . Another point is that should negro soldiers remain in France for any length of time, their stay would give an opportunity for international marriages, which would not be looked upon with favor by either race at home. . . . As a solution to the above problem, I offer the following suggestions: First—That no discharges be given colored soldiers in France. Second—That all colored soldiers now in France be shipped home with the least possible delay. Third—That strictest measures be taken to keep

colored and white soldiers from meeting in places of prostitution while waiting for transportation home.

Source: Walter H. Loving, Confidential Memorandum for General Churchill, Director of Military
Intelligence, November 18, 1918, in National Archives and Records Administration, Washington,
DC, RG 165 War Department: General and Special Staffs—Military Intelligence Division, Case-
file 10218-256.

An Appeal to Black Women, 1917

*Black women provided important services for the troops in the American training
camps as well as those serving overseas. They wrote letters to the men in uniform
to boost their morale and sent them Christmas packages, shaving kits, cigarettes,
chocolate, chewing gum, and magazines. For the soldiers on leave, they hosted
dances, concerts, and dinners. In addition, they organized knitting and sewing
clubs to supply the black troops with much needed clothing items.*

Our Duty
Dear Readers . . . Our men have got to fight and anything that can be done
to help them help others win this war is our duty to do. . . . [I]f you can't knit
then go to the nearest Center and learn; if you feel you can't learn, or don't
want to learn then help buy the yarn that others may knit, who are anxious
to learn. . . .

Ask your grandmother to knit socks. She is usually good at knitting. They
need socks of medium size, evenly and firmly knitted so the finished articles
is without lumps, knots, or ridges to blister the feet in marching. . . . Learn
to knit. But I don't want to knit you say—then learn to sew, learn to hem
sheets properly, and to make pajamas properly, and sew on buttons where you
are told and put tape in correctly. . . .

Then there are the Xmas gifts for the soldier boys. There are three kinds
of kits. Nos. 1-2 and 3 besides the articles contained in either kit you desire
to make, "mirror, metal in case, Safety Razor, Safety Razor blades, Scissors
(preferably folding with pointed ends in sheath. NOT "made in Germany
kind" Shaving Brush and shaving soap are articles especially desired that can
be added to any kit you wish to make or send. Kits number 1 and 2 are for
men on active duty and kit number 3 is for hospital use. Any Red Cross
Chapter will give you directions for making a kit and what articles to equip
it with and will tell you explicitly what not to use and what not to buy. Personal Equipment of Enlisted Men are issued by the War Department. Help
our boys to help whip the "HUNS" by doing your bit. Every little bit helps.
Visit the nearest Center and find out what you can do, then DO IT.

Our men have been drafted and they are going to do their duty as best they can. . . . Few of our men are asking to be exempted. They want the world to know that our race possesses men that any country need be proud of. . . . Petty quarrels with those we love, slights and wounds are all forgotten, we are thinking now of our duty. We haven't time to fret or worry. What's the use anyway? Effort, achievement, honest pride and success, these are the things that we are working to accomplish now, these are the worth while things.

The call may come today—tomorrow. How do we know when, for our men and our boys to answer the Government's call. Boys now, but they will soon prove that they have a man's courage and a man's strength though they lack a few of his years. They are fighting for freedom of speech, freedom to live a man's life as well as for a Nation's Honor. Let us help him to do it all, by knitting and sewing and helping the Red Cross and showing our boys that we are with them heart and hand.

Source: Margaret Black, "Women's Department," *Baltimore Afro-American*, 3 November 1917, 7.

General Charles C. Ballou's Bulletin No. 35, 1918

In the spring of 1918, a black sergeant stationed with the Ninety-Second combat Division in Camp Funston, Kansas, purchased a movie theater ticket in nearby Manhattan. When the white manager assigned him to a segregated seating area, the black soldier complained to his white commander. General Charles C. Ballou ordered an investigation, which revealed that the theater owner had violated state laws that prohibited segregation, and requested the proprietor's prosecution. However, Ballou also issued a bulletin, in which he admonished black soldiers to avoid racial friction and "to refrain from going where their presence will be resented." African Americans were outraged when the black press published the bulletin and the government became increasingly concerned about racial unrest.

Bulletin No. 35
Headquarters Ninety-second Division
   Camp Funston, Kansas
   March 28, 1918

1. It should be well known to all colored officers and men that no useful purpose is served by such acts as will cause the "color question" to be raised. It is not a question of legal rights, but a question of policy, and any policy that tends to bring about a conflict of races, with its

resulting animosities, is prejudicial to an important interest of the colored race.

2. To avoid such conflict the Division Commander has repeatedly urged that all colored members of his command, and especially the officers and non-commissioned officers, should refrain from going where their presence will be resented. In spite of this injunction, one of the Sergeants of the Medical Department has recently precipitated the precise trouble that should be avoided, and then called on the Division Commander to take sides in a row that should never have occurred, and would not have occurred had the Sergeant placed the general good above his personal pleasure and convenience. This Sergeant entered a Theater, as he undoubtedly had a legal right to do, and precipitated trouble by making it possible to allege race discrimination in the seat he was given. He is strictly within his legal rights in this matter, and the theater is legally wrong. Nevertheless the sergeant is guilty of the greater wrong in doing *anything*, no matter how legally correct, that will provoke race animosity.

3. The Division Commander reports that the success of the Division . . . is dependent upon the good will of the public. The public is nine-tenths white. White men made the Division, and they can break it just as easily if it becomes a trouble maker.

4. All concerned are again enjoined to place the general interest of the Division above personal pride and gratification. Avoid every situation that can give rise to racial ill-will. Attend quietly and faithfully to your duties and don't go where your presence is not desired. . . .

By command of Major General Ballou
Allen J. Greer
Lieutenant Colonel, General Staff,
Chief of Staff

Source: Emmett J. Scott, *Scott's Official History of the American Negro in the World War* (n.p., 1919), 97–98.

Resolutions Adopted by the Conference of Black Editors, 1918

In response to growing concerns about low morale among African Americans, the government invited the editors of the most influential black newspapers to attend a three-day conference in the nation's capital. Between June 19 and 21, 1918, black representatives met with various government officials, including the Secretary of War, to discuss allegations of black disloyalty. The black editors insisted that not German propaganda, but poor race relations, particularly lynchings, were responsible for the growing discontent among African Americans. Following the conference, the participants adopted a series of resolutions that assured the Wilson administration of the unwavering loyalty and patriotism of African Americans. However, black representatives also urged the federal government to address racial grievances.

We, the thirty-one representatives of the Negro press . . . wish to confirm, first of all, OUR UNALTERABLE BELIEF THAT THE DEFEAT OF THE GERMAN GOVERNMENT AND WHAT IT TODAY REPRESENTS IS OF PARAMOUNT IMPORTANCE TO THE WELFARE OF THE WORLD IN GENERAL AND TO OUR PEOPLE IN PARTICULAR.

We deem it hardly necessary, in view of the untarnished record of Negro Americans, to reaffirm our loyalty to our country and our readiness to make every sacrifice to win this war. We wish, however, as students and guides of public opinion among our people, to use our every endeavor to keep these 12,000,000 people at the highest pitch, not simply of passive loyalty, but of active enthusiastic and self-sacrificing participation in the war.

We are not unmindful of the recognition of our American citizenship in the draft, of the appointment of Colored officers, of the designation of Colored advisers to the government departments and to other indications of a broadened public opinion; nevertheless we believe today that justifiable grievances of the Colored people are producing not disloyalty, but an amount of unrest and bitterness which even the best efforts of their leaders may not be able always to guide, unless they can have the active and sympathetic cooperation of the national and state governments. German propaganda among us is powerless, but the apparent indifference of our own government may be dangerous.

The American Negro does not expect to have the whole Negro problem settled immediately; he is not seeking to hold up a striving country and a distracted world by pushing irrelevant personal grievances as a price of loyalty; he is not disposed to catalog, in this tremendous crisis, all his complaints and disabilities; he is more than willing to do his full share in helping win the war for democracy and he expects his full share of the fruits thereof—but he is today compelled to ask for that minimum in consideration which will enable him to be an efficient fighter for VICTORY.

Source: "Newspaper Men and Leaders in Important Conference," *Chicago Defender*, 6 July 1918, 4.

W. E. B. Du Bois Urges African Americans to "Close Ranks," 1918

In the wake of the black editors conference, W. E. B. Du Bois published his "Close Ranks" editorial in the NAACP's Crisis magazine. In it Du Bois urged African Americans to support the nation's war effort and forgo the struggle for equal rights for the duration of the war. Many African Americans, particularly members of the black press, were disturbed by Du Bois's uncharacteristic endorsement of accommodation. Since the editorial appeared shortly after the government-sponsored black editors conference, black newspapers charged that Du Bois had sold out to the Wilson administration and betrayed his race. Criticism of Du Bois further escalated when the black press discovered that he had applied for an Army commission in the same week his editorial appeared in the Crisis.

Close Ranks

This is the crisis of the world. For all the long years to come men will point to the year 1918 as the great Day of Decision, the day when the world decided whether it would submit to military despotism and an endless armed peace—if peace it could be called—or whether they would put down the menace of German militarism and inaugurate the United States of the World.

We of the colored race have no ordinary interest in the outcome. That which the German power represents today spells death to the aspirations of Negroes and all darker races for equality, freedom and democracy. Let us not hesitate. Let us, while this war lasts, forget our special grievances and close our ranks shoulder to shoulder with our own white fellow citizens and the allied nations that are fighting for democracy. We make no ordinary sacrifice, but we make it gladly and willingly with our eyes lifted to the hills.

War Saving Stamps

A correspondent writes us: "Has there been put in operation any effective machinery for bringing our twelve million colored citizens, especially those living in the Southern States, into this great national movement for Thrift and Economy, represented by the War Savings Stamp movement? This movement is to have a profound effect on the character of the American people; millions of prodigal, shiftless Americans are going to learn their first lessons in Thrift and Economy through buying Thrift Stamps and War Savings Stamps. It is obvious that our colored citizens should share to the full the benefits as well as the responsibilities of the movement.

"It is a voluntary effort. Thousands of voluntary committees are working to inculcate the lessons of Thrift and inspire voluntary purchase of stamps."

We are glad to say that such a movement has begun. Various organizations are taking hold and the National Association for the Advancement of Colored People will use its more than 30,000 members in 108 branches to push this splendid movement.

Remember, June twenty-eight is National War Savings Day!

Source: "Close Ranks," *Crisis* (July 1918), 111.

President Woodrow Wilson Condemns Mob Violence, 1918

Race leaders had urged the president to speak out against lynchings and other racial violence since the start of the war. They were particularly disappointed when Wilson failed to condemn the atrocities committed during the bloody race riot that had erupted in East St. Louis in July of 1917. It was not until the summer of 1918, a year after the riot, that the president finally issued a statement condemning mob violence. By then, the government had become increasingly concerned about alleged subversive activities of German agents, who were exploiting racial violence to undermine black support of the war.

A Statement to the American People

July 26, 1918

My Fellow Countrymen: I take the liberty of addressing you upon a subject which so vitally affects the honor of the Nation and the very character and integrity of our institutions that I trust you will think me justified in speaking very plainly about it.

I allude to the mob spirit which has recently here and there very frequently shown its head amongst us, not in any single region, but in many and widely separated parts of the country. There have been many lynchings, and every one of them has been a blow at the heart of ordered law and humane justice. No man who loves America, no man who really cares for her fame and honor and character, or who is truly loyal to her institutions, can justify mob action while the courts of justice are open and the governments of the States and the Nation are ready and able to do their duty. We are at this very moment fighting lawless passion. Germany has outlawed herself among the nations because she has disregarded the sacred obligations of law and has made lynchers of her armies. Lynchers emulate her disgraceful example. I, for my part, am anxious to see every community in America rise above that level with pride and fixed resolution which no man or set of men can afford to despise.

We proudly claim to be the champions of democracy. If we really are . . . let us see to it that we do not discredit our own. I say plainly that every American who takes part in the action of a mob or gives it any sort of countenance is no true son of this great Democracy, but its betrayer. . . . How shall we commend democracy to the acceptance of other peoples, if we disgrace our own by proving that it is, after all, no protection to the weak? . . .

I therefore earnestly and solemnly beg that the governors of all the States, the law officers of every community, and above all, the men and women of every community in the United States, all who revere America and wish to keep her name without stain or reproach, will cooperate—not passively merely, but actively and watchfully—to make an end of this disgraceful evil. It cannot live where the community does not countenance it.

I have called upon the Nation to put its great energy into this war and it has responded. . . . I now call upon it, upon its men and women everywhere, to see to it that its laws are kept inviolate, its fame untarnished. Let us show our utter contempt for the things that have made this war hideous among the wars of history by showing how those who love liberty and right and justice and are willing to lay down their lives for them upon foreign fields stand ready also to illustrate to all mankind their loyalty to the things at home which they wish to see established everywhere as a blessing and protection to the peoples who have never known the privileges of liberty and self-government. I can never accept any man as a champion of liberty either for ourselves or for the world who does not reverence and obey the laws of our own beloved land, whose laws we ourselves made. He has adopted the standards of the enemies of his country, whom he affects to despise.

Woodrow Wilson

Source: Arthur S. Link, ed., *The Papers of Woodrow Wilson* vol. 49 (Princeton, NJ: Princeton University Press, 1985), 97–98.

Government Concerns about the Demobilization of Black Troops, 1918

After the war, military officials became concerned about reintegrating black soldiers into civilian society. White Southerners, they feared, would respond with violence to black veterans, particularly those still wearing their uniforms. To assure the peaceful demobilization of black troops as well as the safety of black soldiers, some military officials suggested close collaboration between the Army and representatives of Southern governments. However, the Wilson administration failed to heed their advice and many black veterans faced angry white mobs.

Statement

1. The writer has received within the past few days a number of disquieting reports in personal letters, and in personal interview with Southern visitors in Washington, involving one phase of the work of demobilization. It is not quite clear in my mind whether this problem is one for Military Intelligence or the Morale Branch of the army, but it is self-evident that it should be given attention in some official quarter, and the work should be started ahead of the homeward flow of troops from Europe.

2. I refer specifically to the matter of converting the negro soldiers into civilians once more, and the strong probability that there will be numerous racial clashes in the South unless this matter is properly handled, and a campaign of preparedness diplomatically conducted.

3. Some of the Southern citizens with whom I have talked—and they are not alarmists—do not believe that negro troops should be brought into the South as such; that their homecoming should be as individuals, and not in uniform, if this can possibly be avoided. This, of course, appears to be the extreme view, and at the same time a denial of the right accorded by the War Department to discharged soldiers—wearing of the uniform for a period of three months after discharge.

4. While the problem reverts to the states after negro soldiers leave the service, at the same time there is a growing belief in the South that the federal government should not leave it wholly to the states; that plans should be formed now whereby this prospective trouble will be reduced to a minimum, and it can only be accomplished though close cooperation and thorough understanding between Federal and state authorities before the negroes return.

5. It is needless to point out that the negro soldier returning from France will not be the same sort of negro he was before donning the uniform. The Military Intelligence Division is well acquainted with the new ideas and social aspirations our negro troops have gathered in France, and particularly from his association with the French demi monde. Obviously, if he attempts to carry those ideas back into the South . . . an era of bloodshed will follow as compared with which the history of reconstruction will be mild reading, indeed.

6. I am advised that in at least one Southern state, Alabama, steps are already being taken to meet this problem; that the Governor of that state recently called a secret conference of citizens for its discussion. . . . As to just how Alabama intends to deal with the question, I am not advised.

7. Any person familiar with the South, and its ever-present race problem need not be reminded that the negro soldier strutting about in uniform three months after his discharge will always be a potential danger, especially if he happens to be of the type inclined to impudence and arrogance . . .

Conclusion

8. . . . I am thoroughly convinced that this question deserves immediate consideration, and would respectfully offer this suggestion:

(a) That officers who are thoroughly conversant with the South, and particularly the negro problems, be detailed to visit the Governors of the several Southern states, hold confidential interviews, and ascertain what plans, if any, the state authorities are forming to deal with the problem.

(b) That ways and means of securing the adoption of a policy of tolerance and conservatism toward the returning negro soldiers be discussed, and a system of propaganda planned that will instill into the minds of whites and blacks alike a proper attitude on the subject. In this work, I am quite sure, the press of the South will give hearty cooperation. . . .

(c) Enlist the negro clergy in the work. The negro has no political leaders. His preacher is always his surest and safest guide. . . .

9. To defer action on this matter would be akin to locking the stable door after the horse has been stolen. If those in authority wait until the negro troops have been actually returned and demobilized, it will then be everlastingly too late. Speaking now as a citizen who knows the negro and the troubles that have beset his pathway in the upward climb from slavery, I feel it would be a gross injustice to the race to turn the negro soldiers loose without some precautions being taken, both for their restraint and their protection. They went into the army willingly, and have served faithfully. If many of them have had false ideas instilled into their minds during the period of service it is more a misfortune than their fault. Also, it should be borne in mind that thousand of those negroes who return home will not be trouble-makers, yet they are likely to become the innocent sufferers for the ignorance, arrogance, and wrong aspirations of others. They were ready and willing to sacrifice their lives in time of war. Certainly, they should be protected in time of peace.

Source: F. Sullens to Major Brown, November 30, 1918, Casefile 10218-289, in *Federal Surveillance of Afro-Americans, 1917–1925*, ed. Theodore Kornweibel (Frederick, MD: University Publications of America, 1985), reel 21, frames 175–77.

Returning to Racism

Following World War I, African Americans hoped that, after they had helped "to make the world safe for democracy," the nation could no longer deny them civil rights. However, instead of receiving equal rights, they faced white hostility. The number of lynchings increased from sixty-three in 1918 to seventy-seven in 1919, and race riots erupted in numerous cities throughout the country. The following editorials demonstrate the different attitudes of blacks and whites in the aftermath of the war. Mississippi governor Theodore Bilbo expressed the beliefs of many white Southerners, who insisted on maintaining white supremacy and advocated violence to uphold the racial status quo. African Americans, as illustrated by Du Bois's editorial, were not willing to accept Jim Crow and were determined to fight racism, segregation, and discrimination.

Mississippi Governor Theodore Bilbo Issues "Creed of South," 1919

Mob violence is deplored by all thoughtful citizens, and, as governor of the state, I have done everything in my power to enforce the law in an orderly way. However, it is practically impossible, without great loss of life, especially at the present time, to prevent lynching of Negro rapists when the crime is committed against the white women of the South.

There is considerable feeling and bitter resentment on the part of the white people of the South brought about by the attempt of the Negro Race to seek social and political equality. This desire on the part of the Negro seems to have increased since the world war by the social reception and familiarity with the Negro soldiers by a certain class of white women in France. Fuel is added to the flames by the Negro propaganda through the Northern Negro press. Certain Negro newspapers have been circulated in the South urging that the only solution of the race question is intermarriage of the races. . . .

The attempted interference of certain Negro associations of the North in the adjustment of the race question in the South is resented by the Southern white man, and, in my judgement, is doing more harm than good. This is strictly a white man's country, with a white man's civilization, and any dream on the part of the Negro Race to share social and political equality will be shattered in the end. If the Northern Negro lover wants to stop Negro lynching in the South, they must first get the right conception of the proper relation that must necessarily exist between the races and teach and train the Negro Race along these lines and in this way remove the cause of lynching. The better class of whites and blacks of the South understand each other, and if let alone they will be able to solve their own problems and will live together on proper and peaceful terms.

Source: *Chicago Defender*, 12 July, 1919, 1.

W. E. B. Du Bois, "Returning Soldiers," 1919

We are returning from war! The *Crisis* and tens of thousands of black men were drafted into a great struggle. For bleeding France and what she means and has meant and will mean to us and humanity and against the threat of German race arrogance, we fought gladly and to the last drop of blood; for America and her highest ideals, we fought in far-off hope; for the dominant southern oligarchy entrenched in Washington, we fought in bitter resignation. For the America that represents and gloats in lynching, disfranchisement, caste, brutality, and devilish insult—for this, in the hateful upturning and mixing of things, we were forced by vindictive fate to fight, also.

But today we return! . . . We sing: This country of ours, despite all its better souls have done and dreamed, is yet a shameful land.

It *lynches*.

And lynching is barbarism of a degree of contemptible nastiness unparalleled in human history. Yet for fifty years we have lynched two Negroes a week, and we have kept this up right through the war.

It *disfranchises* its own citizens.

Disfranchisement is the deliberate theft and robbery of the only protection of poor against rich and black against white. The land that disfranchises its citizens and calls itself a democracy lies and knows it lies.

It encourages *ignorance*.

It has never really tried to educate the Negro. A dominant minority does not want Negroes educated. It wants servants, dogs, whores, and monkeys. . . .

It *steals* from us.

It organizes industry to cheat us. It cheats us out of our land; it cheats us out of our labor. It confiscates our savings. It reduces our wages. It raises our rent. It steals our profit. It taxes us without representation. It keeps us consistently and universally poor, and then it feeds us on charity and derides our poverty.

It *insults* us.

It has organized a nation-wide and latterly a world-wide propaganda of deliberate and continuous insult and defamation of black blood wherever found. . . . And it looks upon any attempt to question or even discuss this dogma as arrogance, unwarranted assumption and treason.

This is the country to which we Soldiers of Democracy return. This is the fatherland for which we fought! But it is *our* fatherland. It was right for us to fight. The faults of *our* country are *our* faults. Under similar circumstances, we would fight again. But by the God of Heaven, we are cowards and jack-asses if now that that war is over, we do not marshal every ounce of our brain and brawn to fight a sterner, longer, more unbending battle against the forces of hell in our own land.

We *return*.

We *return from fighting*.

We *return fighting*.

Make way for Democracy! We saved it in France, and by the Great Jehovah, we will save it in the United States of America, or know the reason why.

Source: Du Bois, W. E. B., "Documents of the War," *Crisis* (May 1919), 13–14.

The Red Summer of 1919

Postwar white resistance to racial progress was not limited to the South. In the summer of 1919, numerous race riots erupted in the North, where black migrants and returning black and white soldiers competed for jobs and housing. The racial unrest resulted in so much bloodshed that the NAACP's field secretary, James Weldon Johnson, called it the "Red Summer." The most deadly of the riots occurred in Chicago, where black and white residents fought for thirteen days, causing the death of fifteen whites and twenty-three African Americans and the destruction of over a million dollars worth of property.

The Chicago Race Riot of 1919—"Orgy of Hate"
Defender Reporter Faces Death in Attempt to Get Facts of Mob Violence; Hospitals Are Filled With Maimed Men and Women
For fully four days this old city has been rocked in a quake of racial antagonism, seared in a blaze of red hate flaming as fiercely as the heat of day—each hour ushering in new stories of slaying, looting, arson, rapine, sending the awful roll of casualties to a grand total of 40 dead and more than 500 wounded, many of them perhaps fatally. . . .

Stores and Offices Shut
Victims lay in every street and vacant lot. Hospitals are filled: 4,000 troops rest in arms, among which are companies of the old Eighth regiment while the inadequate force of police battle vainly to save the city's honor.

Fear to Care for Bodies
Undertakers on the South Side refused to accept bodies of white victims.
White undertakers refused to accept black victims. Both for the same rea-
sons. They feared the anger of the grief stricken mourners.

Every little while bodies were found in some street, alley or vacant lot—
and no one sought to care for them. Patrols were unable to accommodate
them because they were being used in rushing live victims to hospitals. Some
victims were dragged to a mob's "No Man's Land" and dropped. . . .

Hospitals Filled with Maimed
Provident hospital, 36th and Dearborn streets, situated in the heart of the
"black belt," as well as other hospitals in the surrounding districts, are filled
with the maimed and dying every hour, every minute, every second finds
patrols backed up and unloading the human freight branded with the red
symbol of this orgy of hate. Many victims have reached the hospitals, only to
die before kind hands could attend to them. So pressing as the situation became that schools, drug stores and private houses are being used. Trucks,
drays and hearses are being used for ambulances.

Monday Sees "Reign of Terror"
. . . Monday morning found the thoroughfares in the white neighborhoods
throated with a sea of humans—everywhere—some armed with guns, bricks,
clubs and an oath. The presence of a black face in their vicinity was the signal
for a carnival of death and before any aid could reach the poor, unfortunate
one, his body reposed in some kindly gutter, his brain spilled over a dirty pavement. Some of the victims were chased, caught and ragged into alley and lots,
where they were left for dead. In all parts of the city, white mobs dragged from
surface cars, black passengers wholly ignorant of any trouble, and set upon
them. An unidentified woman and a 3 month old baby were found dead on the
street at the intersection of 17th street and Wentworth avenue. She had attempted to board a car there when the mob seized her, beat her, slashed her
body into ribbons and beat the baby's brains out against a telegraph pole. Not
satisfied with this, one rioter severed her breasts, and a white youngster bore it
aloft on a pole, triumphantly, while the crowd hooted gleefully. All the time,
this was happening, several policemen were in the crowd, but did not make any
attempt to make rescue until too late.

Kill Scores Coming from Yards
Rioters operating in the vicinity of the stockyards . . . attacked scores of
workers—women and men alike returning from work. Stories of these out-

rages began to flutter into the black vicinities and hysterical men harangued their fellows to avenge the killings—and soon they, infected with the insanity of the mob, rushed through the streets, drove high powered motor cars or waited for street car which they attacked with gunfire and stones. . . .

Police employed in the disturbed sections were wholly unable to handle the situation. When one did attempt to carry out his duty he was beaten and his gun taken from him. The fury of the mob could not be abated. Mounted police were employed but to no avail.

35th Vortex of Night's Rioting
With the approach of darkness the rioting gave prospects of being continued throughout the night. Whites boarded the platforms and shot through the windows of the trains at passengers. Some of the passengers alighting from cars were thrown from the elevated structure, suffering broken legs, fractured skulls, and death. . . .

Police were shot. Whites were seen to tumble out of automobiles, from doorways and others places, wounded or suffering from bruises, inflicted by gunshot, stones or bricks. A reign of terror literally ensued. Automobiles were stopped, occupants beaten and machines wrecked. . . .

Tiring of street fights, rioters turned to burning and looting. . . . The homes of blacks isolated in white neighborhoods were burned to the ground and the owners and occupants beaten and thrown unconscious in the smoldering embers. Meanwhile rioters in the "black belt" smashed windows and looted shops of white merchants on State street. . . .

Toward midnight quiet reigned along State street under the vigilance of 400 policemen and scores of uniformed men of the 8th Regiment. . . .

Source: "Ghastly Deeds of Rioters Told," *Chicago Defender*, 2 August 1919.

Poet Claude McKay Encourages the Use of Violence, 1919

Jamaican born poet Claude McKay wrote his poem "If We Must Die" during the Chicago Race riot. At that time, he worked as a waiter on a railroad that serviced New York, Philadelphia, Pittsburgh, and Washington, D.C.—cities that had attracted large numbers of black migrants during the war. He later recalled that several of his black coworkers secretly carried guns to protect themselves against white violence. McKay's poem, first published in the Liberator *in July 1919, reflected the disillusionment and anger of African Americans following World War I and their growing determination to resist white racism by all means necessary. McKay's "If We Must Die" not only attracted the attention of African Americans but also the*

Department of Justice which investigated the radical poet as a threat to national security.

If We Must Die, 1919
Claude McKay

If we must die, let it not be like hogs
Hunted and penned in an inglorious spot
While round us bark the mad and hungry dogs
Making their mock at our accursed lot.
If we must die, Oh, let us nobly die,
So that our precious blood may not be shed
In vain; then even the monsters we defy
Shall be constrained to honor us though dead
Oh, kinsman! We must meet the common foe;
Though far outnumbered, let us still be brave,
And for their thousand blows deal one death blow!
What though before us lies the open grave?
Like men we'll face the murderous, cowardly pack,
Pressed to the wall, dying, but fighting back!

Source: *Senate Documents*, vol. 12, 66th Congress, 1st Session, May 19–November 19, 1919 (Washington, DC: Government Printing Office, 1919), 167.

~

Notes

Notes to Introduction

1. Crisis (July 1918), 111.
2. Crisis (September 1918), 217.

Notes to Chapter 1

1. "More Slavery at the South," *Independent* 72, 25 (January 1912).
2. Quoted in George Edmund Haynes, "Conditions among Negroes in the Cities," *Annals of the American Academy of Political and Social Science* (September 1913), 112.
3. Darlene Clark Hine and Kathleen Thompson, *A Shining Thread of Hope: The History of Black Women in America* (New York: Broadway Books, 1998), 183.
4. Nancy J. Weiss, "The Negro and the New Freedom: Fighting Wilsonian Segregation," *Political Science Quarterly* (March 1969), 64.
5. Quoted in Christine A. Lunardini, "Standing Firm: William Monroe Trotter's Meeting with Woodrow Wilson, 1913–1914," *Journal of Negro History* (Summer 1979), 43.

Notes to Chapter 2

1. Quoted in U.S. Department of Labor, Office of the Secretary, Division of Negro Economics, *Negro Migration in 1916–1917* (New York: Negro Universities Press, 1919), 107.
2. *Times-Picayune*, 15 December 1916.
3. Greenville, South Carolina, *Piedmont*, quoted in W. E .B. Du Bois, "The Migration of the Negroes," *Crisis* (June 1917), 65.

4. Quoted in U.S. Department of Labor, Office of the Secretary, Division of Negro Economics, *Negro Migration in 1916–1917* (New York: Negro Universities Press, 1919), 31.

5. *Southwestern Christian Advocate*, 5 April 1917.

6. Quoted in *Norfolk New-Journal and Guide*, 24 March 1917, 4.

7. "The National Urban League Discusses 'Migration' Question," *Cleveland Advocate*, 9 December 1916, 1.

8. Emmett J. Scott, "Additional Letters of Negro Migrants of 1916–1918," *Journal of Negro History* 4 (October 1919), 461.

9. Quoted in Roi Ottley, *The Lonely Warrior: The Life and Times of Robert S. Abbott* (Chicago: Henry Regnery Company, 1955), 170.

10. *Christian Recorder*, 31 August 1916.

11. Elaine Latzman Moon, *Untold Tales, Unsung Heroes: An Oral History of Detroit's African American Community, 1918–1967* (Detroit: Wayne State University Press, 1994), 94.

12. "Some Don'ts," *Chicago Defender*, 17 May 1919, 2.

Notes to Chapter 3

1. Francis J. Grimké, *The Collected Works of Francis J. Grimké*, ed. Carter G. Woodson (Washington, DC: Associated Publishers, 1942), vol. 3, 26.

2. Jeanette Keith, *Rich Man's War, Poor Man's Fight: Race, Class, and Power in the Rural South during the First World War* (Chapel Hill: University of North Carolina Press, 2004), 43.

3. *Chicago Defender*, 28 April 1917, 3.

4. *Crisis* (April 1917), 270–71.

5. *Crisis* (June 1917), 59.

6. George S. Schuyler, *Black and Conservative: The Autobiography of George S. Schuyler* (New Rochelle, NY: Arlington House Publishers, 1966), 88.

7. *Cleveland Gazette*, 18 August 1917.

8. Quoted in *Crisis* (July 1917), 138.

9. *Philadelphia Tribune*, 1 September 1917, 4.

10. *Crisis* (October 17, 1917), 284–85.

11. Newton D. Baker to Emmett J. Scott, November 30, 1917, reprinted in Emmett J. Scott, *Scott's Official History of the American Negro in the World War* (Chicago: Homewood Press, 1919), 59.

12. Quoted in Emmett J. Scott, "The Participation of Negroes in World War I: An Introductory Statement," *Journal of Negro Education* 12 (Summer 1943), 290.

Notes to Chapter 4

1. "Personal Experiences of a Black Veteran in World War I: An Interview with Eugene B. Bailey, New Castle, Indiana," compiled and edited by Wayne L. Sanford (Indianapolis: Indiana Historical Society, Military History Section, 1982), 5; "8th

Illinois Regiment Gets Big Send-Off," *Baltimore Afro-American*, 8 September 1917, 1; and Letter to W. E. B. Du Bois, February 25, 1918, W. E. B. Du Bois Papers, box 54, Fisk University, Nashville, Tennessee.

2. Quoted in *Baltimore Afro-American*, 30 August 1918, 4.

3. Harry Haywood, *Black Bolshevik* (Chicago: Liberator Press, 1978), 45.

4. Diary of Ralph D. Taylor, January 3, 1918, diary in possession of the author.

5. Quoted in Mark Ellis, *Race, War, and Surveillance: African Americans and the United States Government during World War I* (Bloomington: Indiana University Press, 2001), 90.

6. Newton D. Baker to W. E. B. Du Bois, December 13, 1917, *The Papers of W. E. B. Du Bois, 1803 (1877–1963) 1965* (New York: Microfilming Corporation of America, 1981), reel 5.

7. Emmett J. Scott, *The American Negro in the World War* (n.p., 1919), 95.

8. Charles H. Williams, *Sidelights on Negro Soldiers* (Boston: B. J. Brimmer Co., 1923), 26.

9. U.S. Congress, House, Hearing before the Committee on Education, H.R. 6490, 65th Cong., 2d sess., 4 March 1918, 8.

10. "Illiteracy and the War," *New York Age*, 30 March 1918, 4.

11. Harrison J. Pinkett to Miss Ovington, January 19, 1918, W. E. B. Du Bois Papers, box 56, Fisk University, Nashville, Tennessee.

12. "Personal Experiences of a Black Veteran in World War I," 14.

Notes to Chapter 5

1. Diary of Ralph D. Taylor, April 14, 1918, diary in possession of the author.

2. Ely Green, *Ely: Too Black, Too White* (Amherst: University of Massachusetts Press, 1970), 360.

3. Ibid., 368.

4. Quoted in "The Colored Soldier in the US Army: World War I," memorandum for Colonel Ralph L. Tate, 19 May 1942, Carlisle Barracks.

5. Diary of Ralph D. Taylor, May 27, 1918, diary in possession of the author.

6. Addie W. Hunton and Kathryn M. Johnson, *Two Colored Women with the American Expeditionary Forces* (Brooklyn: Eagle Press, 1920), 184.

7. *Afro-American*, 11 July 1919, p.4.

8. Diary of Ralph D. Taylor, September 21, 1918, diary in possession of the author.

9. *New York Times*, 7 February 1918, 9.

10. *Afro-American*, 17 October 1919, 4.

11. Corporal Reuel M. Jordan, "The Plight of the Ninety-Second Division," n.d., W. E. B. Du Bois Papers, Fisk University, Nashville, Tennessee, box 56.

12. Ralph W. Tyler Sr. to George A. Myers, January 26, 1919, George A. Myers Papers, Ohio Historical Society, box 17, folder 4.

13. Green, *Ely: Too Black, Too White*, 391.

14. *Afro-American*, 2 May 1919, 1.

15. W. E. B. Du Bois, "An Essay Toward a History of the Black Man in the Great War," *Crisis* (June 1919), 72.

Notes to Chapter 6

1. W. E. B. Du Bois, "Close Ranks," *Crisis* (July 1918), 111.

2. Emmett J. Scott, *Scott's Official History of the American Negro in the World War* (Chicago: Homewood Press, 1919), 97–98.

3. *Crisis* (December 1917), 85.

4. Scott, *Scott's Official History*, 92.

5. Joel E. Spingarn to Colonel Marlborough Churchill, Chief, Military Intelligence Branch, June 22, 1918, in *Federal Surveillance of Afro-Americans, 1917–1925*, ed. Theodore Kornweibel (Frederick, MD: University Publications of America, 1985), reel 19, frame 732.

6. *New York Times*, 7 July 1918, 58.

7. *Philadelphia Tribune*, 6 July 1918, 1.

8. Spingarn to Churchill, in *Federal Surveillance of Afro-Americans*, reel 19, frame 733.

9. Arthur H. Fleming, Chief of Section, Council of National Defense, "Organization of Negroes," 24 July 1918, National Archives and Records Administration, Washington, DC, RG 4, box 591.

Notes to Epilogue

1. John R. Williams, "A Trench Letter," 1918, W. E. B. Du Bois Papers, Fisk University, Nashville, Tennessee, box 56.

2. *Philadelphia Tribune*, 14 September 1918, 4.

3. "Minutes of the Meeting of the Board of Directors," 9 April 1917, *Papers of the NAACP Part 1, 1909–50: Meetings of the Board of Directors, Records of Annual Conferences, Major Speeches, and Special Reports*, reel 1, frame 536.

4. Newton D. Baker to Emmett J. Scott, 30 November 1917, published in *Afro-American*, 8 December 1917, 4.

5. F. Sullens to Major Brown, November 30, 1918, Casefile 10218-289, in *Federal Surveillance of Afro-Americans, 1917–1925*, ed. Theodore Kornweibel (Frederick, MD: University Publications of America, 1985), reel 21, frames 175–77.

6. Quoted in John B. Cade, *Twenty-Two Months with "Uncle Sam": Being the Experiences and Observations of a Negro Student Who Volunteered for Military Service against the Central Powers from June, 1917, to April, 1919* (Atlanta, GA: Robinson-Cofer Co., 1929), 125.

7. *Chicago Defender*, 12 July 1919, 1.

8. Quoted in Jane and Harry Scheiber, "The Wilson Administration and the Wartime Mobilization of Black Americans," *Labor History* 10, (Summer, 1969), 449

9. *Crisis* (May 1919), 13–14.

10. Walter Howard Loving to director, Military Intelligence, 18 March 1919, in Walter Howard Loving Papers, Moorland-Spingarn Research Center, Howard University, Washington, D.C., box 113-1, no. 12.

~

Bibliographic Essay

Many scholars have explored various aspects of the African American experience during World War I. Much of the scholarship has focused on racial conditions during the war, the relationship between African Americans and the Wilson administration, the impact of the wartime migration, the role of the black press, and black military service.

Studies that examine racial conditions in the South prior to and during the war include C. Vann Woodward's classic *The Strange Career of Jim Crow* (1955; repr., New York: Oxford University Press, 2001); John Dittmer, *Black Georgia in the Progressive Era, 1900–1920* (Urbana: University of Illinois Press, 1977); Joel Williamson, *The Crucible of Race: Black-White Relations in the American South Since Emancipation* (New York: Oxford University Press, 1984); Neil R. McMillen, *Dark Journey: Black Mississippians in the Age of Jim Crow* (Urbana: University of Illinois Press, 1989); Leon F. Litwack, *Trouble in Mind: Black Southerners in the Age of Jim Crow* (New York: Alfred A. Knopf, 1998); and Steven Hahn, *A Nation under Our Feet: Black Political Struggles in the Rural South from Slavery to the Great Migration* (Cambridge, MA: Harvard University Press, 2003).

Urban black communities are discussed in Mark R. Schneider, *Boston Confronts Jim Crow, 1890–1920* (Boston: Northeastern University Press, 1997); Earl Lewis, *In Their Own Interest Race, Class and Power in Twentieth-Century Norfolk, Virginia* (Berkeley: University of California Press, 1991); Joe William Trotter Jr., *Black Milwaukee: The Making of an Industrial Proletariat* (Urbana: University of Illinois Press, 1988); George C. Wright, *Life Behind a Veil: Blacks in Louisville, Kentucky, 1865–1930* (Baton Rouge: Louisiana State University Press, 1985); Thomas L. Philpott, *The Slum and the Ghetto: Neighborhood Deterioration and Middle-Class Reform, Chicago 1880–1930* (New York: Oxford University Press, 1978); James Borchert, *Alley Life in Washington: Family, Community, Religion, and Folklife in the City, 1850–1970* (Urbana: University of Illinois Press, 1980); Alan H Spear,

Black Chicago: The Making of Negro Ghetto, 1890–1920 (Chicago: University of Chicago Press, 1967); and Gilbert Osofsky, *Harlem: The Making of a Ghetto, Negro New York 1890–1930* (New York: Harper & Row, 1963).

Other books that illustrate racial conditions during the Jim Crow era include Christopher Waldrep, *African Americans Confront Lynching: Strategies of Resistance from the Civil War to the Civil Rights Era* (Lanham, MD: Rowman & Littlefield, 2009) and W. Michael Byrd and Linda A. Clayton's, *An American Health Dilemma: A Medical History of African Americans and the Problem of Race*, 2 vols. (New York: Routledge, 2002). For the experience of black women during the Jim Crow era see Tera W. Hunter, *To 'Joy My Freedom: Southern Black Women's Lives and Labors after the Civil War* (Cambridge, MA: Harvard University Press, 1997) and Jacqueline Jones, *Labor of Love, Labor of Sorrow: Black Women, Work and the Family, from Slavery to the Present* (New York: Basic Books, 1985). For black efforts to obtain education see James D. Anderson, *The Education of Blacks in the South 1860–1935* (Chapel Hill: University of North Carolina Press, 1988). Studies that analyze class divisions within the black community are Willard B. Gatewood, *Aristocrats of Color: The Black Elite, 1880–1920* (Bloomington: Indiana University Press, 1990) and Jacqueline M. Moore, *Leading the Race: The Transformation of the Black Elite in the Nation's Capital, 1880–1920* (Charlottesville: University Press of Virginia, 1999).

The impact of the wartime migration is captured in numerous contemporary reports and studies, including Carter G. Woodson, *A Century of Negro Migration* (Washington, DC: Association for the Study of Negro Life and History, 1918); U.S. Department of Labor, *Negro Migration in 1916–1917* (Washington, DC: Government Printing Office, 1919); Emmett J. Scott "Letters of Negro Migrants of 1916–1918," *Journal of Negro History* 4 (July 1919): 290–340, "Additional Letters of Negro Migrants of 1916–1918," *Journal of Negro History* 4 (October 1919): 412–75, and *Negro Migration during the War* (New York: Oxford University Press, 1920); Thomas J. Woofter Jr., *Negro Migration: Changes in Rural Organization and Population of the Cotton Belt* (New York: W.D. Gray, 1920); and Donald Henderson, "The Negro Migration, 1916–1918," *Journal of Negro History* 6, 4 (1921): 383–409.

Scholarly analyses of the Great Migration include Robert B. Grant's, *The Black Man Comes to the City: A Documentary Account from the Great Migration to the Great Depression, 1915–1930* (Chicago: Nelson-Hall Company, 1972); Florette Henri, *Black Migration: Movement North, 1900–1920* (Garden City, NY: Anchor Books, 1976); Sam Marullo, "The Migration of Blacks to the North, 1911–1918," *Journal of Black Studies* 15 (1985): 291–306; Carol Marks, *Farewell—We're Good and Gone: The Great Black Migration* (Bloomington: Indiana University Press, 1989) and "Black Workers and the Great Migration North," *Phylon* 46 (1985): 148–61; Alferdteen Harrison, ed., *Black Exodus: The Great Migration from the American South* (Jackson: University Press of Mississippi, 1991); Joe William Trotter Jr., ed. *The Great Migration in Historical Perspective: New Dimensions of Race, Class, and Gender* (Bloomington: Indiana University Press, 1991) and "African Americans in the City: The Industrial Era, 1900–1950," *Journal of Urban History* 21 (1995): 438–57; Milton C. Sernett, *Bound for the Promised Land: African American Religion and the Great Migration* (Durham, NC: Duke University Press, 1997); Eric Arnesen, *Black Protest and the Great Migration: A Brief History with Documents* (Boston: Bedford/St.

Martin's Press, 2003); and James N. Gregory, *The Southern Diaspora: How the Great Migrations of Black and White Southerners Transformed America* (Chapel Hill: University of North Carolina Press, 2005). A good reference source is Steven A. Reich, *Encyclopedia of the Great Black Migration*, 3 vols. (Westport, CT: Greenwood Press, 2006).

For insight into the impact of the Great Migration on specific cities see Kenneth L. Kusmer, *A Ghetto Takes Shape: Black Cleveland, 1870–1930* (Urbana: University of Illinois Press, 1976); Peter Gottlieb: *Making Their Own Way: Southern Blacks' Migration to Pittsburgh, 1916–1930* (Urbana: University of Illinois Press, 1987); James R. Grossman, *Land of Hope: Chicago, Black Southerners, and the Great Migration* (Chicago: University of Chicago Press, 1989); Kenneth L. Kusmer, ed., *The Great Migration and After, 1917–1930* (New York: Garland Publishing, 1991); Richard W. Thomas, *Life for Us Is What We Make It: Building Black Community in Detroit, 1915–1945* (Bloomington: University of Indiana Press, 1992); and Kimberley L. Phillips, *AlabamaNorth: African-American Migrants, Community, and Working-Class Activism in Cleveland, 1915–45* (Urbana: University of Illinois Press, 1999).

For an overview of the Urban League's efforts to assist African Americans see Arvarh E. Strickland, *History of the Chicago Urban League* (Urbana: University of Illinois Press, 1966); Guichard Parris and Lester Brooks, *Blacks in the City: A History of the National Urban League* (Boston: Little, Brown and Company, 1971); Nancy J. Weiss, *The National Urban League: 1910–1940* (New York: Oxford University Press, 1974); Jesse Thomas Moore Jr., *A Search for Equality: The National Urban League, 1910–1961* (University Park: Pennsylvania State University Press, 1981); and Touré F. Reed, *Not Alms but Opportunity: The Urban League and the Politics of Racial Uplift, 1910–1950* (Chapel Hill: University of North Carolina Press, 2008).

Studies focusing on the Wilson administration's relationship with African Americans are Henry Blumenthal, "Woodrow Wilson and the Race Question," *Journal of Negro History* 48, 1 (January 1963): 1–21; Rayford Logan, *The Betrayal of the Negro: From Rutherford B. Hayes to Woodrow Wilson* (1965; repr., New York: Da Capo Press, 1997); Jane L. and Harry N. Scheiber, "The Wilson Administration and the Wartime Mobilization of Black Americans, 1917–1918," *Labor History* 10, 3 (1969): 433–458; Nancy J. Weiss, "The Negro and the New Freedom: Fighting Wilsonian Segregation," *Political Science Quarterly* 84, 1 (March 1969): 61–79; Morton Sosna, "The South in the Saddle: Racial Politics during the Wilson Years," *Wisconsin Magazine of History* 54 (Fall 1970): 30–49; Jonathan Rosenberg, *How Far the Promised Land? World Affairs and the American Civil Rights Movement from the First World War to Vietnam* (Princeton, NJ: Princeton University Press, 2006) and "For Democracy, Not Hypocrisy: World War and Race Relations in the United States, 1914–1919," *International History Review* 21, 3 (September 1999): 592–625; Nicholas Patler, *Jim Crow and the Wilson Administration: Protesting Federal Segregation in the Early Twentieth Century* (Boulder: University Press of Colorado, 2004); and Eric S. Yellin, "In the Nation's Service: Racism and Federal Employees in Woodrow Wilson's Washington" (PhD diss., Princeton University, 2008).

The war's impact on black industrial employment is discussed in George E. Haynes, "The Effect of War Conditions on Negro Labor," *Proceedings of the Academy of Political*

Science 8, 2 (1919): 165–78 and *Negro Migration: Its Effect on Family and Community Life in the North* (Indianapolis: Bobbs-Merrill, 1924); U.S. Department of Labor, Division of Negro Economics, *The Negro at Work during the World War and during Reconstruction* (Washington DC: Government Printing Office, 1921); and Lorenzo J. Green and Carter G. Woodson, *The Negro Wage Earner* (New York: Russell & Russell, 1930). For the role of George E. Haynes in the Labor Department's Division of Negro Economics, see Henry P. Guzda, "Social Experiment of the Labor Department: The Division of Negro Economics," *Public Historian* 4, 4 (Fall 1982): 7–37.

Numerous studies examine the role of the black press and its editors; the most comprehensive is William G. Jordan, *Black Newspapers and America's War for Democracy, 1914–1920* (Chapel Hill: University of North Carolina Press, 2001). Other books and articles include Lester M. Jones, "The Editorial Policy of the Negro Newspapers of 1917–1918 as Compared with That of 1941–1942," *Journal of Negro History* 29 (1944): 24–31; Roi Ottley, *The Lonely Warrior: The Life and Times of Robert S. Abbott* (Chicago: Henry Regnery Company 1955); Theodore Kornweibel Jr., *No Crystal Stair: Black Life and the Messenger, 1917–1928* (Westport CT: Greenwood Press, 1975); Carolyn A. Stroman, "The *Chicago Defender* and the Mass Migration of Blacks, 1916–1918," *Journal of Popular Culture* 15 (1981): 62–67; James R. Grossman, "Blowing the Trumpet: The *Chicago Defender* and Black Migration during World War I," *Illinois Historical Journal* 78 (1985): 82–96; Mark Ellis, "America's Black Press, 1914–18," *History Today* 41, 9 (September 1991): 20–27; and Alfred Lawrence Lorenz, "Ralph W. Tyler: The Unknown Correspondent of World War I," *Journalism History* 31, 1 (2005): 2–12.

Memoirs, autobiographies, and biographies of contemporaries who were involved in the struggle for civil rights are crucial for an understanding of race relations during the war. Among the most important ones are James Weldon Johnson, *Along This Way: The Autobiography of James Weldon Johnson* (New York: Viking Press, 1933); Walter White, *A Man Called White: The Autobiography of Walter White* (New York: Viking Press, 1948); Elliott M. Rudwick, *W. E. B. Du Bois: Voice of the Black Protest Movement* (1960; repr., Urbana: University of Illinois Press, 1982); George S. Schuyler, *Black and Conservative: The Autobiography of George S. Schuyler* (New Rochelle, NY: Arlington House Publishers, 1966); W. E. B. Du Bois, *The Autobiography of W. E. B. Du Bois: A Soliloquy on Viewing My Life from the Last Decade of Its First Century* (New York: International Publishers, 1968); Stephen R. Fox, *The Guardian of Boston: William Monroe Trotter* (New York: Atheneum, 1970); Harry Haywood, *Black Bolshevik: Autobiography of an Afro-American Communist* (Chicago: Liberator Press, 1979); Genna Rae McNeil, *Groundwork: Charles Hamilton Houston and the Struggle for Civil Rights* (Philadelphia: University of Pennsylvania Press, 1983); David Levering Lewis, *W. E. B. Du Bois: Biography of a Race, 1868–1919* (New York: Henry Holt, 1993); Jennifer D. Keene, "W. E. B. Du Bois and the Wounded World: Seeking Meaning in the First World War for African Americans," *Peace and Change* 26 (April 2001): 135–52; Jacqueline M. Moore, *Booker T. Washington, W. E. B. Du Bois, and the Struggle for Racial Uplift* (Lanham, MD: Scholarly Resources, 2003); and Kenneth Robert Janken, *Rayford W. Logan and the Dilemma of the African-American Intellectual* (Amherst: University of Massachusetts Press, 1993) and *White: The Biography of Walter White, Mr. NAACP* (New York: New Press, 2003).

Other studies that examine race leaders and organizations involved in the wartime civil rights struggle are Charles F. Kellogg, *NAACP: A History of the National Association for the Advancement of Colored People Vol.1, 1909–1920* (Baltimore: Johns Hopkins University Press, 1967); B. Joyce Ross, J. E. *Spingarn and the Rise of the NAACP, 1911–1939* (New York: Atheneum, 1972); Robert L. Zangrando, *The NAACP Crusade against Lynching, 1909–1950* (Philadelphia: Temple University Press, 1980); Kevin K. Gaines, *Uplifting the Race: Black Leadership, Politics, and Culture in the Twentieth Century* (Chapel Hill: University of North Carolina Press, 1996); and Carolyn Wedin, *Inheritors of the Spirit: Mary White Ovington and the Founding of the NAACP* (New York: Wiley, 1997).

For racial violence during the war see United States Congress, House of Representatives, Special Committee to Investigate the East St. Louis Riots, "Report of the Special Committee Authorized by Congress to investigate the East St. Louis Riots" (Washington, DC: Government Printing Office, 1918); Elliott M. Rudwick, *Race Riot at East St. Louis July 2, 1917* (Carbondale: Southern Illinois University Press, 1964); Vincent P. Franklin, "The Philadelphia Race Riot of 1918," *Pennsylvania Magazine of History and Biography* 99 (1975): 336–50; Robert V. Haynes, *A Night of Violence: The Houston Riot of 1917* (Baton Rouge: Louisiana State University Press, 1976); Herbert Shapiro, *White Violence and Black Response: From Reconstruction to Montgomery* (Amherst: University of Massachusetts Press, 1988); C. Calvin Smith, "The Houston Riot of 1917, Revisited," *Houston Review* 13, 2 (1991): 85–102 and "On the Edge: The Houston Riot of 1917 Revisited," *Griot* 10 (Spring 1991): 3–12; Charles L. Lumpkins, *American Pogrom: The East St. Louis Race Riot and Black Politics* (Athens: Ohio University Press, 2008); and Lee Kenneth, "The Camp Wadsworth Affair," *South Atlantic Quarterly* 74, 2 (Spring 1975): 197–211.

The most comprehensive study of the draft is John Whiteclay Chambers II, *To Raise an Army: The Draft Comes to Modern America* (New York: Free Press, 1987). For a discussion of African Americans and the draft see Campbell C. Johnson, "The Mobilization of Negro Manpower for the Armed Forces," *Journal of Negro Education* 12, 3 (Summer 1943): 298–302; Emmett J. Scott, "The Participation of Negroes in World War I: An Introductory Statement," *Journal of Negro Education* 12, 3 (Summer 1943): 288–97; Paul T. Murray, "Blacks and the Draft: A History of Institutional Racism," *Journal of Black Studies* 2, 1 (1971): 57–76; and James Mennell, "African-Americans and the Selective Service Act of 1917," *Journal of Negro History* 84, 3 (Summer 1999), 275–87. For draft opposition see Theodore Kornweibel Jr., "Apathy and Dissent: Black America's Negative Responses to World War I," *South Atlantic Quarterly* 80, 3 (Summer 1981): 322–38; Gerald E. Shenk, *"Work or Fight!": Race, Gender, and the Draft in World War I* (New York: Palgrave Macmillan, 2005) and "Race, Manhood, and Manpower: Mobilizing Rural Georgia for World War I," *Georgia Historical Quarterly* 81 (Fall 1997): 622–62; and Jeanette Keith, "The Politics of Southern Draft Resistance, 1917–1918: Class, Race, and Conscription in the Rural South," *Journal of American History* 87, 4 (2000): 1335–61, as well as her superb *Rich Man's War, Poor Man's Fight: Race, Class, and Power in the Rural South during the First World War* (Chapel Hill: University of North Carolina Press, 2004).

Contemporary accounts of black military participation, including those of African Americans soldiers and whites who served with them, are William S. Bradden, *Under Fire with the 370th* (Chicago: Self-published, n.d.); Emmett J. Scott, *Scott's Official History of the American Negro in the World War* (Chicago: Homewood Press, 1919); W. E. B. Du Bois, "An Essay Toward a History of the Black Man in the Great War," *Crisis* (June 1919): 63–87; Kelly Miller, *Kelly Miller's History of the World War for Human Rights* (1919; repr. New York: Negro Universities Press, 1969); W. Allison Sweeney, *History of the American Negro in the Great World War* (Chicago: Cuneo-Henneberry, 1919); *A Pictorial History of the Negro in the Great War, 1917–1918* (New York: Touissant Pictorial, 1919); Obidah M. Foster, *The Modern Warfare and My Experiences in France* (Washington, DC: The Goines Printing Co., 1919); Royal A. Christian, *Roy's Trip to the Battlefields of Europe: Being the Diary of Royal A. Christian, Confidential Messenger to Colonel Moorhead C. Kennedy, Deputy Director-General of Transportation American Expeditionary Forces in the World War* (Chambersburg, PA: Press of J.R. Kerr, 1920); Major Warner A. Ross, *My Colored Battalion: Dedicated to the American Colored Soldier* (Chicago: Warner A. Ross, Publisher, 1920); Arthur Furr and Monroe Mason, *The American Negro Soldier with the Red Hand of France* (Boston: The Cornhill Co., 1921); Chester D. Heywood, *Negro Combat Troops in the World War: The Story of the 371st Infantry* (Worcester, MA: Commonwealth Press, 1928); John B. Cade, *Twenty-Two Months with "Uncle Sam": Being the Experiences and Observations of a Negro Student Who Volunteered for Military Service against the Central Powers from June 1917 to April 1919* (Atlanta, GA: Robinson-Cofer Co., 1929); Napoleon B. Marshall, *The Providential Armistice: A Volunteer's Story: Military Sketch of Captain Napoleon B. Marshall* (Washington, DC: Liberty League, 1930); Arthur W. Little, *From Harlem to the Rhine* (New York: Corvici, 1936); Ely Green, *Ely, Too Black, Too White* (Amherst: University of Massachusetts Press, 1970); Charles H. Williams, *Sidelights on Negro Soldiers* (Boston: B. J. Brimmer Co., 1923); and Tracey Lovette Spencer, James E. Spencer Jr., and Bruce G. Wright, "World War I as I Saw It: The Memoir of an African American Soldier," *Massachusetts Historical Review* 9 (2007): 134–65.

The best book on black soldiers in World War I is Arthur E. Barbeau and Florette Henri, *The Unknown Soldiers: Black American Troops in World War I* (Philadelphia: Temple University Press, 1974). For a general survey of African Americans in the military see Bernard C. Nalty, *Strength for the Fight: A History of Black Americans in the Military* (New York: Free Press, 1986). A very useful collection of documents can be found in Morris J. McGregor and Bernard C. Nalty, *Blacks in the United States Armed Forces: Basic Documents*, vol. 4, *Segregation Entrenched, 1917–1940* (Wilmington, DE: Scholarly Resources, 1981). An excellent reference source is Jonathan D. Sutherland, *African Americans at War: An Encyclopedia* (Santa Barbara, CA: ABC Clio, 2004). Other studies that focus on various aspects of the black military experience include Bruce White, "The American Military and the Melting Pot in World War I," in *War and Society in North America*, ed. J. L. Granatstein and R. D. Cuff (Toronto: Thomas Nelson & Sons, 1971): 37–51; Jack D. Foner, *Blacks and the Military in American History: A New Perspective* (New York: Praeger Publishers, 1974); Marvin Fletcher, *The Black Soldier and Officer in the United States Army, 1891–1917* (Columbia: University of Missouri, Press, 1974); Hal S. Chase, "Struggle for Equality: Fort Des Moines Training Camp for Colored Officers, 1917," *Phylon*, 39, 4 (1978): 297–310; Gerald W. Patton, *War and Peace: The Black Officer in the American*

Military, 1915–1941 (Westport, CT: Greenwood Press, 1981); Garna L. Christian, *Black Soldiers in Jim Crow Texas, 1899–1917* (College Station: Texas A&M University Press, 1995); Reid Badger, *A Life in Ragtime: A Biography of James Reese Europe* (New York: Oxford University Press, 1995); Steven A. Reich, "Soldiers of Democracy: Black Texans and the Fight for Citizenship, 1917–1921," *Journal of American History* 92 (March 1996): 1478–1504; Michael L. Cooper, *Hell Fighters: African American Soldiers in World War I* (New York: Dutton, 1997); Bill Douglas, "Wartime Illusions and Disillusionment: Camp Dodge and Racial Stereotyping, 1917–1918," *Annals of Iowa* 57 (1998): 111–34; James N. Leiker, *Racial Borders: Black Soldiers along the Rio Grande* (College Station: Texas A&M University Press, 2002); Bill Harris, *The Hellfighters of Harlem: African-American Soldiers Who Fought for the Right to Fight for Their Country* (New York: Carroll and Graf, 2002); Jennifer D. Keene, *Doughboys, the Great War, and the Remaking of America* (Baltimore: Johns Hopkins University Press, 2001), "Protest and Disability: A New Look at African American Soldiers during the First World War," in *Warfare and Belligerence: Perspectives in First World War Studies*, ed. Pierre Purseigle (London: Brill Academic Publishers, 2005): 215–41, "A Comparative Study of White and Black American Soldiers during the First World War," *Annales de Demographie Historique* 1 (2002): 71–90, and "Intelligence and Morale in the Army of a Democracy: The Genesis of Military Psychology during the First World War," *Military Psychology* 6, 4 (1994): 235–53; Stephen L. Harris, *Harlem's Hell Fighters: The African-American 369th Infantry in World War I* (Washington, DC: Brassey's, 2003); Frank E. Roberts, *The American Foreign Legion: Black Soldiers of the 93d in World War I* (Annapolis, MD: Naval Institute Press, 2004); Richard Slotkin, *Lost Battalions: The Great War and the Crisis of American Nationality* (New York: Henry Holt, 2005); Robert J. Dalessandro, et al., *Willing Patriots: Men of Color* (Altglen, PA: Schiffer Military History, 2009). A very engaging journalistic account of the 369th Infantry Regiment is Peter N. Nelson's *A More Unbending Battle: The Harlem Hellfighters' Struggle for Freedom in WW I and Equality at Home* (New York: Basic Civitas Books, 2009). The propaganda film *The Training of Colored Troops* can be accessed at http://www.realmilitaryflix.com/public/524. cfm. For a discussion of the film see Thomas Winter, "The Training of Colored Troops: A Cinematic Effort to Promote Nation Cohesion," in *Hollywood's World War I*, ed. Peter C. Rollins and John E. O'Connor (Bowling Green, OH: Bowling Green State University Press, 1997): 13–25. Information about Colonel Charles Young can be found in Robert E. Greene, *Colonel Charles Young: Soldier and Diplomat* (Washington, DC: R.E. Greene, 1985) and David P. Kilroy, *For Race and Country: The Life and Career of Colonel Charles Young* (Westport, CT: Praeger , 2003).

The experience of black soldiers in France is illustrated in W. E. B. Du Bois, "The Negro Soldier in Service Abroad during the First World War," *Journal of Negro Education* 12, 3 (Summer 1943): 324–34; Yves-Henri Nouailhat, *Les Américains à Nantes et St. Nazaire, 1917–1919* (Paris: Les Belle Lettres, 1972); Felix James, "Robert Russa Moton and the Whispering Gallery in France after World War I," *Journal of Negro History* 62 (July 1977): 235–42; Tyler Stovall, *Paris Noir: African Americans in the City of Light* (Boston: Houghton Mifflin 1996) and "The Color Line Behind the Lines: Racial Violence in France during the Great War," *American Historical Review* 103 (June 1998):

737–69; and Jennifer D. Keene, "French and American Racial Stereotypes during the First World War," in *National Stereotypes in Perspective: Frenchmen in America: Americans in France*, ed. William Chew (Amsterdam: Rodopi Press, 2001): 261–81. A particularly insightful study of the impact of military service on black masculinity is Adriane Lentz-Smith, *Freedom Struggles: African Americans and World War I* (Cambridge, MA: Harvard University Press, 2009).

For the wartime services of the YMCA and the YWCA see Addie W. Hunton and Kathryn M. Johnson, *Two Colored Women with the American Expeditionary Forces* (Brooklyn, NY: Eagle Press, 1920); Nina Mjagkij, *Light in the Darkness: African Americans and the YMCA, 1852–1946* (Lexington: University Press of Kentucky, 1994); Susan Kerr Chandler, "'That Biting, Stinging Thing Which Ever Shadows Us': African-American Social Workers in France During World War I," *Social Service Review* 69, 3 (1995): 498–514; and Nancy Marie Robertson, *Christian Sisterhood, Race Relations, and the YWCA, 1906–46* (Chicago: University of Illinois Press, 2007).

Scholars who have explored the home-front experience of African Americans have largely focused on black support of the war and opposition to it as well as the government's effort to suppress dissent. For interpretations of W. E. B. Du Bois's "Close Ranks" editorial see Mark Ellis, "'Closing Ranks' and 'Seeking Honors': W. E. B. Du Bois in World War I," *Journal of American History* 79 (June 1992): 96–124; William G. Jordan, "'The Damnable Dilemma': African-American Accommodation and Protest during World War I," *Journal of American History* 81 (March 1995): 1562–83; and Mark Ellis, "W. E. B. Du Bois and the Formation of Black Opinion in World War I: A Commentary on 'The Damnable Dilemma,'" *Journal of American History* (March 1995): 1584–90. For government surveillance of African Americans see Mark Ellis, *Race War and Surveillance: African Americans and the United States Government during World War I* (Bloomington: Indiana University Press, 2001) and "Federal Surveillance of Black Americans during the First World War," *Immigrants & Minorities*, 12, 1 (March 1993): 1–20; Wray R. Johnson, "Black American Radicalism and the First World War: The Secret Files of the Military Intelligence Division," *Armed Forces & Society* 26, 1 (1999): 27–54; and Theodore Kornweibel Jr., *"Investigate Everything": Federal Efforts to Compel Black Loyalty during World War I* (Bloomington: Indiana University Press, 2002). Information about Walter Howard Loving can be found in Claiborne T. Richardson, "The Filipino-American Phenomenon: The Loving Touch," *Black Perspective in Music* 10, 1 (Spring 1982): 3–28.

For a discussion of the role of black women see William J. Breen, "Black Women and the Great War: Mobilization and Reform in the South," *Journal of Southern History* 44 (August 1978): 421–40 and Nikki Brown, *Private Politics and Public Voices: Black Women's Activism from World War I to the New Deal* (Bloomington: Indiana University Press, 2006). Jennifer D. Keene examines government propaganda efforts among African Americans in "Images of Racial Pride: African American Propaganda Posters in the First World War," in *Picture This! Reading World War I Posters*, ed. Pearl James (Lincoln: University of Nebraska Press, 2009): 207–40.

Information about returning black soldiers, the eruption of postwar racial violence, and the memory of the war in the black community can be found in The Chicago Commission on Race Relations, *The Negro in Chicago: A Study of Race Relations and a Race Riot* (Chicago: University of Chicago Press, 1922); Arthur I. Waskow, *From Race Riot to Sit-In, 1919 and the 1960s a Study in the Connections between Conflict and Violence* (Garden City, NJ: Doubleday, 1966); William M. Tuttle Jr. *Race Riot: Chicago in the Red Summer of 1919* (New York: Atheneum, 1970); Hyesung Hwang, "World War I and the New Negro," *Journal of North American Studies* 1 (1995): 43–68; Mark R. Schneider, *"We Return Fighting": The Civil Rights Movement in the Jazz Age* (Boston: Northeastern University Press, 2002); Chad L. Williams, "Vanguards of the New Negro: African American Veterans and Post-World War I Racial Militancy," *Journal of African American History* 92 (Summer 2007): 347–70; and Jennifer D. Keene, "The Memory of the Great War in the African American Community," in *Unknown Soldier: The American Expeditionary Forces in Memory and Remembrance*, ed. Mark Snell (Kent, OH: Kent State University Press, 2008): 60–79.

Despite the wealth of scholarship, historians have not yet given adequate attention to the African American experience during World War I. We still know very little about the government's propaganda and mobilization efforts among black civilians and black community responses to it. Moreover, the recruitment of black officer candidates and their training at the Des Moines Officers Training Camp deserves further scholarly inquiry. Also lacking are biographies of Emmett J. Scott, George E. Haynes, Walter H. Loving, Addie W. Hunton, and Ralph W. Tyler, which could provide important insights into the wartime experience of African Americans.

Index

Abbott, Robert S., 32–35, 47, 55, 125, 132, 133, 151, 167. *See also* migration; press, black; Washington conference of race leaders in 1918
African Methodist Episcopal church. *See* churches, black
Aix-Les-Bain, 118–119
Akron, Ohio, 26, 27
Alabama, 24, 26, 28, 34, 89, 95
Albany, Georgia, 38
Amenia Conference, x, 57
American Colonization Society, 25
American Distinguished Service Cross, 113
American Expeditionary Forces, 85, 105, 108, 175–177
American Library Association, 93. *See also* Young Men's Christian Association
American Protective League, 124
Aristocrats of Color. *See* elites, black
Arkansas, 24, 34
armistice, 113, 115
Army. *See* United States Army, black troops

Arundel-on-the-Bay, Maryland, 12
Association for the Study of Negro Life and History, ix
Association of Colored Women's Clubs, 44. *See also* Dunbar-Nelson, Alice
Atlanta, 8, 10, 11, 17, 33, 137
Atlantic City, New Jersey, 12
Atwell, Ernest T., xiv, 139–140. *See also* United States Food Administration

Bailey, Eugene B., 81
Baltimore, 8, 10
Baltimore Afro-American. See press, black
Ballou, Charles C., xii, 60–61, 72, 104, 112–113, 114, 126–127, 131, 183–184. *See also* black officers training camp; combat units, black
Baker, Newton D.: appoints Emmett J. Scott, 69–70, 71, 72; creates black combat divisions, xix, 72, 141–142; endorses black officers training camp, xix, 56, 58–59, 71, 142; enforces military segregation, xi, 71, 88–89, 127; initiates draft, 52–53; meets with race leaders, x, 69, 71,

132–134; on Charles Young, 63, 64;
responds to Houston Mutiny, 69;
visits troops in France, 114–115. *See
also* black officers training camp;
combat units, black; draft; labor
battalions, black; National Guard
units, black; soldiers, black; Scott,
Emmett J.; Spingarn, Joel E.; training
camps; United States Army, black
troops; United States War
Department; Wilson, Woodrow
Baptist church. *See* churches, black
Barnes, W. Harry, 141
Bilbo, Theodore, 143, 191
Bill of Particulars, 136. *See also*
Washington conference of race
leaders in 1918
Bingham, E. G., 61. *See also* black
officers training camp
Birmingham, 8, 28
The Birth of a Nation, ix, 21–22, 48–49
black officers training camp: black press
opposed to, 55, 59, 161–167, 183;
campaign for, 51, 54–56, 59, 166–
168; commissions received at, xii,
70–72; creation of, x, xi, xix, 58–61;
famous graduates of, 61; training at,
60–61; white southern opposition to,
59. *See also* Baker, Newton D.;
Ballou, Charles C.; Du Bois, W. E.
B.; Historically Black Colleges and
Universities; National Association
for the Advancement of Colored
People; officers, black; press, black;
Spingarn, Joel E.; United States
Army, black troops; Young, Charles
Bliss, Tasker H., 70
boll weevil, ix, 24
Bordeaux, 100
Bouldin, G. W., 125. *See also* subversion
Bowles, Eva D., 91–92. *See also* Young
Women's Christian Association
Bostick, Texas, 84

Boston, 8, 122
Boston Guardian. See press, black;
Trotter, William Monroe
Boyd, Henry Allen, 132
Brest, 100, 114
Brown v. Board of Education, 61
Brownsville incident, 66–67. *See also*
Houston Mutiny
Bruce, Roscoe Conkling, 132
Buchanan v. Warley, xii, 41
Buffalo, New York, 27, 143
Buffalo Soldiers, xix, 105
Bullard, Robert Lee, 112–113
Bulletin No. 35, xii, 126–127, 131,
183–184. *See also* Ballou, Charles C.
Bureau of Colored Troops, xviii

Cabaniss George W., 56. *See also* black
officers training camp
Camp Pontanezen. *See* Brest
Camp Reader for American Soldiers, 96.
See also Young Men's Christian
Association
camps in the United States. *See* training
camps
Carnegie, Andrew, 17
Central Committee of Negro College
Men, 55–56, 59. *See also* black
officers training camp
Challes-les-Eaux, 119
Chambéry, 119
Charleston, South Carolina, 90
Chase, Calvin, 134
Chicago, 8, 10, 25, 26, 27, 32–34, 40,
45, 47, 49, 82, 134, 143. *See also*
Chicago race riot
Chicago Defender. See press, black
Chicago race riot, xv, 144–145, 146–
147, 193–195
Christian Recorder. See press, black
Christian, Royal, 85
churches, black, 7, 30, 35, 37, 40, 44–
45, 47, 52, 64, 123, 132, 146

Cincinnati, 8, 27
Circle for Negro War Relief, 123
Civil War, xvii, xviii, xix, 1, 12, 13, 19, 20, 26, 33, 48
civilian home front support, xx, 123, 122–123, 137–140, 141, 186. *See also* morale; Red Cross; women; Young Men's Christian Association; Young Women's Christian Association
Cleveland, 26, 27, 37, 45, 49
Cleveland Gazette. See press, black
Cleveland Advocate. See press, black
"Close Ranks" editorial. *See* Du Bois, W. E. B.
Colored Man No Slacker, 130. *See also* Committee on Public Information; morale
Colored Medical Officers Training Camp, xi, 61, 70, 72. *See also* black officers training camp
Colored Officers Training Camp. *See* black officers training camp
Columbus, Ohio, 8, 27, 45, 91–92
Columbus Dispatch, 137
combat units, black: casualties of, 110–111, 112–113; draftees in, xi, 51, 54, 70, 71–72, 111, 112; engaged in battle, 109–111, 112; French interaction with, 99, 106–109, 114, 175–177, 181–182; German propaganda aimed at, xiv, 111, 177–179; medals received by, 113; Ninety-Second Infantry Division, xii, xiii, xix, 72, 73, 99, 104, 106, 112–113, 114, 126, 178, 183; Ninety-Third Infantry Division (Provisional), xii, xix, 72, 73, 99, 103–112, 172; 366th Infantry, 95; 368th Infantry xiv; 369th Infantry, xii, xiv, 103, 104–105, 106, 108, 111–112, 143, 144, 145; 370th Infantry, xiii, xiv, 103, 111, 172; 371st Infantry, xiii, xiv, 103, 113; 372nd Infantry, xii, xiv, 103, 106,

107, 111; training of, 112. *See also* black officers training camp; draft; labor battalions, black; National Guard units, black; soldiers, black; training camps; United States Army, black troops
Commission on Interracial Cooperation, xiv, 143
Commission on Training Camp Activities, 91. *See also* Young Men's Christian Association; Young Women's Christian Association
Commissioner of Education, 94
Committee of 100 Colored Citizens on the War, 56. *See also* black officers training camp
Committee of One Hundred, 130. *See also* morale
Committee on Public Information, xiv, 130–134, 136, 137. *See also* morale; subversion
Congressional Medal of Honor, 113
Connecticut, xix
convict-lease-system 6
Council of National Defense, xiii, 137
courts-martial, xii, 113, 170. *See also* Houston Mutiny
Craig, Arthur U., 139. *See also* subversion; United States Food Administration
"Creed of the South." *See* Bilbo, Theodore
Creel, George, 131, 132, 136. *See also* Committee on Public Information; Washington conference of race leaders in 1918
Crisis. See Du Bois, W. E. B.; National Association for the Advancement of Colored People; press, black
Crispus Attucks Circle, 122
Croix de Guerre, 113
Curtis, Helen, 103. *See also* Young Men's Christian Association

Damaged Goods, 96. *See also* Spingarn, Arthur, B.; venereal disease

Davis, Benjamin O., 60

De Priest, Oscar, ix, 147

Debs, Eugene V., 19

Delaware, 8

delinquents, 76, 77, 80

Dennison, Franklin A., 81, 103, 111. *See also* combat units, black; National Guard units, black; officers, black; soldiers, black

Department of Labor. *See* United States Department of Labor

deserters, 77, 80

Des Moines, Iowa, black officers training camp. *See* black officers training camp

Detroit, 26, 27, 44, 45, 46, 49

Dillard, James H., 127. *See also* United States Department of Labor

The Disgrace of Democracy, 66, 164–166. *See also* Miller, Kelly

District of Columbia, xix, 52

Division of Negro Economics. *See* United States Department of Labor

Dixon, Thomas, 21

Dockery, Albert B., 63. *See also* Young, Charles

"Double V," 147

Douglass, Charles R., 12, 58

Douglass, Frederick, 12, 58

draft: black response to, 51, 52, 54, 80–81, 141; composition of draft boards, 74–75; exemption of blacks from, 53, 77; initiation of, x, xviii, 52–54; racial bias of, 54, 74–77, 80, 123; racial quotas of, xi, 54, 70, 76; registration for, xi, xiii, 73–75, 76, 78–79; southern white response to, 53, 70, 75, 76, 77. *See also* labor battalions, black; soldiers, black; training camps

Drake University, Iowa, 60

Du Bois, W. E. B.: applies for Army commission, xiii, 135–136; attends Washington conference of race leaders in 1918, 132–134; campaigns for black officers training camp, 54, 57–58, 166–168; editor of *Crisis*, 18, 54, 58, 115, 135–136; government surveillance of, 125; health problems of, 57, 135; on education, 16, 17; protests discrimination, 44, 58, 71, 115–116, 120; supports war, xvii, xviii, xix, 58; urges blacks to close ranks, xiii, xvii, xx, 122, 135–136, 186; visits France, xiv, 115–116. *See also* black officers training camp; National Association for the Advancement of Colored People; press, black; Spingarn, Joel E.; Washington conference of race leaders in 1917 and 1918; Young, Charles

Duluth, Minnesota, 83

Dunbar, Paul Laurence, 62, 139

Dunbar-Nelson, Alice, xiii, 137–138, 140

Durham, North Carolina, 14

Dyer, Leonidas C., 66, 134, 136

East St. Louis, Illinois, xi, xx, 27, 49–50, 64–66, 71, 122, 123, 161–164, 187

elites, black, 12–13, 34, 43–44, 48

Espionage Act of 1917, xi, 125. *See also* subversion

Europe, Jim Reese, 108, 111, 143

Exodusters. *See* Singleton, Benjamin "Pap;" Wells-Barnett, Ida B.

Farmers and Laborers Protective Association, 81

Federal Bureau of Investigation, 124

Fifteenth Amendment, 4, 135

Fisk University, Tennessee, 55, 128, 137

Fletcher, Ben, 81
Florida, 24, 26, 85
Food Administration. *See* United States
 Food Administration
Fort Brown, Texas, 66–67
Fort Huachuaca, Arizona, 62, 63
Four Minute Men, 130. *See also*
 Committee on Public Information;
 morale
Fourteenth Amendment, 135
French High Commission, 132

Garrison, William Lloyd, 20
Gary, Indiana, 26, 27
Garvey, Marcus, x, 146
General Erwin, 114
General Amnesty, 5
General Order No. 7, 69
Georgia, 19, 24, 26, 28, 32, 34, 38, 76,
 85, 89
grandfather clause, 5, 22
Great Migration. *See* migration
Great Northern Drive, 34. *See also*
 Abbott, Robert S.; migration; press,
 black
"A Greeting to our Colored Soldiers,"
 143
Green, Ely, 90–91, 100–101, 113, 115,
 116, 120, 179–180. *See also* labor
 battalions, black
Green, John E., 60
Green Corn Rebellion, 81
Greer, Allen J., 184
Griffith, D. W., ix, 21, 48
Grimké, Archibald H., 56, 132
Grimké, Francis J., 52
Gruening, Martha, 170. *See also*
 Houston Mutiny
Guinn v. U.S., ix, 22

Haiti, 62
Hall, Charles E., 128. *See also* United
 States Department of Labor

Hampton Institute, Virginia, 32, 55, 59,
 95, 1397
Harlem Hellfighters, 112, 143, 144. *See
 also* combat units, black; National
 Guard units, black; soldiers, black
Haynes, George E., xiii, 128–130, 140.
 See also United States Department of
 Labor; Washington conference of
 race leaders in 1918
Hayward, William, 103, 106, 111–112.
 See also combat units, black; National
 Guard units, black; soldiers, black
Historically Black Colleges and
 Universities, 14–15, 30, 32. *See also*
 black officers training camp;
 Hampton Institute; Howard
 University; Fisk University;
 Morehouse College, Tuskegee
 Institute; Wilberforce University
Hoboken, New Jersey, xiv, 99
Homestead Act, 25
Hoover, Herbert, 139. *See also* United
 States Food Administration
Hope, John, 92, 119. *See also* Young
 Men's Christian Association
Hope, Lugenia Burns, 92. *See also* Young
 Women's Christian Association
hostess houses. *See* Young Women's
 Christian Association
Houston, Charles Hamilton, 61. *See also*
 black officers training camp
Houston Mutiny, xi, xii, xiii, xiv, 66–68,
 89, 124, 125, 134, 137, 170–172. *See
 also* Baker, Newton D.; Brownsville
 incident; National Association for
 the Advancement of Colored
 People; press, black; United States
 War Department; United States
 Army, black troops
Howard University, Washington, D.C.,
 15, 55, 57, 58, 59, 66, 70, 93, 125,
 137, 169
Hughes, Charles E., 22

Hunton, Addie W., 103, 120. *See also* Young Men's Christian Association
Hurley Edward N., 132

"If We Must Die," xiv, 146, 195–196
Ildlewild, Michigan, 12
Illinois, xix, 8, 10, 11, 18, 25, 26, 27, 32–34, 40, 45, 47, 49, 82, 134, 143. *See also* Chicago race riot; East St. Louis, Illinois
Indianapolis, 8, 27
Inter-Allied games, 117
Jacksonville, Florida, 28
Jeanes-Slater Fund for Negro Education, 128. *See also* United States Department of Labor
Jennifer, William, 128. *See also* United States Department of Labor
Jim Crow laws, 1, 6–7, 10
Johnson, Henry, 111–112, 127
Johnson, James Weldon, x, 57, 144, 193. *See also* National Association for the Advancement of Colored People
Johnson, Kathryn M., 103. *See also* Young Men's Christian Association
Jones, Eugene Kinckle, 158. *See also* National Urban League
Jonesboro, Arkansas, 83
Jordan, Reuel M., 114
Justice Department. *See* United States Department of Justice

Kansas, 25, 126
Kansas City, 8, 27
Kentucky, xviii, 8, 62, 92
Knights of Columbus, 91
Ku Klux Klan, ix, 144

labor battalions, black: composition of, 51, 73, 86–87, 89; in France, 99–104, 106, 116, 117–118; racial abuses of, 100–101, 102, 113–114. *See also*

Baker, Newton D.; draft; Scott, Emmett J.; training camps; venereal disease; Young Men's Christian Association; Young Women's Christian Association
Laclede, Missouri 105
Lake Mohonk Conference, 15
leave areas. *See* Young Men's Christian Association
Letterman General Hospital, California, 62, 63. *See also* Young, Charles
Le Blanc, Joseph, 108
Liberia, 25, 60, 62
Lincoln, Abraham, xviii, 11, 18, 19
literacy test, 5
Little, Arthur W., 110, 111–112. *See also* combat units, black; National Guard units, black
Logan, Rayford W., 107, 116
Long, Howard, 61
Louisiana, 24, 25, 26, 29, 76, 132
Louisville, 8, 9, 24, 93
Loving, Walter Howard, 95, 116, 124–125, 130, 131, 134, 174, 181. *See also* morale; press, black; Spingarn, Joel E., subversion
lynching. *See* racial violence

Macon, Georgia, 38
Madden, Martin B., 134
Manhattan, Kansas, 126
Marines. *See* United States Marine Corps
Marshall, Thurgood, 61
Maryland, xviii, xix, 8, 71
Massachusetts, xix
May, Charlie, 101
McKay, Claude, xiv, 146, 195–196
Means, Wilhelmina Lewis, 44
Médailles Militaires, 113
medals. *See* combat units, black
Meharry Medical College, Tennessee, 15, 70

Memphis, 8
Meridian, Mississippi, 35
The Messenger. See press, black
Methodist church. *See* churches, black
middle class, black, 13–14, 44–46, 48,
   147, 157, 160
migration: black response to, 29–30,
   32–35, 37, 39–40, 42–48, 155–157;
   economic opportunities during, xx,
   23, 24, 121; experience of migrants
   during, 31, 35– 41, 151–152, 153–
   155; impact of labor agents on, 24,
   26–29, 31, 35, 152–153; North
   affected by, xx, 23, 24–27, 40–47,
   157–161; pre-World War I, 8, 11,
   24–25, 41; South affected by, 27–29,
   37–38; white response to, 28–29,
   31–32, 34–35, 38–39, 49; women's
   role in, 26, 35, 36–37, 38, 44. *See
   also* National Urban League;
   population, black northern;
   population, black southern; press,
   black; United States Department of
   Labor
military casualties, 110–111, 112–113,
   116–118
Military Intelligence Branch. *See*
   subversion
Miller, Clifford L., xii
Miller, Kelly, 56, 66, 71, 161–162
Milwaukee, Wisconsin, 45
Mine Eyes Have Seen the Glory, 137. *See
   also* Dunbar-Nelson, Alice
Mississippi, 24, 25, 26, 29, 35, 76, 113,
   143
Missouri, xviii, 8
Mobile, Alabama, 27, 37
Montgomery, Alabama, 28, 90
Moores, Merrill, 136
Moorland, Jesse E., 93. *See also* Young
   Men's Christian Association
morale, xx, 123–1275, 127–131, 138,
   140, 145, 174, 177, 181. *See also*

subversion; Washington conference
   of race leaders in 1918
Morehouse College, Georgia, 55, 92,
   119, 137
Moton, Robert R., xiv, 30, 55–56, 69–
   70, 115, 125, 132, 179–180. *See also*
   Scott, Emmett. J.; Tuskegee Institute;
   Washington, Booker T.; Washington
   conference of race leaders in 1918
Murphy, John H., 132

NAACP. *See* National Association for
   the Advancement of Colored People
Nashville, 8, 15, 25, 132
Nashville Globe. See press, black
National Association for the
   Advancement of Colored People
   (NAACP): Charles Young and, 63–
   64; growth following World War I,
   xxi, 147; organizes Silent Parade, xi,
   xx, 64–66; position on black officers
   training camp, x, 54–58; relationship
   with Woodrow Wilson, x, 18–22,
   64–66, 141; response to East St.
   Louis riot, 49–50, 161–164; response
   to Houston Mutiny, 170–172. *See
   also* black officers training camp; Du
   Bois, W. E. B.; Spingarn, Joel E.;
   United States Department of Labor;
   Washington conference of race
   leaders in 1917
National Bar Association, 61
National Colored Soldiers' Comfort
   Committee, 123, 137
National Defense Act of 1916, 54
National Guard units, black: xix, 52,
   62, 72, 73, 81, 90; Eighth Illinois,
   81, 83–84, 103, 111, 172–173;
   Fifteenth New York Volunteer
   Infantry, 103, 143; First Separate
   Battalion of the District of
   Columbia, x, 52; Ninth Ohio, 62.
   See also combat units, black; soldiers,

black; training camps; United States Army, black troops
National Independent Political League. See Trotter, William Monroe
National Liberty Congress, xiii, 134–135
National Liberty Loan Campaigns, 122, 141
National Negro Business League, 17, 137
National Negro Conference, 127
National Urban League, x, xii, 30–31, 40, 45–48, 157–161. See also migration; United States Department of Labor
Navy. See United States Navy
Negro Migration in 1916–17. See United States Department of Labor
New Jersey, 19, 92
"New Negro," 146
New Orleans, 8, 9, 29, 47, 82
Newark, New Jersey, 26, 27
Newport, Virginia, 12
Newport News, Virginia, xiv, 90, 99
New York, xix, 15, 103
New York Age. See press, black
New York City, 8, 10, 11, 18, 25, 26, 27, 40, 45, 65–66, 104, 111, 123, 143, 144, 195
Niagara Movement, 18
Ninety-Second Infantry Division. See combat units, black
Ninety-Third Infantry Division (Provisional). See combat units, black
Ninth Cavalry. See United States Army, black troops
North Carolina Mutual Life Insurance Company, 14
nurses. See Red Cross; United States Army Nurses Corps

officers, black, 71, 72, 104, 110, 111, 113. See also black officers training camp
Ohio, xix, 28, 62, 64

Oklahoma, 24, 81
Our Colored Fighters, 130. See also Committee on Public Information; morale
Ovington, Mary White, 58
Owen, Chandler, xi, xiii, 80–81, 125

Pan-African Congress, 146
Pennsylvania, 36, 85
Pershing, John J., 62, 105, 111, 131, 142
Pershing Stadium, 117
Philadelphia, 8, 10, 25, 26, 27, 31, 40, 45, 88, 122, 195
Philadelphia Tribune. See press, black
Pinchback, P. B. S., 132
Pinkett, Harrison J., 95
Pittsburgh, 8, 27, 45, 129, 195
Pittsburgh Courier. See press, black
Plan of San Diego, 124. See also subversion
Plattsburg, New York, 54, 91
Plessy v. Ferguson, 7
Pocahontas, 104–105. See also troop transports
poll tax, 5
population, northern black: crime among, 42–43, 45, 48; diet of, 9, 42, 43, 47; health of, 42, 48; living and working conditions of, 1, 7–12, 23–24, 32, 36, 40–43, 156–157; women, 9, 36–37. See also migration; National Urban League
population, Southern black: children, 2–4, 149; diet of, 3–4, 9, 43, 47; education of, 4, 15–16, 150; health of, 3, 4, 9–10; living and working conditions of, 1–4, 6–11, 37–38, 149–151; women 2–3, 9, 36–37. See also migration; National Urban League
Portland, Oregon, 82
Post, Louis F., 127. See also United States Department of Labor

Post Office Department, 124, 125. *See also* press, black

Powell, Adam Clayton, 64

Presbyterian church. *See* churches, black

press, black: critical of "Close Ranks" editorial, 135–136; critical of Woodrow Wilson, 33, 65–66, 121; coverage of Charles Young, 63, 64; government surveillance of, xx, 125–126; position on black officers training camp, 55, 59; protests *The Birth of a Nation*, 21–22; response to Houston Mutiny, 68; role in black community, 14, 32–34; praises appointment of Emmett J. Scott, 71. *See also* Abbott, Robert S.; Committee on Public Information; Du Bois, W. E. B; migration; Trotter, William Monroe; Tyler, Sr., Ralph W.; Washington conference of race leaders in 1917 and 1918

propaganda. *See* Committee on Public Information; morale; subversion

Pullman Company, 33

Queen, Hallie E., 125

racial violence, xx, xxi, xiv 1, 5–6, 11, 14, 20, 29, 33, 49, 89–90, 93, 118, 122, 131, 136, 143, 181, 187–188, 193–195. *See also* Brownsville incident; Chicago race riot; East St. Louis, Illinois; Houston Mutiny; Red Summer

Randolph, A. Philip, xi, xiii, 80–81, 125

Red Cross, xx, 82, 117, 122, 133, 138–140, 141

Red Summer, xv, 144, 190–191, 193. *See also* Chicago race riot

restrictive covenant, 10, 40, 41

Richmond, Virginia, 8, 9

Roberts, Needham, 111–112, 127

Rodenberg, William, 66

Roosevelt, Franklin D., 132

Roosevelt, Theodore, 17, 19, 92

San Antonio Inquirer. *See* press, black

Saratoga Springs, New York, 12

Savannah, Georgia, 8, 28, 38

Schuyler, George S., 61, 88. *See also* black officers training camp

Scott, Emmett J.: attends Amenia Conference, 57; Committee on Public Information and, 137; organizes Washington conference of race leaders in 1918, 130–135; relationship with Alice Dunbar-Nelson, 137–138; work for War Department, xii, xiv, 69–70, 71–72, 88, 115–116, 126–127, 145–146. *See also* Baker, Newton D.; combat units, black; Du Bois, W. E. B.; labor battalions, black; morale; Moton, Robert R.; National Guard units, black; press, black; soldiers, black; training camps; United States Department of Labor

Secret Information Concerning Black American Troops, xiii, 175–177

Secretary of War. *See* Baker, Newton D.

Sedition Act of 1918, xiii, 125

Selective Service Act of 1917. *See* draft

send-off celebrations, 82–83. *See also* draft

Service of Supply. *See* labor battalions, black

sharecropping, 2, 3, 15, 74

Shreveport, Louisiana, 122

Silent Parade. *See* East St. Louis, Illinois; National Association for the Advancement of Colored People

Simmons, Roscoe Conkling, 130. *See also* Loving, Walter Howard; morale

Singleton, Benjamin "Pap," 24–25

slackers, 74, 80, 102
Smiley, J. Hockley, 32. *See also* Abbott, Robert S.; press, black
Soldier's First Book, 96. *See also* Young Men's Christian Association
soldiers, black: challenge discrimination, 83–84, 88, 174–175; demobilization of, 145, 188–190; health of, 75, 76, 84–85, 86, 95–96; literacy rates of, 87–88, 94–96; number of, 73, 76–77; off-duty hours of, 88–89, 90–96, 122–123; pay of, 77; segregation of, 51, 58, 71, 72, 123; southern white opposition to, xix, 68–71, 77; training and equipment of, 71, 86–87; victory parades and, xiv, 143–144; volunteers, 52, 73; white abuses of, 85, 86, 88. *See also* black officers training camp; combat units, black; draft; labor battalions, black; National Guard units, black; training camps; United States Army, black troops; Young Men's Christian Association; Young Women's Christian Association
Soldiers Comfort Unit, 122
The Souls of Black Folk, 17. *See also* Du Bois, W. E. B.
South Carolina, 24, 26, 28, 76, 81, 85
Spanish-American War. *See* United States Army, black troops
Spanish influenza, 93, 116, 138
Spartanburg, South Carolina, xi, 89–90, 104
Spingarn, Arthur B., 95–96, 119. *See also* National Association for the Advancement of Colored People; venereal disease
Spingarn, Joel E., x, 54–58, 131, 135–136, 168. *See also* black officers training camp; Du Bois, W. E. B.; National Association for the Advancement of Colored People; subversion

Splendid Little War. *See* United States Army, black troops
Springfield, Illinois, 11, 18
St. Louis, 8, 26, 27, 45, 49, 134, 143
St. Nazaire, 100–102, 116
St. Paul, Minnesota, 139
State Department. *See* United States Department of State
stevedores. *See* labor battalions, black
Stone Mountain, Georgia, ix
Stowers, Freddie 113
Student Army Training Corps, 137, 140
subversion: alleged German activities among blacks, 52, 121, 124–125, 132, 174; government investigations of, 70, 115, 124–125, 131, 135–136, 139. *See also* Committee on Public Information; Loving, Walter Howard; morale; Spingarn, Joel E.; Trotter, William Monroe

Taft, William Howard, 126
Talented Tenth, 17, 18, 61. *See also* Du Bois, W. E. B.
Tampa, Forida, 30
Taylor, Ralph D., 106, 108, 110, 111. *See also* combat units, black; National Guard units, black
Tennessee, xix, 8, 88
Tenth Cavalry. *See* United States Army, black troops
Terrell, Mary Church, 57
Terrell, Robert Church, 132
Texas, 25, 29, 81, 84. *See also* Brownsville incident; Houston Mutiny
The Training of Colored Troops, 130. *See also* Committee on Public Information; morale
Thirteenth Amendment, 1, 135
"To Make the World Free," 130. *See also* Committee on Public Information; morale

Toledo, Ohio, 27
training camps: arrival of black soldiers in, xi, 82, 84–85; Camp Alexander, Virginia, 86, 90, 93; Camp Dodge, Iowa, 59, 93, 95; Camp Funston, Kansas, 126, 183; Camp Grant, Illinois, 89; Camp Hill, Virginia, xii, 86, 95; Camp Jackson, South Carolina, 87; Camp Lee, Virginia, xii, xiv, 85; Camp Logan, Texas, 67, 170, 172; Camp Meade, Maryland, xiii, 71, 85–86, 89, 173–174; Camp Merritt, New Jersey, xiii, 93, 104; Camp Mills, New York, xi, 89; Camp Pike, Arkansas, 89; Camp Shelby, Mississippi, 95; Camp Sheridan, Alabama, 90; Camp Sherman, Ohio, 93; Camp Stuart, Virginia, 90–91; Camp Taylor, Kentucky, 92, 93; Camp Travis, Texas, 94; Camp Upton, New York, xii, 89, 92; Camp Wadsworth, South Carolina, xi, 89, 104; conditions in, 85–86, 88–89, 127, 173–174; location of, 84; racial unrest in, 89–90, 93. See also black officers training camp; draft; Houston Mutiny
Travelers Aid Society, 40
trench warfare, 109–111
troop transports, 99–100, 104–105, 172–173
Trotter, William Monroe, ix, 19–21, 22, 125, 131, 134–135. See also Du Bois, W. E. B.; press, black; subversion
Tupes, Herschel, 111
Tuskegee Institute, Alabama, 17, 30, 55, 57, 59, 69, 125, 137. See also Moton, Robert R.; Scott, Emmett J.; Washington, Booker T.
Twenty-Fourth Infantry. See United States Army, black troops
Twenty-Fifth Infantry. See United States Army, black troops

Tyler, Sr., Ralph W., xiv, 115, 132, 137, 140. See also Committee on Public Information; morale; press, black
Tyler, Texas, 84

United States Army, black troops: in Hawaii, xix, 52; in Mexico, xix, 52, 62, 105, 172; in Philippines, xix, 52, 60, 62, 68, 124; in Spanish–American War, xvii, xix, 65, 92, 105, 172; Ninth Cavalry, xix, 51, 62, 73; prior to World War I, xvii, xviii, xix, 60, 62, 66–67, 73, 92, 105, 124; Tenth Cavalry, xix, 51, 62, 73, 101, 105; Twenty-Fifth Infantry, xix, 51, 66, 73, 101, 170–172; Twenty-Fourth Infantry, xi, xix, 51, 60, 66–68, 73, 89. See also Baker, Newton D.; combat units, black; draft; labor battalions, black; National Guard units, black; soldiers, black; training camps; United States War Department
United States Army Medical Corps, 61
United States Army Nurses Corps, xiv, 138–139, 140, 142
United States Department of the Interior, 131
United States Department of Justice, 124
United States Department of Labor, xii, xiii, 31, 35, 42, 127–130, 149–150, 152–155
United States Department of State, 124
United States Food Administration, xiv, 137, 139–140
United States Marine Corps, 102, 124
United States Military Academy, West Point, 62, 105
United States Navy, xix, 132, 133
United States Sanitary Corps, 95–96
United States Secretary of War. See Baker, Newton D.
United States Shipping Board, 132

United States War Department: establishes Student Army Training Corps, 137, 140, 143; position on black officers training, 56–59, 61; racial policy of, 51–52, 69, 71, 72, 127, 141, 149; response to Houston Mutiny, 67–71. *See also* Baker, Newton D.; combat units, black; draft; labor battalions, black; National Guard units, black; Scott, Emmett J.; training camps

United War Savings Stamps, 122, 141, 186

Universal Negro Improvement Association, 146

vagrancy laws, 6, 38

Vann, Robert L., 132. *See also* press, black

venereal disease, 85, 95–96, 102–103, 106, 132. *See also* Spingarn, Arthur B.; Young Men's Christian Association

Vicksburg, Mississippi, 122

Villard, Oswald Garrison, 20

Virginia, 8, 19, 28, 32

Waldron, J. Milton, 56. *See also* black officers training camp

Walker, Madame C. J., 147

war bond drives, xx, 141

War Department. *See* United States War Department

Washington, D.C., 8, 10, 15, 55, 58, 64, 122, 125, 132, 195

Washington Bee. See press, black

Washington, Booker T.: death of, ix, 18, 57, 69; disciples of, 29–30, 57, 69, 130; on racial advancement, 16–17, 44, 135; use of Tuskegee Machine, 18, 69. *See also* Du Bois, W. E. B.; Moton, Robert R.; Scott, Emmett J.; Tuskegee Institute

Washington conference of race leaders in 1917, x, 58, 169–170

Washington conference of race leaders in 1918, xiii, 122, 131–135, 136–137, 142, 184–185

Washington, Jesse, x, 29

"We Return Fighting," xiv, 191–193

Wells-Barnett, Ida B., 25, 125

West Point. *See* United States Military Academy, West Point

Wilberforce University, Ohio, 62

Williams, Eugene, xv, 144–145

Williams, John R., 141

Wilmington, N. C., 11

Wilson, Sidney, 88

Wilson, William B., 127. *See also* United States Department of Labor

Wilson, Woodrow, ix, xvii, xviii, 19–22, 23; appoints racial advisors, 122, 127, 137, 139–140, 142; concerns about black morale, xx, 64, 123–125, 127–129; condemns mob violence, xiii, 122, 136, 142, 187–188; response to Houston mutiny, xiii, 134, 137, 142; United States War Department and, 52–53, 56, 63. *See also* Baker, Newton D.; East St. Louis, Illinois; morale; press, black; Trotter, William Monroe; Washington conference of race leaders in 1918

women, 2–3, 9, 25, 26, 35, 36–37, 38, 57, 58, 103, 123, 125, 137–140, 149, 150–151, 182–183. *See also* Red Cross; Young Women's Christian Association

Wood, Leonard, 54–55. *See also* black officers training camp

Woodson, Carter G., ix

work or fight laws, 128–129

World War II, 149

World's Columbian Exposition, 32

wounded soldiers. *See* military casualties

Y-huts. *See* Young Men's Christian Association
Young, Charles, xi, xiii, xiv, 58, 60, 62–64, 105–106, 124, 134, 140, 143, 166. *See also* black officers training camp; Pershing, John J; United States Army, black troops
Young Men's Christian Association (YMCA): black contributions to, 122; location of YMCA huts in American military camps, 84; response to wartime migration, 40, 44; services in training camps, x, xx, 74, 91, 93–96, 173–174; services in France, xx, 103, 104, 114, 118–120; services on troop transports, 100. *See also* Young Women's Christian Association
Young Women's Christian Association: black contributions to, 122; location of YWCA hostess houses in American military camps, 84; response to wartime migration, 40, 44; services in American training camps, xx, xii, 91–93, 138. *See also* women; Young Men's Christian Association
Young Men's Hebrew Association, 91
Youngstown, Ohio, 27, 45

~

About the Author

Nina Mjagkij is professor of history at Ball State University in Muncie, Indiana. She is the author of the award-winning *Light in the Darkness: African Americans and the YMCA, 1852–1946* and editor of *Organizing Black America: An Encyclopedia of African American Associations.*